GOD'S OUTRAGEOUS CLAIMS

Resources by Lee Strobel

The Case for Christ

The Case for Christ audio

The Case for Christ—Student Edition (with Jane Vogel)

The Case for Christmas

The Case for Christmas audio

The Case for a Creator

The Case for a Creator audio

The Case for a Creator—Student Edition (with Jane Vogel)

The Case for Easter

The Case for Faith

The Case for Faith audio

The Case for Faith—Student Edition (with Jane Vogel)

The Case for Faith Visual Edition

Experiencing the Passion of Jesus (with Garry Poole)

Inside the Mind of Unchurched Harry and Mary

Surviving a Spiritual Mismatch in Marriage
(with Leslie Strobel)

Surviving a Spiritual Mismatch in Marriage audio

What Jesus Would Say

UPDATED EDITION

LEE STROBEL

GOD'S OUTRAGEOUS CLAIMS

DISCOVER
WHAT THEY MEAN
FOR YOU

ZONDERVAN™

GRAND RAPIDS, MICHIGAN 49530 USA

WILLOW
Willow Creek Resources

ZONDERVAN™

God's Outrageous Claims
Copyright © 1997, 2005 by Lee Strobel

This title is also available as a Zondervan audio product. Visit www.zondervan.com/audiopages for more information.

Requests for information should be addressed to:

Zondervan, *Grand Rapids, Michigan 49530*

ISBN-13: 978-0-310-26775-1
ISBN-10: 0-310-26775-7

International Trade Paper Edition

Interior design by Beth Shagene

Printed in the United States of America

05 06 07 08 09 10 11 /❖DCI/ 17 16 15 14 13 12 11 10 9 8 7 6 5 4 3 2

CONTENTS

AN INTRODUCTION TO GOD'S SURPRISES

*O*ver there, on the hillside—can you hear him? He's turning everything upside down again. He's rewriting all the rules. Oh, man,
he's headed for trouble now! You can't say things like that and get away
with it. He's talking about God as if he knows him. About life as if he
understands it. About hope as if he has some. About a better way—a narrow way. And look at the people. They can't help but listen, even when he
stuns them. Somehow they know: this Jesus speaks the truth.

Outlandish. Extraordinary. Astonishing.

Often when Jesus speaks, he says something that leaves us mut-
tering, "That's *outrageous*."

Lose your life to save it. The first will be last. The meek will in-
herit the earth. Rejoice in persecution. Pray for your enemies. It's
better to give than receive. Turn the other cheek. Humble yourself
to be exalted. Incredible!

Jesus tells us to forgive when we'd rather retaliate, to love when
it feels so good to hold a grudge, to serve when we'd prefer to indulge ourselves, to include when we'd rather shun, to obey when
we want to rebel, to have a child's faith when we pride ourselves on
being smart, and to believe even when we're pestered by doubts.
Amazing!

This Jesus sees potential in us that we don't see in our wildest
dreams. He detects qualities in us that we would never think we

have. He has faith in us that we lack in ourselves. He sees truths about us that can give us hope and confidence.

God's astounding claims about you and me are sprinkled throughout the pages of Scripture. There are assertions about how we can grow in virtue, relate to others with authenticity, earn a living with integrity, and make a difference even in the midst of a culture that's unraveling at the seams. When I come across one of these nuggets, I can't help but shake my head in wonder.

That's what this book is about—a sampling of thirteen phenomenal claims that the Bible makes about us. If we take them seriously and open ourselves to God's activity, we can discover new insights into who we are and new principles as to how we can live with courage and conviction.

In fact, it's no exaggeration to say that God's claims can change the entire trajectory of your life. At least, that's what happened to me. Over time these discoveries helped move me from being a stone-hearted, atheistic journalist to becoming a committed follower of Jesus. My world has been turned inside out—and looking back, I wouldn't want it any other way.

This isn't a book to read passively. It's not a collection of feel-good platitudes that offer easy answers. You'll find much of it encouraging, some of it challenging, but all of it intensely practical. After all, that's what God is like. He doesn't just give us wisdom; he gives us wisdom that *works*.

And he speaks with compassion: "For surely I know the plans I have for you, says the LORD, plans for your welfare and not for harm, to give you a future with hope."[1]

God has made some claims about you. Outrageous claims. Read them with fresh eyes and a willing heart and let them begin to transform your attitudes, your outlook, your values—and your life.

THERE'S FREEDOM
IN FORGIVING
YOUR ENEMIES

Associated Press reporter Terry Anderson was held hostage in Lebanon for nearly seven years. He was chained to a wall in a filthy, spider-infested cell. He suffered through sickness. He endured mental torture. He longed for his family. He was ground down by the dull ache of incessant boredom.

Through it all, he was given one book—the Bible—and as he devoured it in a search for words of hope, he came across what appeared to be outrageous words of hopeless naïveté: "You have heard that it was said, 'Love your neighbor and hate your enemy,'" Jesus told a crowd. "But I tell you: Love your enemies and pray for those who persecute you."[1]

Can you imagine how outlandish that command must have seemed to Anderson after spending 2,455 mind-numbing days in cruel captivity? Love *whom*? Pray for *whom*? Show kindness toward those who brutalized me? Exhibit compassion toward those who callously extended none to me? Is Jesus a cosmic comedian or merely a starry-eyed idealist?

Finally Anderson was released on December 4, 1991. Journalists clustered around and peppered him with questions. They wanted to know what his ordeal had been like. They wanted to know his plans for the future. But then one reporter called out the question that stopped Anderson in his tracks: "Can you forgive your captors?" What an easy question to pose in the abstract; what a profound issue to ponder honestly amid the grim reality of harsh injustice.

Anderson paused. Before the words of his response could come out of his mouth, the Lord's Prayer coursed through his mind: "Forgive us our sins, for we also forgive everyone who sins against us."[2]

Then this victim of undeserved suffering spoke. "Yes," he replied, "as a Christian, I am required to forgive—*no matter how hard it may be.*"[3]

Often it *is* hard. So hard, in fact, that Jesus' decree to love and pray for our opponents is regarded as one of the most breathtaking and gut-wrenching challenges of his entire Sermon on the Mount, a speech renowned for its outrageous claims. There was no record of any other spiritual leader ever having articulated such a clear-cut, unambiguous command for people to express compassion to those who are actively working against their best interests.

Jesus has done it again!

But wait. Hold on a moment. Maybe this command isn't so outlandish after all. Perhaps it's actually a prescription that benefits both those who forgive and those who are forgiven. Maybe there are a host of benefits that come with fostering an atmosphere of grace rather than an environment of maliciousness.

The truth is, God's wisdom works. Choosing to forgive instead of hate can turn out to be one of our greatest blessings in disguise—if we understand how this extraordinary principle works.

THE RIVALS AROUND US

Love my enemies? I don't have any *enemies*—do you? Nobody has ever shoved a machine gun under my chin and herded me into a dank cell for seven years. Nobody has ever brutalized me the way Terry Anderson was abused.

But even in the civilized United States, we *do* have enemies. To one degree or another we all have adversaries or opponents toward whom we feel animosity.

He may be the owner of a competing business who's stealing your best customers, and if you're honest, you'll admit that you hate him for putting your livelihood in jeopardy. She may be a colleague who's fighting against you — all too successfully — for bonuses and advancement. He may be the midlevel executive who's firmly entrenched above you in the corporate structure, and you resent him because he's blocking your way to the top.

If you're management, your adversary may be the union, or vice versa. Your enemy might be the people who hold opposing views on abortion or homosexuality, and you've gone beyond disagreeing with their opinions to despising them as people. It might be a teacher who refuses to cut you any slack. Or the girlfriend who broke your heart. Or the father who stunted your self-esteem. Or a former friend who broke your confidence and spilled your secrets to the world. Or the ex-spouse who trashed your marriage. Or the recalcitrant employee who just won't get on board with your policies. Or the classmate whose popularity eclipses yours. Or the colleague who is reaping all the recognition that *you* deserve.

When I was a journalist at the *Chicago Tribune*, I had plenty of enemies. They were reporters at the *Sun-Times*, the *Daily News*, and the various broadcast stations who would strive to beat me to stories. I felt intense malice toward them because in order for them to succeed, they had to cause me to fail. Even now that I'm a Christian author and speaker — although I'm terribly embarrassed to admit this — I sometimes jealously view others as opponents if they turn a better phrase or score higher with audiences. Such can be the depth of my own sinful pettiness.

We *all* have rivals. In fact, let me press the issue further by asking you to get specific: Who are the adversaries in *your* life?

What are their names? Actually bring one of their faces into your mind, because I don't want us to stay merely in the realm of the hypothetical. Let's talk about real people, real relationships, real conflict—and the road toward real healing.

WHAT'S LOVE GOT TO DO WITH IT?

Exactly what do you need to do about that person you've brought into your mind? It's too general just to say that you're supposed to love him or her. Should you stop competing with this individual? Should you become best buddies or golfing partners? Should you go on Caribbean cruises together? Should you treat him or her like a son or daughter?

Jesus was very precise in choosing a word for "love" that doesn't imply emotion as much as it suggests attitude and action. As difficult as it sounds, he's urging us to have a humble, servant demeanor toward people who are our adversaries. To look for the best in them and offer help as they need it. To have a sense of goodwill and benevolence toward them in spite of their lack of the same toward us. To pray for their welfare and the well-being of their families. Even though we may continue to compete with them, we are to do so fairly and respectfully, not maliciously as if we're trying to destroy them.

Technically, we aren't being asked to *like* the other person, because that would require an emotion that we sometimes can't conjure up, despite our best intentions. But in effect we are to treat them *as though* we like them—because that's a decision of our will. We don't have to approve of what they are, what they've done, or how they conduct their affairs, but we are to love *who* they are—people who matter to God, just like you and me. People who have failed but who are eligible for God's forgiving grace.

In fact, the Bible says, "But God demonstrates his own love for us in this: While we were still sinners, Christ died for us."[4]

Amazingly, God's response to our rebellion against him wasn't to declare war on us as his enemies. Instead, he returned love for evil so the path could be paved for us to get back on good terms with him. And that's the kind of love he wants us to extend to those who have crossed us.

But if you are mentally focusing on a particular rival right now, then my guess is that a one-word question has just popped into your mind: "Why? Why should I return goodwill for ill will?"

For those who are followers of Jesus, the answer is simple: he said that this is the pattern of living he wants his people to pursue. And that's enough. We have confidence that he would never ask us to do anything that would ultimately work to our detriment.

But even beyond that, there are tremendous payoffs for following this ostensibly outrageous command. Although our motive shouldn't be to get something in return, the truth is that there's a lot to be gained. In fact, these next few pages are going to focus on the extraordinary psychological, physical, relational, spiritual, and kingdom benefits that accrue when we resolve to forgive our adversaries.

THE PSYCHOLOGICAL BENEFIT: HEALING OUR MIND AND EMOTIONS

"For as he thinks within himself," says the Bible, "so he is."[5] In other words, people who entertain bitter thoughts and exhibit an angry attitude toward their enemies often become bitter and angry people. They become a hostage to their own hate. They don't hold a grudge as much as the grudge holds them in its claws.

This was true for Elizabeth Morris, a woman from a small Kentucky town who told me about her remarkable metamorphosis from an angry and embittered woman into someone who experienced the freedom of becoming a grace giver.

Elizabeth described how she had been sitting up late in the evening two days before Christmas in 1982, waiting for her son, Ted, to come home from his temporary job at a shopping mall. He had just completed his first semester at college and was working to get some extra money during the Christmas break.

But at 10:40 p.m., Elizabeth got the telephone call that all parents fear. "Mrs. Morris, this is the hospital," said the voice. "Your son has been in an accident."

As it turned out, another young man who had been driving drunk—in fact, whose blood-alcohol level was three times the legal limit—had crossed the highway's center line and smashed head-on into Ted's car. The drunk driver was only slightly injured, but before the night was over, eighteen-year-old Ted Morris was dead.

Elizabeth and her husband, Frank, were devastated. Ted was their only child, a well-behaved son with a bright future, and suddenly he was gone. The Morrises' anger escalated when the twenty-four-year-old man who killed Ted was given probation for the crime. Elizabeth told me that the hatred within her was like a wildfire sweeping down a dry canyon, consuming every part of her.

She began replaying the mental videotape of that night like a horror movie, over and over again. She ached for revenge. Sometimes she would fantasize about driving down the street and encountering Tommy Pigage, the man who killed her son. She would imagine hitting him with her car, pinning him up against a tree, and watching him suffer in agony as she slowly crushed him to death.

She spent a lot of her spare time actually tracking Tommy to see if she could catch him violating the terms of his probation, so he would be sent to prison. Over time her bitterness and negative attitude began to drive a wedge between her and her husband. It began to chase away her friends. It drained away her ability to laugh and enjoy life.

And that's the psychological reason why forgiveness makes so much sense. Acrid bitterness inevitably seeps into the lives of people who harbor grudges and suppress anger, and bitterness is always a poison. It keeps your pain alive instead of letting you deal with it and get beyond it. Bitterness sentences you to relive the hurt over and over. Elizabeth described it as a cancer that was eating away at her from the inside.

She desperately wanted help, but it was some time before she discovered the only cure. Elizabeth came to the realization that her heavenly Father also had lost his only Son. And yet when Jesus was suffering on the cross—before he died as payment for Elizabeth's own wrongdoing—he looked at the merciless soldiers who were in charge of torturing him and said, "Father, forgive them, for they do not know what they are doing."[6]

That's when Elizabeth knew it was time for her—*as an act of her will*—to offer forgiveness to the man who killed her only son. So that's what she did. And over time as her attitude began to change, not only was she rescued from her caustic bitterness but she and her husband were actually able to build a relationship with their son's killer. In fact, it was their friendship that influenced Tommy Pigage to begin following Jesus and turn his life around.

As unbelievable as it sounds, Elizabeth's husband, a part-time preacher, ended up baptizing Tommy, and as Tommy emerged from beneath the water, symbolizing the renewal of his life through Christ, they hugged and sobbed. Later he presided at Tommy's wedding. The Morrises began riding to church every Sunday with Tommy and his wife, and together they worshipped the God of the second chance.

How were the Morrises able to do all that? Because their animosity toward Tommy, the killer, had been replaced by their acceptance of Tommy, the person who matters to God. And the result has been a personal peace that goes beyond human understanding.

"I can't tell you how good it felt to get on with life, to laugh again, to finally shake free from that anchor of hate that weighed me down," Elizabeth told me.[7]

That's one of the greatest benefits of forgiving those who have harmed us.

THE PHYSICAL BENEFIT: NEUTRALIZING OUR LIFE-THREATENING ANGER

In my conversations with Elizabeth Morris, she made a casual comment that seemed extreme at first but that I later came to recognize as being chillingly accurate. "I think in the long run," she said, "it would have destroyed me if I hadn't forgiven Tommy."

By now I've seen enough scientific studies to conclude that bitterness and bottled-up anger don't just mess with our minds but also threaten our very lives. Declared an article in the *New York Times*: "Researchers have gathered a wealth of data lately suggesting that chronic anger is so damaging to the body that it ranks with—or even exceeds—cigarette smoking, obesity, and a high-fat diet as a powerful risk factor for early death."

In one study at the University of Michigan, a group of women was tested to see who was harboring long-term suppressed anger. Then all the women were tracked for eighteen years, and the outcome was startling: the women with suppressed anger were three times more likely to have died during the study than those who didn't have that kind of bitter hostility. A similar study was performed over twenty-five years on males who were graduates of the medical school at the University of North Carolina. The results showed that the physicians with hidden hostilities died at a rate that was six times greater than those who had more forgiving attitudes.

There's plenty of anecdotal evidence, too. One woman who helped victims of German atrocities recover after World War II noticed an amazing phenomenon among her patients. Those who developed forgiving attitudes toward their enemies were able to rebuild their lives despite their injuries. But the patients who were steeped in bitterness remained invalids.

The medical evidence is clear and mounting. It's no exaggeration to say that bitterness is a dangerous drug in any dosage and that your very health is at risk if you stubbornly persist in being unforgiving.

THE RELATIONAL BENEFIT: HOLDING OUT HOPE OF RECONCILIATION

At the height of the Cuban Missile Crisis, as the tension was building toward what could have been the outbreak of World War III, Soviet Premier Nikita Krushchev sent an urgent communiqué to President John F. Kennedy. In part, the message said,

> You and I should not now pull on the ends of the rope in which you have tied a knot of war, because the harder you and I pull, the tighter the knot will become. And a time may come when this knot is tied so tight that the person who tied it is no longer capable of untying it, and then the knot will have to be cut. What that would mean I need not explain to you, because you yourself understand perfectly what dread forces our two countries possess.[8]

In effect, when you make the decision to return good for evil, you're choosing to stop yanking on the rope of conflict and making the knot in your relationship so tight that it can never be untied. By simply dropping your end of the cord, you're loosening the tension and preserving the possibility that the still-loose knot might somehow be untangled by the two of you. This maintains the hope—however faint—that reconciliation might someday occur.

As you think of the adversary whose face you've brought into your mind, you might be tempted to rule out any likelihood of ever having a civil relationship with him or her. But don't write off anything too quickly.

"There were probably some Christians who hated Saul when he was filled with malice and breathing threats and murder against the church," said David Dockery and David Garland in *Seeking the Kingdom*. "Who would have guessed that he would become the apostle Paul,... preaching ... love and forgiveness? The one who treats us as our enemy today may become our brother or sister tomorrow. Jesus says to treat them today as our brother and sister."[9]

Hatred writes people off; love holds out hope.

THE SPIRITUAL BENEFIT: BEING FORGIVEN AS WE FORGIVE OTHERS

Jesus told the story of a king who decided to balance his books by collecting the money that people owed him. So he summoned a servant whose debt totaled ten million dollars, and sternly ordered him to pay up. The man pleaded poverty.

In those days, the king had the authority to sell a person and his family into slavery to recoup a debt, or to throw the debtor into prison until his relatives paid up. In this instance, when the king threatened to sell the servant, his family, and all his possessions as a way of regaining at least part of what was owed, the servant fell on his knees and pleaded, "Be patient with me, and I will pay back everything."

Of course, there was no way he was ever going to come up with ten million dollars. But because the king was merciful and took pity on the begging servant, he did an amazing thing: he gave him a second chance. The debt was summarily wiped off the books.

But that's not the end of the story. The servant, who should have been brimming with a grateful attitude, soon came across a fellow worker who owed him a paltry twenty dollars. The forgiven servant demanded payment, clutching the debtor by the throat and choking him. "Be patient with me," the man gasped, "and I will pay you back." Sound familiar? But the first servant refused. Instead, he had the man thrown into prison to suffer until the debt was repaid.

When word of this encounter made its way back to the king, he was incensed. "You wicked servant," he said to the worker he had forgiven. "I canceled all that debt of yours because you begged me to. Shouldn't you have had mercy on your fellow servant just as I had on you?"

With righteous indignation, the king then threw him into prison until he could repay the entire ten million dollars—which meant he was doomed to a lifetime in the dungeon.

Here's the kicker: "This," Jesus said, "is how my heavenly Father will treat each of you unless you forgive your brother from your heart."[10]

People who hear this story bristle at the fundamental unfairness of the man who had been forgiven much but who himself forgave nothing. His gross insensitivity violates our sense of equity and justice. Someone once called his actions "a moral monstrosity."

Yet if the thought of someone acting so unjustly makes us angry, doesn't it make sense that God would get upset with those who have received his priceless forgiveness but then harbor petty grudges against others, plot revenge against those who have harmed them, and adamantly refuse to forgive the wrongs of adversaries?

Jesus was very straightforward about this. After teaching his followers the Lord's Prayer—which includes the request that God forgive our wrongdoing as we have forgiven our opponents—Jesus concludes by saying, "But if you do not forgive men their sins, your Father will not forgive your sins."[11]

This means that an ongoing relationship with God can become severely strained by a refusal to extend forgiveness to those who have inflicted harm. People cannot be tightly connected with God, experience his favor flowing freely into their life, or have an optimal relationship with him, and at the same time be stubbornly unforgiving toward others. After all, think of what such people are doing: trivializing the suffering that Jesus went through to extend his forgiveness to them.

So if you're a follower of Jesus but you feel distant from him during this era of your life, if you're having difficulty resting easy in his forgiveness, could it be because you're blatantly refusing to let go of your animosity toward another person—maybe even the very person I asked you to picture in your mind?

THE KINGDOM BENEFIT: OUR FORGIVENESS ATTRACTS OTHERS

"If you love those who love you, what reward will you get?" Jesus asked.[12] There's nothing particularly commendable about loving those who already care about us. Everybody does that. But when someone offers love to a person who has been an enemy, the world takes notice. People are pointed toward God as being the only source of motivation for this kind of outrageous compassion.

People certainly took notice when a thirty-three-year-old victim of a heinous crime appeared in an Indiana courtroom. The previous year, a twenty-two-year-old man had broken into her apartment, shot her in the chest, struck her with a revolver, sexually assaulted her, then put a pillow over her head and pulled the trigger once more. Miraculously she survived, because her forearm blocked the bullet.

The assailant was captured and convicted, and the victim was invited to speak at his sentencing. I'm sure that Judge Paula Lopassa expected her to angrily denounce this brutal defendant and indignantly demand the harshest possible penalty.

But the victim was a Christian, and although she said the defendant needed to be incarcerated as punishment and to protect society, she also told the judge, "I'm not after vengeance or retribution.

They won't change what's happened, and they'll only poison me. I want to help this man. He's mildly retarded, he obviously needs help, and I want to make sure he gets that help for his own sake and so he can be a free man again someday. I don't want him to suffer; I've suffered enough for the both of us. I want what's best for him. And, with God's help, I want to forgive him."

With that, tears began running down the judge's face! She actually broke down sobbing. I'll tell you what: I've covered scores of criminal cases as a legal affairs journalist, but I've never seen a judge weep in open court.

When she regained her composure, Judge Lopassa said, "The reason I'm crying is because of her forgiving nature. It's unusual for the victim of such a vicious crime to have such a forgiving attitude. And I think that she's reflecting all the best that there is in human nature."

This unexpected attitude of the crime victim pointed the judge and defendant toward God as being the only possible motivator for her compassionate response. As A. M. Hunter said, "To return evil for good is the devil's way; to return good for good is man's; to return good for evil is God's."

PURSUING THE P-E-A-C-E PROCESS

Forgiving enemies runs absolutely contrary to every impulse of human nature. When people are hit, their knee-jerk response is to hit back—*harder*. So if we're going to try to follow this outlandish claim, we clearly need some help.

"If it is possible," said the apostle Paul, "as far as it depends on you, live at peace with everyone."[13] That's God's ultimate goal—peace, reconciliation, and community between people and between people and him. So I'm going to use the word *peace* and go through what I call the "p-e-a-c-e process"—a plan whose five steps each begin with a letter from that word.

But let me pause for a moment to explain something. Through-out this book, I'm going to take time wherever possible to offer some action steps based on biblical teaching and my own experiences as a Christian. If we're going to become more like Jesus, it's critically important that we get extremely practical by exploring the "how-tos." However, I don't mean to suggest that we can solve everything if we just follow the right formula. These are merely steps that I've found helpful in my own spiritual life and that I hope you'll experiment with.

With that in mind, here's the p-e-a-c-e process, an approach that has proven invaluable to me over the years as I've tried to follow God's outrageous directive to love my enemies.

Seeking God's Assistance

The *p* in p-e-a-c-e stands for *pray*. That means, first, praying for ourselves, which involves going to God and honestly expressing our emotions, whether it's to say, "I don't feel like loving my opponent" or "I don't know how to forgive my enemy" or "I'll never be able to love my adversary unless you give me the power to do it."

If you're having trouble letting go of your animosity or bitterness, tell God about it. Admit your reluctance and ask him to help you deal with your resentment, hostility, and anger. Ask God for the capacity to love the person you don't even like.

This made all the difference to Adolph Coors IV, a member of the famous Colorado beverage family whose father was ambushed and murdered when Adolph was fourteen years old. Many years later Adolph became a follower of Jesus, and he realized he needed to forgive the man who had shown no mercy toward his dad.

"I knew I wasn't capable of this kind of forgiveness," Adolph said during a talk I heard a while back. "It was beyond me. But I found the answer in the Bible, in the fourth chapter of Philippians, the thirteenth verse, which assured me that I could do all things through Jesus Christ, who gives me strength."

Adolph found out that we can siphon strength from God to do what we know is right but which we lack the capacity to accomplish on our own. A lot of times that's the only way we're going to be capable of forgiving.

So Adolph brought the matter to God in prayer and made a decision of his will to take a concrete step toward forgiveness by driving toward the penitentiary to meet with his dad's killer. By the time he got there, Christ had provided him with the strength he needed to follow through. And once Adolph managed to extend forgiveness to his father's killer, his own emotional healing really began.

But in addition to praying for ourselves, we need to pray for our enemies, too. "Pray for those who persecute you," urges Jesus.[14] Ask God to safeguard their health, to bless their families, to encourage them, and to help them see their own need for God. "This is the supreme demand," said Dietrich Bonhoeffer, the Christian leader who suffered under the Nazis and was eventually executed. "Through the medium of prayer we go to our enemy, stand by his side, and plead for him to God."

When you do that, here's what you'll discover: your attitude toward your opponent will begin to change. I've learned from first-hand experience that you can't pray for people for very long and still hate them.

I remember being exasperated, as a newspaper editor, by a problem employee who always seemed anxious to undercut my authority and challenge my leadership. After I caught myself becoming increasingly vengeful and spiteful toward him (which, incidentally, only escalated his own antipathy toward me), I decided to begin praying for him, even though I didn't feel like it at first.

Over time the very act of going before the Father on his behalf softened my attitude. As I prayed for his well-being, I actually began to care deeply about him. And with that new attitude, I was able to start returning good for evil, and this is what eventually won him over.

So how about the adversary you have pictured in your mind? Can you begin praying for him or her? Or if you can't quite bring yourself to do that yet, can you at least go to God and tell him that you're going to need his strength to move toward forgiveness? This is a spiritual prerequisite to taking the next four steps.

Radically Shifting Our Perspective

The first *e* in p-e-a-c-e reminds us to *empathize* with others, which means to see our enemy from a completely different perspective.

Normally, we evaluate the worth of people based on their relationship to *us*. Can they help us? Can they hurt us? But when we choose instead to see them from the perspective of their value to God, we begin to recognize that they have supreme worth because they bear God's image, even though it's distorted and obscured by sin. When we start seeing them as people who matter to God, they begin to matter more to us.

We don't have to condone what they've done to us. Certainly, Elizabeth Morris didn't trivialize what Tommy Pigage did to her son. But what she did was to forgive Tommy Pigage, the *person* — she forgave him because he's etched with the likeness of God and because he matters to God every bit as much as she does. She didn't affirm what Tommy did but she affirmed him as an individual, the handiwork of the Creator of the universe.

William Barclay relates a wonderful rabbinic story that emphasizes how much God values all those he has created, even though they've strayed into sin. In this ancient tale, the angels of heaven begin to noisily rejoice as the waters of the Red Sea cave in on the Egyptian soldiers and drown them as they pursue the Israelites. Amid their celebration, God lifts his hand to stop them. "The work of my hands are sunk in the sea," God says sternly, *"and you would sing?"*[15]

The Bible confirms, in Ezekiel 33:11, that God takes no pleasure in the demise of evil people. So if God could have compassion toward those ill-intentioned Egyptians, pause for a moment and think about the opponent you've brought to mind. Ask yourself, "What does this person look like from God's perspective?" Can you look beyond his or her behavior and get a glimpse of why he or she matters to God? As Ralf Luther said, "To love one's enemy does not mean to love the mire in which the pearl lies, but to love the pearl that lies in the mire."

Dropping Our End of the Rope

We also need to take specific action steps to extend compassion to our opponents. That's why the *a* in p-e-a-c-e stands for *act*. The Bible says, "Do good to those who hate you."[16]

If a business competitor beats you out for a contract, send a note offering your congratulations. If a former spouse falls on hard times, be generous in providing assistance. If your adversaries require help moving or fixing a flat tire or need to borrow something, go to their aid. I admit that these are outrageous responses, but they're the very kind that God wants us to make.

In addition, taking a step of action also means calling a ceasefire in the war of words. "Bless those who curse you," Jesus said.[17] This means deciding that when another person shoots bitter words your way, you'll fight the urge to retaliate, and instead respond with kind and considerate language. As difficult as it seems, we need to resist the temptation to traffic in rumors, gossip, or unfair criticism.

So about that opponent in your mind: can you commit to keeping alert for opportunities to serve him or her? Can you drop your end of the rope in your verbal tug-of-war? Those acts of kindness go a long way toward dismantling barriers of animosity, because when we make the choice to act in someone's best interests, over time we find that our hard-hearted viewpoint toward them—and their opinion of us—invariably begins to improve.

Sometimes we just can't bring ourselves to take an action step of forgiveness. To do so, we need help from beyond ourselves. You'll gain some practical assistance in the chapter entitled "Outrageous Claim #5: God Can Give You Power as Power Is Needed," which deals with how we can tap into God's power when we're feeling particularly powerless to do what we know he wants us to do.

Owning Our Side of the Conflict

The *c* in p-e-a-c-e urges us to *confess*: more often than not, we share part of the blame for pushing a person into the role of being our enemy. Sometimes it's our own jealousy, our own stubbornness, our own ambition, or our own bad attitude that has contributed—at least in part—to the rift between us.

There is a direct connection between confession and healing.[18] And when we objectively assess the situation and candidly admit to ourselves—and then to God and our adversary—that we share some of the blame, that can be a big step toward healing the effects of hate.

That's what happened in Mississippi, when a group of blacks and whites got together to engage in a constructive dialogue after years of suspicion and animosity between them. At one point a young African-American pastor stood. "There have been nearly seven hundred lynchings in the state of Mississippi, but I have never heard a white pastor preach against racism," he said. "I need to know—*why?*"

Tension seized the room. Finally an older white pastor stood. He could have angrily tried to defend his record. He could have engaged in an elaborate rationalization. He could have stubbornly denied doing anything wrong.

But instead he said, "I guess that question falls to me. To tell you the truth, it was fear. I was just afraid. *We* were afraid—afraid of our people and of the consequences. So we just stood by. And the truth is, I don't know how to make it right. I'd like to go back, but we can't. All I can do is tell you—I'm sorry. *I'm sorry.*"

With that the two former adversaries walked toward each other and embraced. There wasn't a dry eye in the room. And God was pleased.

Few things accelerate the peace process as much as humbly admitting our own wrongdoing and asking forgiveness. That tells our adversaries that we're so serious about dealing honorably with the friction between us that we're willing to go beyond pride and self-interest to confess that yes, we do own some of the responsibility for the rift.

What about the adversary in your mind? Be honest: are you at least partly responsible for the conflict between you? And if you are, shouldn't you take the step of seeking forgiveness for that?

Looking for an Example

The apostle Paul urged, "Be imitators of God,"[19] and so the second *e* in p-e-a-c-e represents the word *emulate*. Whenever we're not sure how to love an enemy, whenever we hesitate because we're perplexed over how to proceed, whenever we wonder if we've gone far enough in our effort to reconcile, we can look at the example of Jesus and model ourselves after him. He set the ultimate standard, as illustrated by this compelling observation from British pastor John Stott:

> Jesus seems to have prayed for his tormentors actually while the iron spikes were being driven through his hands and feet; indeed, the imperfect tense [of the biblical account] suggests that he kept praying, kept repeating his entreaty, "Father, forgive them; for they know not what they do." *If the cruel torture of crucifixion could not silence our Lord's prayer for his enemies, what pain, pride, prejudice, or sloth could justify the silencing of ours?* [20]

We cannot excuse ourselves by claiming that Jesus is divine and that therefore we can never be expected in our human nature to be as generous with our forgiveness as he is. For when the bloodied apostle Stephen was being brutally stoned to death after having proclaimed Jesus as the Messiah, his last words as he fell to his knees were, "Lord, do not hold this sin against them."[21]

How was Stephen able to so magnanimously forgive the very people who were hurling rocks at him? There's a clue a few verses earlier: Stephen was empowered by the Holy Spirit.[22]

The only way we can ever really emulate Christ is by yielding ourselves to the Spirit's influence in our life and allowing him to produce the love, joy, peace, patience, kindness, goodness, faithfulness, gentleness, and self-control that the Bible promises he will manifest over time in the followers of Jesus.[23]

LEAPING THE LAST TWO BARRIERS

Jesus' teaching about forgiving our enemies is among his most challenging and difficult. In fact, someone once said that if forgiving your enemies comes too easily, you probably haven't forgiven them at all. You've just mouthed hollow words, and you haven't actually invited your heart to change.

So as you struggle to implement his instructions, as I have in my own life, I hope the p-e-a-c-e process will prove helpful. But we're not finished yet. We haven't explored all the important aspects of this outrageous claim.

When I was studying journalism at the University of Missouri, my professors drilled into me the six basic questions that a reporter must ask in pursuing any story: who, what, where, when, why, and how. And spiritually speaking, those are good questions to ask ourselves as well.

We've already looked at *who* our enemies are, *what* we are being asked to do, *why* this outrageous claim makes sense, and *how* we can implement forgiveness through the p-e-a-c-e process. However, that leaves us with two questions—*when* and *where*. But I'm going to reserve those for you to answer.

So here's your assignment: one more time, bring that adversary into your mind. Can you picture the person's face? Now, the rest is up to you, along with God's enabling power and presence in your life. You decide when and where you're going to implement the p-e-a-c-e process with them—for your own sake, for their sake, and for the sake of God's kingdom.

YOU CAN EVEN LEARN TO FORGIVE YOURSELF

The year was 1966. The location was Vietnam. A twenty-two-year-old American soldier named Marshall and four others in his unit were on a reconnaissance mission that would change their lives forever.

You might have seen their story portrayed in the 1989 movie *Casualties of War*. The film depicted how the five soldiers came upon a hut while on patrol. Four of them kidnapped a young Vietnamese woman, forced her to walk barefoot and without food or water for an entire day, and then sexually assaulted her. Later she was killed.

Despite repeated attempts by the four to coerce Marshall into participating in the atrocities, he steadfastly refused. But he blamed himself for his inability to prevent the woman's brutalization. Even though he blew the whistle on the other four soldiers and three of them ended up in prison, Marshall has been haunted by his role in the incident ever since.

In an interview more than twenty years after he left Vietnam, Marshall said he'll have to live with what happened for the rest of his life. Then he said something especially revealing: "I think God forgives. But God is more forgiving to us than we are to ourselves."[1]

The year was 1965. The scene was a second-grade classroom in Illinois. The teacher had a mean streak and would sometimes humiliate the children when they did something wrong.

One day a little girl named Marilyn was acting immaturely. To embarrass her, the teacher put a frilly bonnet on Marilyn's head and instructed the class to make fun of her for acting like a baby. The teacher appointed a girl named Kelly to lead the humiliation, and she gave Kelly a baby bottle to wave in Marilyn's face as Marilyn cried with shame.

"Yes, Marilyn, you have to take the bottle, because you're a baby!" Kelly taunted. "The teacher says so!"

More than a quarter of a century later, Kelly was still feeling so much guilt over the role she played in Marilyn's disgrace that she tried to unburden herself by writing about the incident to a newspaper advice columnist. Despite the passage of time, she was still finding it difficult to forgive herself.

"WHY DON'T I *FEEL* FORGIVEN?"

Let's be clear: not all guilt is bad. The Bible says that one of the Holy Spirit's missions is to convict people of their sin, which is an unpleasant means to a desirable end. When we come face-to-face with our own rebellion against God and are brought to our knees in repentance, we open ourselves up to the forgiveness and grace available through Jesus. We're seized by guilt because, after all, we *are* guilty. But the Bible is quick to assure us, "Therefore, there is now no condemnation for those who are in Christ Jesus."[2]

Yet some remain tortured by guilt, forgiven by the ultimate Judge but seemingly forever condemned by their own one-person jury. Through the years, people have told me about some of their most painful guilty feelings: grief over their failures as a parent, despair over having had an affair, embarrassment over committing a crime, sorrow over a marriage that disintegrated, anguish over hurting another person. So often the refrain is the same: "Why can't I seem to forgive myself? What do I have to do to *feel* forgiven?"

Living under persistent personal indictment can have a corrosive effect on us, by keeping the pain of our past alive. It can eat away at our confidence and erode our self-esteem. It can drain away our optimism and leave us with a profound sense of discouragement.

It would be terrific if there were an easy cure. In fact, several years ago two entrepreneurs marketed a product called Guilt Away, a gag gift that was actually a spray bottle of scented water. "Hounded by nagging guilt?" their advertisement asked. "Then get rid of it the modern way—spray it away with Guilt Away!" The price: only $3.98 a bottle.

But forgiving ourselves isn't that simple. I know, because I've struggled in this area. I've found that there are no magic formulas or quick solutions—but there is hope. God's outrageous claim is that through biblical wisdom and his help, we can finally take significant steps down the road toward healing. After all, once he has forgiven us, there's no need for us to continue to wallow in our own self-condemnation.

As I've explored this area, I've noticed three categories of circumstances in which people find it especially difficult to extend forgiveness to themselves. In the pages that follow, I'm going to explore each of them, one at a time, and consider both the symptoms and a prescription for dealing with them. See if any of these descriptions apply to you or to someone you know.

SELF-ANGER SPECIES #1: EXAGGERATED REACTIONS TO MERE MISTAKES

There was a trend a while back in which some municipalities adopted a "zero tolerance for drugs" policy. That meant they would crack down so hard on illegal substances that if agents found even a smidgen of marijuana or just a trace of cocaine, they would prosecute that individual to the maximum extent of the law.

Similarly, some people with a perfectionistic mind-set have zero tolerance for mistakes in their life. I'm not necessarily referring to moral failings; instead, these are the kinds of everyday errors that all of us commit.

For these people, a faux pas is okay for others but inexcusable for themselves. As a result, when they make a mistake, they're so self-condemning and reluctant to forgive themselves that they get imprisoned in a jail of self-directed anger—and they throw away the key.

If they lose an important phone number, lock themselves out of their car, or accidentally delete something from their computer, they don't say to themselves, "Oops, I goofed. But hey, everybody does it. That's life. No big deal."

Instead, observed Dr. Chris Thurman in his book *The Truths We Must Believe*, these people go ballistic. They're convinced that this minor lapse is just one more bit of conclusive proof that they have no value as an individual.

They overreact by saying, "I didn't just *do* something stupid; I *am* stupid. Only a moron would do what I just did. I'm the biggest idiot in the world! This just shows that I'm a loser. Everybody's going to end up mad at me now. It's intolerable to keep making these kinds of mistakes." And they continue to heap condemnation on themselves.

The more our society pushes the distorted value that excellence is everything, the more some people are going to go beyond the laudable aspects of excellence and get trapped in perfectionism by setting unreasonable personal standards that they can never attain. Studies have shown that perfectionistic people suffer more health setbacks, work problems, anxiety, depression, and low self-esteem than others. In fact, perfectionists on the average earn fifteen thousand dollars a year *less* than others!

What's at the root of all this? Dr. Thurman summarized it this way:

> Some people have extremely strong feelings of shame and inferiority deep within themselves.... They convince themselves if they could just avoid making mistakes, it would drive away those feelings.... Of course, this only exacerbates the problem. They can never be totally successful because each new mistake they make underscores their lack of perfection and thus leads to even more self-abuse and depression. The cycle is vicious and endless.[3]

Defusing Our Self-Condemnation

I used to be convinced that my worth as a person was solely based on what I was able to accomplish. So when I would make an everyday mistake, I was ruthless on myself. To me, this was more than just an inadvertent error; it was another reason why I wouldn't be acceptable to others or to God. It was one more bit of evidence in the case of incompetency I was building against myself.

And that's not uncommon for perfectionists. "Their relationship with God is based on how well they perform," said another psychologist, Dr. David Stoop. "They are drawn to faith in God by an awareness of their 'badness,' but the day-to-day solution to their 'badness' is to try harder and do things perfectly." While the perfectionist may understand that God accepts him on the basis of faith and grace, "that's just the beginning. *He must now prove that he is worthy of that grace.* He must perform in a perfect way."[4]

One of the keys that helped me escape that prison was reading a story about how some religious leaders were trying to bait Jesus into making a mistake. His reply gave me a whole new perspective on myself.

"Is it right to pay taxes to Caesar or not?" they asked. "Should we pay or shouldn't we?"

Jesus asked someone to bring him a coin, which he held up to the crowd. "Whose portrait is this?" he asked. "And whose inscription?"

"Caesar's," they replied.

Said Jesus, "Give to Caesar what is Caesar's and to God what is God's."[5]

When I read this, a lightbulb flashed in my head. Jesus was telling them that the coin was imprinted with the image of the emperor, so at tax time they should go ahead and give it to him. Ultimately it's his. But the clear implication is this: *we are engraved with the likeness of our Creator, and therefore we ultimately belong to him.* We matter to God because his very image is etched into our souls!

Suddenly I realized that *this* was the basis of my value. Though I was tarnished by sin, God nevertheless considered me worth loving. And he was willing to restore me by wiping away my wrongdoing, not on the basis of my personal performance but because he has chosen to be gracious to me. My mistakes didn't destroy the image of God that was inscribed in me, so my errors can't eliminate the reason why I have value in his eyes.

This understanding—that I matter to God no matter what—gave me a healthier perspective and began to defuse the anger that I would direct toward myself for everyday errors. Although dealing with this type of self-anger can be a long and complicated process, this basic revelation can crack open the door to recovery for those who struggle with persistent self-condemnation for their inevitable shortcomings.

SELF-ANGER SPECIES #2: SIMMERING SORROW OVER WRONGS COMMITTED IN YOUR PAST

LaGena Lookabill Greene had a storybook life. Her beauty, brains, and abilities brought her to the finals of America's Junior Miss pageant, earned her a college scholarship in chemistry, landed her on the pages of *Glamour* and *People*, and gained her guest shots in commercials, movies, and television dramas. She credited her strong sense of Southern values with keeping her out of the drug-and-sex fast lane of Hollywood.

But she made one fatal mistake. Wined and dined by a success-ful race-car driver who proposed marriage to her, she gave herself to him during a whirlwind weekend in New York City. It was her one and only sexual encounter.

And that's how she contracted AIDS.

"By engaging in premarital sex, I had not followed God's will for me, and I'm paying for that mistake," she wrote later. *"Forgiv-ing myself was the most difficult part of my spiritual journey."*[6] Like the man I know who jumped into bed with his secretary and ended up losing his wife and kids. Or the lawyer who experimented with cocaine, got sucked into the quicksand of drug abuse, and lost both the respect of his family and his license to practice his profession. Or the county official who never thought anybody would catch him taking kickbacks, until one day the FBI came knocking.

When I was in college during the early 1970s, before I was a Christian, one of my fiancée's friends got pregnant and came to me for advice. "No problem," I said. "I've got the perfect solution. It's easy. No pain, no regrets. Just get an abortion." I even helped arrange for her transportation to New York, where abortion was legal at the time.

Years later when I came to understand the magnitude of what I had done in facilitating the destruction of an unborn child, I tor-tured myself with remorse. How could I have been so cavalierly irresponsible about that kind of decision? How could I have given advice off the top of my head without knowing anything about the subject?

Have you ever felt this sort of self-anger? If so, you have a choice. You can either let it paralyze you or you can let it propel you toward something positive. In my own case, I've not only changed my view toward abortion but I've often challenged people, in both public and private settings, to choose life. Having received God's forgiveness, over time I've been able to pardon myself as well.

In my quest for self-forgiveness, I've found that there are three steps that are particularly helpful: understanding and receiving God's mercy, seeking forgiveness from those we've hurt, and reaching out to friends who care. Let's explore each one.

Understanding God's Vast Forgiveness

People who have difficulty forgiving themselves for their past transgressions usually make one of two mistakes: they imagine their wrongdoing as being so big that it outstrips God's power to forgive, or they picture God's forgiveness as being too small to cover them. On either count, they're simply mistaken.

Your sin can never be so great that it would disqualify you from your Father's forgiveness. Think of it this way: regardless of what you've done, what's the worst possible penalty that society could impose on you? The death penalty, right? No matter what you've done, that's the maximum penalty the world can levy.

Now consider this: Jesus has already suffered the death penalty on your behalf to pay for all of your sin. He has paid the ultimate price. And that's why you can never submit a debt of wrongdoing to Jesus that will come back to you marked "insufficient funds."

As for those who think God's forgiveness is too small, they're usually making the error of thinking that his clemency is like human forgiveness. But clearly it's not.

- People are often reluctant to forgive. But Psalm 86:5 says, "You are kind and forgiving, O Lord, abounding in love to all those who call to you."
- People forgive but don't forget, so when you get in a heated argument, they're apt to throw your past transgressions into your face to gain a strategic advantage. Yet Isaiah 43:25 says, "I, even I, am he who blots out your transgressions, for my own sake, and remembers your sins no more."
- People forgive minor annoyances but sometimes refuse to pardon major hurts. However, Isaiah 1:18 assures us, "Though your sins are like scarlet, they shall be as white as snow; though they are red as crimson, they shall be like wool."
- People put conditions on their forgiveness. But Isaiah 55:7 says, "Let the wicked forsake his way and the evil man his thoughts. Let him turn to the LORD, and he will have mercy on him, and to our God, for he will freely pardon."
- People may forgive one or two mistakes, but then they'll draw the line and say, "That's it, no more." However, Lamentations 3:21–23 says, "Yet this I call to mind and therefore I have hope: Because of the LORD's great love we are not consumed, for his compassions never fail. They are new every morning; great is your faithfulness."
- People forgive but hold a grudge. "For I will forgive their wickedness," the Lord said in Jeremiah 31:34, "and will remember their sins no more."

You can readily see how confusing God's compassion for human forgiveness could contribute to our inability to forgive ourselves. For instance, if I thought my mistakes were going to remain in the forefront of God's mind, ready to be used like a club against me in the future, wouldn't that keep them alive in my mind, too?

If my sins were too gross for God to handle, wouldn't that mean the guilt would fall back on my shoulders? If I were to keep making the same mistake over and over, wouldn't I max out God's clemency? And if God puts conditions on his forgiveness, doesn't that mean I have to convince him how sorry I am by moping around under a mountain of shame?

But let me say it again: *God's forgiveness isn't like human forgiveness.* Its scope, its completeness, and its availability far outstrip the ability of people to forgive. Said the apostle John, "If we confess our sins, [God] is faithful and just and will forgive us our sins and purify us from all unrighteousness."[7]

All throughout history, the size of people's sin has never been the issue with God; the issue has always been whether people were willing to humble themselves and come clean with him about their guilt.

After struggling with self-forgiveness for quite a while, here's the conclusion reached by AIDS-stricken LaGena Lookabill Greene: "I know Jesus is willing to pardon even our worst failures, *and knowing that he's forgiven me, I can forgive myself.*"

Read and reread the Scriptures I've just cited. Mark these verses in your Bible. Pray through them. Refer to them in the morning when you get up and at night before you go to bed. Memorize them. Go over and over them until you *own* them. Saturate your mind with the truth of God's forgiveness so it begins to register deep inside your heart. Dwell on it so it drowns out the voices of condemnation that seek to sentence you to a punishment that you don't have to suffer.

That's an important step toward finally feeling forgiven, but I want to add this: forgiveness doesn't depend on our feelings. When we turn our sin over to Christ, we're forgiven because God says we are, regardless of whether we feel anything. So our attitude shouldn't be, "I'll believe I'm forgiven when I feel it." Instead, it ought to be, "I believe I'm forgiven because God says it's true."

Over time as we increasingly see ourselves as forgiven individuals, that feeling of being forgiven will follow. And I'll tell you what: when the reality of God's forgiveness reaches the end of that sometimes difficult and circuitous path from our head (where we understand it) to our hearts (where we experience it emotionally), it's a breathtaking experience.

Seeking Forgiveness from Those We've Hurt

Sometimes the reason we have difficulty forgiving ourselves is because we've never brought closure to our wrongdoing by asking the person we've harmed to forgive us. In effect, we've received *vertical* or divine forgiveness from God, but we don't feel forgiven, because we lack *horizontal* or relational forgiveness from the individual we've hurt.

For instance, maybe you can't forgive yourself for the way you let down your children. That regret might be staying alive because you've never gone to them, apologized, and asked them to forgive you. Or perhaps you trashed a relationship, and the reason you can't shake that nagging sense of guilt is because you've never tried to reconcile. The wounds of your past remain open because you haven't tried to heal them through making things right with whomever you've wronged.

Jesus takes this so seriously that he said if you're on your way to church and realize that you've got a rift in a relationship, you should first go to be reconciled with that person and then go worship. Why was he so concerned about that? Because our relationship with God is impeded when we stubbornly refuse to handle our relational problems with integrity. The apostle John said, "Whoever loves God must also love his brother."[8]

But let's be honest: apologizing runs against the grain of just about every instinct we have. We tend to get deterred by stubborn roadblocks in our path, including:

- *The self-deception barrier.* We say to ourselves, "C'mon, I haven't hurt anyone. I only play one role in life, and that's victim."

- *The self-defense barrier.* We say, "Okay, I may have hurt some-one, but look at what he did to *me*. Besides, he started it!"
- *The self-interest barrier.* We say, "If I admit stuff to you, then you'll have something on me, and that will give you power over me that I don't want you to have."
- *The self-doubt barrier.* We say, "If I ask forgiveness for having hurt you in a way that you may not be fully aware of, I'll be admitting that my image of being such a great guy isn't true. And if people find out what I'm really like, they won't care for me."
- *The self-protection barrier.* We say, "I'm just plain afraid of the embarrassment of asking forgiveness. I'm fearful of the other person's anger toward me."
- *The self-importance barrier.* We say, "Why should I humble *myself* and ask anyone else's forgiveness?"

All of these barriers tempt us to take a U-turn on the road toward seeking forgiveness. But if you choose a detour, I'll tell you what you'll find, because I've taken that route before: you'll encounter a path paved with guilt that will continue to gnaw at you, you'll find relational potholes that will never get fixed, and you'll find frustration because your spiritual life will get stuck.

But if you pursue reconciliation, the benefits can be tremendous, as a woman testified in a letter to a syndicated advice columnist. She said that when she was a teenager, she carelessly trashed her relationship with her mother, who was raising her alone since her father died. She ended up jumping into a relationship with a man who became physically abusive. She was scared and embarrassed, not knowing where to turn.

"Guess where I went?" she asked. "Back to my mother. We did a lot of talking and I did a lot of apologizing. We rebuilt the bridges I had burned. During the next four years, my mother became my best friend. When she retired, I didn't have enough money for a big gift, so I gave her an invitation to have lunch with me every Tuesday. As it turned out, the gift I thought I was giving my mother, I gave to myself. My mother died six months after she retired; the memories from our lunches are treasures."

This is how she concluded: *"I live in peace now—at peace with myself for having righted things with my mom."*

We can experience that kind of peace—that blissful absence of self-accusation—when we seek to rebuild bridges as she did. But there are some cautions to consider.

Be prepared for the possibility that your efforts to reconcile won't be well received by the people you've hurt.

They may not give you a hug and kiss after you've admitted how you harmed them. They may vent anger and spew ugly accusations. They may say, "After what you did to me, how can you expect me to forgive you?" For some, hate is their hobby—they enjoy despising you and they don't want to give that up. Those are risks we must assume. The apostle Paul told us, "If it is possible, *as far as it depends on you*, live at peace with everyone."[9] Remember that you're only responsible for your actions, not their reactions.

Don't inadvertently hurt someone else in your effort to apologize.

Red flags ought to pop up if your wrongdoing involved adultery, promiscuity, or other misconduct in which asking forgiveness at this time could do more harm than good. For instance, if you've had an affair with another man's wife and he isn't even aware of it, you can see that trying to apologize to him could cause great damage. If you fathered a child out of wedlock, it might not be in the child's best interest for you to suddenly burst onto the scene. The timing of each situation needs to be carefully considered. A good approach is that if there's any possibility of hurting someone, sit down with a wise Christian friend and get some godly advice.

If the person you hurt is now dead or unavailable for you to talk to, don't give up.

You can still proceed with the process. Sometimes writing a letter, even though it will never be read by the other person, can help ease your guilt. For instance, this note was found at the Vietnam Memorial in Washington, D.C., along with the faded photograph of a Vietnamese soldier and his young daughter:

Dear Sir,

For twenty-two years I have carried your picture in my wallet. I was only eighteen years old that day that we faced one another on that trail in Chu Lai, Vietnam. Why you didn't take my life I'll never know. You stared at me for so long, armed with your AK-47, and yet you did not fire. Forgive me for taking your life. I was reacting just the way I was trained, to kill V.C....

So many times over the years I have stared at the picture of you and your daughter. Each time my heart and guts would burn with the pain of guilt. I have two daughters myself now.

I perceive you as a brave soldier defending his homeland. Above all else, I can now respect the importance that life held for you. I suppose that is why I am able to be here today. It is time for me to continue the life process and release my pain and guilt.

Forgive me, Sir.[10]

Writing that kind of letter can contribute to a tremendous sense of cleansing. But I want to tell you something from personal experience: your regret can be compounded if you fail to act. I found that out years ago with my dad.

When I was a senior in high school, I was in an era of all-out rebellion against my father. That spring I was involved in lying to him, stealing from him, intentionally misleading him, and sneaking around behind his back to do what he had specifically ordered me not to. When he found out about it, he was really hurt. Everything came to a climax in a big confrontation during which harsh words were spoken and I ended up leaving home.

I eventually returned, but my dad and I glossed over our conflict rather than dealing with it. Over the years, I found that I was having difficulty forgiving myself for the way I had wronged him. I felt guilt and remorse, and yet I always found reasons not to come right out and ask his forgiveness.

Sometimes I'd rationalize it away, saying to myself, "*He's* got some things *he* should apologize for." Sometimes it would be a matter of pride: "Why should *I* go crawling to *him*?" Sometimes I'd just put it off: "I can always handle it later, right?"

But there was no later. Though I thought he had many years left, my dad died at age sixty-four.

Just before his burial, I asked for some time to be alone with him. I stood in the room at the funeral parlor, in front of the open casket. After a long period of silence, I finally managed to whisper the words I desperately wished I had spoken many years earlier: "I'm sorry, Dad."

Please take my advice: *if there are people you've wronged, go to them*. Whether it's a son or daughter, a mother or father, a sister or brother, a former friend or colleague—don't get detoured by rationalizations. Don't trip over your pride. Don't think about what *they* need to apologize to *you* for. Go to them, write them a letter, call them on the phone, and clean up your side of the relationship. Do it for your sake as well as theirs.

And let God use that to help you move toward forgiving yourself.

Reach Out and Touch Someone

Another way God flows a sense of forgiveness into our lives is through secure and trusting relationships with other Christians, who can put our feelings of guilt into perspective.

I'm talking about someone who will listen to us admit our mistakes, and say, "You think *that's* something? Listen to how I messed up last week!" Or someone who will tell you, "Look, I've done the same thing myself" or "I know how you feel; I've been tempted to do that, too."

These friends don't minimize or casually dismiss what we've done, but they encourage us to receive God's forgiveness, they commiserate with us, and they help us see that we're not alone. And they conclude the conversation by saying, "You know, in the end it really doesn't matter what you've done. It won't change the fact that you still matter to God, and you still matter to me."

The Bible tells us, "Therefore confess your sins to each other and pray for each other so that you may be healed."[11] God can use this kind of relationship to help resolve our sense of guilt.

Even so, some people need more than just a good listener. These individuals are magnets for guilt. They have a deep-seated habit of blaming themselves for anything bad that happens in their general vicinity, whether they deserve it or not. They're the type who gets robbed in Central Park and feels terrible because they didn't have a second watch to give the mugger! Often this mind-set is part of a pattern that started early in life when they were raised by critical parents who were never satisfied with anything they did.

Just as God often decides to work through a skilled surgeon to heal someone of physical disease, sometimes God chooses to work through pastors and Christian counselors to heal people by helping them unravel the hidden motivations behind their behavior. If you chronically heap unwarranted blame on yourself, the most spiritual thing you can do is seek out a trained Christian professional to help you short-circuit that tendency.

And of course, all of us need to reach out to the God who wants to bear our burdens. We need to ask him to bring us to the point where even though we still may remember the wrongs of our past, the pain has finally been dulled and the blame has been eased.

That's what it means to forgive ourselves.

SELF-ANGER SPECIES #3: GNAWING REGRETS OVER MISSED OPPORTUNITIES

The time had finally come—the moment that all parents anticipate with simultaneous dread and excitement. Our first child, Alison, was moving away to college.

Leslie and I stood with her on the campus of the University of
Illinois in Champaign, and we cried together. Of course, many of
the tears were good ones. We were proud of her and enthusiastic
about this thrilling time in her life. But I have to admit that some
of my tears flowed out of a sense of regret.

When Alison was a little girl, I spent virtually all of my time
at the newspaper office and not much with her. So I cried that
day over the missed opportunities that can never be recaptured:
the unhurried afternoons at the playground that never occurred,
the special moments of her sitting on my knee that rarely took
place, the leisurely reading of books together that almost never
happened. I wept because of the choices I had made. I was mourn-
ing the "might-have-beens."

Every time we choose to go down a particular road in life, we
forfeit other opportunities. In the end we often beat ourselves up
over the decisions we made. In fact, studies have shown that people
ache more over what they *failed to do* than what they actually *did*.

You can just imagine Charlie Brown sixty years from now as a
bitter old man, torturing himself with the question, "Why didn't
I have the guts to ask out that little red-haired girl? She's the only
one I've really loved! Maybe life would have turned out differently."

Or the teenager who says, "Why didn't I take the path of chas-
tity rather than promiscuity? Think of all the pain I would have
avoided." A recent poll showed that a majority of sexually active
teenagers feel this way.

Or the business executive who looks longingly through his office window and says, "How did I end up chained to a desk in a

job I hate? I love the outdoors; why didn't I pursue a career that I really would have enjoyed?"

Or the person who looks back and says, "Why didn't I take school more seriously? If I had finished college, who knows what I might have accomplished?" Surveys have shown that forgoing educational opportunities is the biggest regret that haunts people.

The Woulda-Coulda-Shoulda Syndrome

People caught in the grips of what psychologist Arthur Freeman calls "woulda-coulda-shoulda thinking" get angry at themselves for the fear of failure, the refusal to take risks, or the shortsightedness that stopped them from going down the "right road" in the first place.

Can you relate to that? Is there some aspect of your life that makes you wince and say, "Why didn't I take another path?" If so, what should you do? One option would be to read various advice books and get some helpful suggestions, such as these:

- Learn from your mistakes so you won't make the same error the next time you make a choice. For instance, if you selected the wrong path because of a lack of assertiveness, you can try to assert yourself more in the future.

- See if you can still jump onto the road that you should have taken in the first place. Perhaps a midcareer change or taking college courses later in life might let you pick up where you left off.

- Avoid dwelling on the past. "Thinking about what went wrong and why it went wrong leads to inaction—to giving up and giving in," Dr. Freeman said. "Thinking about what can be put right, what can be done, what new opportunities can be developed, leads to action, to change, to hope, to a new attitude about life's possibilities."[12]

As the apostle Paul said, "But one thing I do: Forgetting what is behind and straining toward what is ahead, I press on toward the goal to win the prize for which God has called me heavenward in Christ Jesus."[13]

Wisdom That Worked for Me

For me, however, it was two particular bits of biblical counsel that did the most in helping me deal with my regrets over the untaken roads of my past.

First, these words of the apostle Paul helped me by assuring that God can create something positive out of the negative choices I made: "And we know that in all things God works for the good of those who love him, who have been called according to his purpose."[14] This extraordinary verse gave me confidence that regardless of what might have been, God can take what *has* happened and fashion something beneficial from it.

Look at it this way: as you sit there reading this book, you are the sum total of all the life experiences you've gone through. You may wish you had chosen another path, but you didn't. You've been shaped by the many choices you've made, both the smart ones and the dumb ones. And here God is saying that he can take the raw material of who you are right now and customize a future of hope for you.

When I think about my self-centered, self-destructive, profane, angry, and often drunken twenties, I sincerely wish I had taken another route in life. In retrospect, I would much rather have started following Jesus when I was a teenager, so I could have avoided the heartbreak that those years brought to myself and my family. But I didn't, and I can't change that decade. Yet God says that despite my sinful rebellion during those years, he can create something positive from it—and he has.

Because I experienced those raw and turbulent years, now I'm able to sit down with people who are living that same kind of lifestyle and let them know that there's another way. When I tell them there is a God who can rescue them, I have more empathy, more understanding, and more credibility because of what I've gone through myself. And God has flowed satisfaction and fulfillment into my life as I've seen him use the pain of my past to reach people with his message of love and grace.

The second pivotal verse for me was written by the disciple Matthew. These words convinced me that in the future, I could do a better job of making choices that I wouldn't end up regretting later: "But seek first [God's] kingdom and his righteousness, and all these things will be given to you as well."[15]

In other words, if I use a "God-first" grid in making future decisions, I can have confidence that I'll be taking the right roads in life. After all, this is a much healthier decision-making grid than the ones I had used in my past: grids of expedience and instant gratification, of self-advancement and narcissism.

There's an ancient saying: "Love God, and then do whatever you want." That's a succinct description of how to live a life with minimal regrets, because if you *really* love God, you'll put him first, you'll make his priorities your priorities, you'll seek his guidance when making decisions, and you'll follow his commands as you make choices that will lead to the benefit of both yourself and your family. I can tell you that as I've become a Christian and started using that grid, I have a lot fewer regrets that will weigh on me in the future.

EASING THE PAIN OF THE PAST

On May 4, 1983, a fifteen-year-old suburban Chicago teenager got into a fight with her mother over the prom. "I wanted to stay out later than my mom was willing to let me," she recalled later. "I argued my point, said a few words I would later regret, and stomped off angrily to my room."

The next day, she caught a glimpse of her mother sleeping on the couch as she raided her purse for lunch money. But that was the last she would ever see her alive. "I never expected that I would be pulled from my class that day, May 5, 1983, to be told that my mother, who was my best friend, had just been shot and killed by my stepfather."

A flash of anger, a life of regret.

"I had the best mother in the world," she said. "The day I finally got to tell her was Mother's Day, as I was standing over her casket with my sister, saying our last good-byes. All around her were cards filled with words of love and hope that she never got to read. Now it is years later, and the guilt is still strong as ever from that fight on May 4. *It will never go away.*"

Regrets. Self-directed anger. An inability to forgive ourselves for what we've done or failed to do. These can haunt us or even consume us—but as we've seen, there is genuine hope through Jesus Christ.

It's an outrageous claim but it's true: he wants to take us to a place where the mistakes of our past may still make an unwelcome appearance in our mind from time to time but the pain will be eased. The ache will be lessened. They will pale in the shadow of the cross, that ultimate symbol of complete and eternal forgiveness.

That's when we know we've finally forgiven ourselves, even as we've been fully pardoned by Jesus.

YOU CAN SURVIVE THE RAT RACE WITHOUT BECOMING A RAT

I was sitting with my feet up on my desk at the *Chicago Tribune*, leaning back in my swivel chair and soaking in the front-page banner: "Ford Ignored Pinto Fire Peril, Secret Memos Show." My eyes lingered on the bold-faced "Exclusive!" and on my byline atop the article.

I wish I could say that I cared about the people who had burned to death in crashes involving the controversial subcompact Pinto, but I didn't. I was an atheist at the time, concerned only about my own professional advancement, and I knew that this story was going to bolster my career.

I had discovered a cache of secret Ford Motor Company documents while I was checking a court file. Based on those memos and other research, my story detailed how the automaker knew in advance that the Pinto could explode when struck from behind at about twenty miles an hour but decided against improving its safety to save a few dollars per car.

As I was plotting follow-up articles, my phone rang. The caller identified himself as a lawyer who was in the midst of a multi-million-dollar civil lawsuit against Ford.

"Look," he said urgently, "I'm desperate. If I don't get those documents quickly, my lawsuit is going down the drain. That means the families of some people killed in a crash will never be compensated for their loss. Will you make me copies of those memos?"

"Sorry, I can't do that," I replied. "It would be a breach of journalistic ethics for me to help you fight Ford. As a reporter, I've got to maintain neutrality."

"In other words," he said, "you're going to stick by your ethical guidelines even if it means justice will be thwarted and some innocent victims will never get the day in court that they deserve?"

I paused to consider the dilemma, but he must have interpreted my silence as another rejection. "Okay," he said finally. "Here's what I'll do: I'll fly to Chicago tomorrow. Meet me at O'Hare. I'll have a briefcase filled with five thousand dollars in cash. You give me photocopies of the documents, I'll give you the briefcase. Nobody will know."

He let the offer sink in. "What do you say?" he asked.

A CRISIS IN CHARACTER

Ford ultimately was charged with reckless homicide in the fiery deaths of three teenage girls who would have walked away from a rear-end collision if their Pinto hadn't exploded. It was a landmark case: the first time a U.S. corporation had been criminally charged with allegedly designing and marketing a product that was unreasonably dangerous.

Consumer advocate Ralph Nader said it was "a lack of moral courage that put 1.5 million Pintos on the road with that atrocious gas tank." During the company's ensuing nine-week trial, I listened as former Ford executive Harley Copp gave his opinion:

"Ambitions overbalanced ... morality" in the decision to produce the car.

Ford adamantly insisted it had done nothing wrong, and the corporation was acquitted after the judge refused to let jurors see most of the secret Ford memos that I had already published. But the automaker was hit with numerous multimillion-dollar civil lawsuits and suffered a public relations black eye for refusing to improve the Pinto's safety until pressured by the government.[1]

The Pinto controversy, first exposed by countercultural *Mother Jones* magazine, seemed to mark the beginning of an era in which corporate America's ethical image was repeatedly tarnished. During a ten-year period, 115 of the country's largest 500 companies—well-established corporations with well-respected names—were found guilty of serious criminal or civil misconduct.

How did that happen? I don't think these corporate leaders suddenly showed up at the office one day and announced, "Let's violate our commitment to ethics and integrity."

More likely it was the culmination of a long and gradual slide. Colleagues started rationalizing to each other, "It's okay, the competition does the same thing" or "The IRS won't look into that." Corners were cut. Small-scale cheating was overlooked, then tolerated, then subtly encouraged.

And slowly the corporation slipped from asking the question, "What's the right thing to do?" to asking, "What are we legally required to do?" to asking, "What do you think we can get away with?"

THE MEANING OF INTEGRITY

You and I shouldn't be too sanctimonious: this ethical erosion doesn't happen only in corporate boardrooms. The same deterioration can occur in the lives of individuals as they face daily challenges to be fair, honest, law-abiding, and hardworking in the murky environment of the marketplace, where there's a whole lot more ambiguous gray than sharp contrasts of black and white.

And if you're involved in the everyday maelstrom of the working world—as an employee or manager, salesperson or executive, blue-collar or white-collar worker—then you will inevitably face ethical issues. Sooner or later you're going to be tempted to sacrifice your integrity on the altar of commerce.

"The trouble with the rat race," comedian Lily Tomlin quipped, "is that even if you win, you're still a rat." But that doesn't have to be the case. God's outrageous claim is that you can survive the rat race without becoming a rat.

Admittedly, easy answers can be elusive. However, we'll see in this chapter that there are strong motivators for us to maintain our virtue, even in the midst of an economy that seems bent on honoring money over morality, profits over principle, and results over righteousness.

Integrity, the saying goes, begins with "I." It starts with the day-in, day-out ways in which you and I interact with customers and employees, with patients and clients, with bosses and boards of directors. In noting the common root of the words *integrity* and *integer* (or whole number), author Warren Wiersbe observes, "A person with integrity is not divided (that's *duplicity*) or merely pretending (that's *hypocrisy*). He or she is 'whole'; life is 'put together,' and things are working together harmoniously. People with integrity have nothing to hide and nothing to fear. Their lives are open books."[2]

Living Out What We Believe

As Christians, integrity means there should be congruence between our character and our creed, between our beliefs and our behavior. It means loving God with the totality of who we are and allowing our faith to extend to the whole of our life, including our careers. And that's where things get dicey. For instance:

- Christians believe that all people matter to God. But do we really live out that value when we're dealing with coworkers, customers, and competitors?
- Christians talk about humility and say it's better to serve than to be served. But does that show up in how we relate to the people who work for us or in the way we trumpet our accomplishments in our quest for a promotion?
- Christians endorse truth telling. But does that translate into practice when we're selling a product, talking about a rival, promising a delivery date, or cutting a deal?
- Christians preach honesty. But is that always on our mind when we're filling out expense reports or creating an advertising campaign?
- Christians are supposed to exhibit Christ's love to others. But how does that play out in the midst of corporate downsizing or when we're dealing with low-performing employees?
- Christians are expected to treat others as they would want to be treated. But then how do they justify giving less than a full day's work for a full day's pay? (The collective national price tag of sloughing off at work has been put as high as $350 *billion* a year.)[3]

I'm not naive. I'm not suggesting that integrating faith into the workplace is simple, because I know it isn't. In fact, if it were easy, more people would be doing it. But researchers have found that on the average, people who attend church aren't much more ethical than people who don't. One Gallup poll found that 43 percent of unchurched people have pilfered work supplies, while 37 percent of churchgoers have, too.

Obviously, a lot of people are saying one thing while sitting in the pews on Sunday morning and doing something quite different after punching the time clock the following day. Regrettably, for many faith is a weekend proposition, not a weekday reality.

INCURRING THE COSTS OF INTEGRITY

Integrity begins with a decision. And if we're going to choose to have not a fragmented faith that isolates God from our careers but an integrated faith that invites him to work with us, then we need to know in advance what we're getting into. So let's employ a commonly used business tool—a "cost-benefit analysis"—to see whether the benefits of extending our faith to the marketplace outweigh the costs we might incur.

And I want to concede up front that there *will* be costs. "Ethics sound fine, but let's get down to dollars and cents," some people say. "If I don't make up a good story about why I haven't finished this project on time, the client may fire me. Or if I don't phony-up my estimate, I won't get this job. Or unless I gloss over the flaws of the product I sell, I won't get a commission—and my mortgage is due next week."

Those are real-world pressures. This is where we feel our integrity put to the test and where we're tempted to pursue short-term expediency even if it might mean corroding our character or damaging our reputation in the long haul. The Bible says, "Those who sow trouble reap it"[4]—maybe not immediately, but eventually.

Yes, there can be financial costs to exercising integrity in the marketplace. In the end, however, this cost isn't as great as the long-term damage that's caused by sacrificing our character.

And that's not just naive thinking. Many prominent executives agree. "To be a winner," said Albert Carr in the *Harvard Business Review*, "a person must play to win. This does not mean that he must be ruthless, cruel, harsh, or treacherous. On the contrary, the better his reputation for integrity, honesty, and decency, the better his chances for victory will be in the long run."[5]

PAYING THE PRICE OF PRINCIPLE

Not only might we incur financial costs if we refuse to do what's wrong but we also may suffer economic sacrifices if we choose to do what's right. That's what happened to Jack Eckerd, owner of a chain of drugstores across the country, just a few days after he became a Christian.

Eckerd strolled into one of his "family" stores and noticed copies of pornographic magazines for sale. Seeing the situation through the fresh eyes of a new Christian, Eckerd immediately ordered all such periodicals removed from his seventeen hundred stores. When someone asked whether he was taking this action because of his decision to follow Jesus, Eckerd replied, "Of course. Why else would I throw a few million dollars out the window?"[6]

There's no getting around it: sometimes we take a financial hit when we do the right thing. But that's a price of following Jesus.

Another cost we might incur is alienation from our colleagues. For example, if you were to suddenly give the company a check for the personal long-distance calls you've been making on your corporate cellular phone, wouldn't your coworkers look bad by comparison and get angry at you? If they think you're being holier-than-thou, wouldn't that strain your relationship with them and maybe even derail your career?

Some of this fear is overblown. Having integrity doesn't mean you have to become an obnoxious morality enforcer who piously pontificates every time the company sails into murky ethical waters. Many issues can be handled by tactfully suggesting alternatives and working within the system to improve the corporate moral climate over time. One survey showed that only 30 percent of those who took an ethical stand ended up facing any negative consequences.

But when you take a stand, sometimes you stand out. And when you stand out, you might become a target and incur some costs.

So the cost side of our cost-benefit analysis does contain some possible downsides to pursuing integrity. However, the benefit side is crowded with five categories of rewards we can reap when we live out our faith at the work site. I'm going to devote the next few pages to looking at each one of them—the personal, family, business, societal, and spiritual benefits.

PERSONAL BENEFITS: THE ABILITY TO BE FORGETFUL

If you ask someone who lives with biblical integrity to tell you one of the greatest benefits that he or she enjoys, the likely answer will be a clear conscience. "The man of integrity walks securely, but he who takes crooked paths will be found out."[7]

That's a great personal benefit. When we pursue our careers with integrity, we don't have to spend time fretting that someone will uncover our lies. We don't have to endure an ongoing, low-level sense of anxiety about getting caught at something. We don't have to stockpile excuses or dream up rationalizations. We can mail our income taxes on April 15 and sleep like a baby that night.

A friend of mine, Russ Robinson, is committed to pursuing his career as a lawyer with integrity. "One of the biggest benefits has been the ability to be forgetful," he said. "What I mean is that I don't have to struggle to remember when I've told the truth and when I've lied. I don't have to expend a lot of energy trying to keep my stories straight. And that's very liberating!"

FAMILY BENEFITS: TEACHING OUR KIDS BY OUR ACTIONS

The Bible specifically mentions the family benefits we receive when we exercise biblical ethics: "A righteous man who walks in his integrity—how blessed are his sons after him."[8]

Let's face it: kids come prewired with supersensitive hypocrisy detectors. They can spot inconsistency a mile away. And if you're living with a fractured faith, it's only a matter of time before your children will detect the cracks and your credibility will crumble.

For instance, if you're trying to raise them to respect the property of others but they see you ripping off supplies from work, suddenly they start saying to themselves, "Oh, I get it! The real trick is not to get caught."

Or if they hear you on the phone making phony excuses to your boss about why a project isn't finished, they conclude to themselves, "I get it! When you're in a jam, you lie your way out."

It's like the story of the teacher who arranges for a conference with little Johnny's father. "Johnny keeps stealing things from the other kids," she said. "He takes their pens, their paper, their tape—and I can't figure out why."

Johnny's father was puzzled, too. "I can't understand why he'd feel a need to do that," he replied. "Johnny knows I can get him all the supplies he needs from work!"

When we send our kids mixed signals, we get mixed-up kids. We have a choice: we can either confuse them by modeling a life that's conflicting and compartmentalized, or we can model integrity so they can see how our beliefs really do determine our behavior.

BUSINESS BENEFITS: LOVE AS A LEGITIMATE STRATEGY

For years, Kristine Hanson, a Harvard-educated business executive, and Robert Solomon, a philosopher, conducted seminars for businesses, using her real-world marketplace experience and his academic expertise on ethics. This was their conclusion:

> The most successful people and companies are those that take ethics seriously. This is not surprising, since ethical attitudes largely determine how one treats employees, suppliers, stockholders, and consumers, as well as how one treats competitors and other members of the community. Inevitably, this affects how one is

treated in return. Ethical managers and ethical businesses tend to be more trusted and better treated and to suffer less resentment, inefficiency, litigation, and government interference. *Ethics is just good business.*[9]

At a time when most people believe morality in business has been deteriorating, those companies that operate with honesty enjoy definite business benefits.

In fact, I once talked with a business leader who had recently retired from a tremendously successful career as vice president of one of the country's largest corporations. He had been responsible for a division that had more than seventy-five hundred employees, and he was hailed from around the country as an outstanding executive.

"What made you such an effective leader?" I asked.

His reply: he simply took principles from the Bible—concepts like truth telling, conflict resolution, servant leadership, and so on—and put them into action in the marketplace. His big discovery, he said, was that "love is a legitimate business strategy." He proved it by the way he treated his employees and customers. They flourished—and so did he.

This is true on a smaller scale as well. I was talking with a professional person who owns a firm that he operates according to biblical ethics. He conceded that yes, he had lost some clients over the years because he had refused to comply with their demands that he color outside ethical lines. But he said his business has prospered overall because he built a reputation in the community as someone who can be trusted.

When we, as Christians, are known as being commitment keepers, promise fulfillers, and scrupulously ethical businesspeople, then we stand out from society's background noise of deceit, deception, and dishonesty. And that positions us positively in the marketplace.

SOCIETAL BENEFITS: THE INFLUENCE OF A GODLY INDIVIDUAL

Living out our faith in the marketplace is also good for society as a whole. The truth is that the ethical temperature of a company, an industry, or an entire nation will notch up only when individuals make the commitment, one by one, to morality in business.

The truth is that one person *can* make a difference by taking an ethical stand. I saw this illustrated by a friend of mine, who was involved in a business that required frequent interaction with a certain branch of government in Cook County, Illinois. Usually one of his assistants handled those transactions, but one day nobody else was around, so my friend went to the county building himself.

That's when he encountered a petty form of extortion that everyone else had been tolerating for years as merely a cost of doing business. But instead of participating in the illegal activity, my friend simply said, "No, I'm not going to pay off."

He didn't shout or cause a scene; he merely refused to perpetuate the corruption. And this single individual's quiet but decisive action set in motion a chain of events that resulted in a federal grand jury investigation, a government crackdown, and eventually one little corner of county government getting cleaned up.

There's no question that the community benefits when people stand up for morality. For instance, Jack Eckerd's costly decision to stop selling adult magazines reverberated throughout the entire country. After he removed the pornography from his stores, Eckerd wrote to the presidents of other drugstore chains to encourage them to do the same. As a result of his activism and of pressure by Christian organizations, stores began pulling X-rated materials from their shelves or stepping up efforts to keep the material away from children.

"What couldn't be accomplished by passing laws or fighting in courts was accomplished when a man gave his life to Christ and surrendered to his Lordship," said Charles Colson, a friend of Eckerd's. "Don't tell me one man can't make a difference!" [10]

SPIRITUAL BENEFITS: DRAWING CLOSER TO GOD

Of all the benefits we receive when we maintain biblical ethics in the marketplace, the most significant are the spiritual ones.

When your loyalty is to God on weekends but only to the bottom line on weekdays, you're driving a wedge between yourself and God. It would be like saying to your spouse, "As long as I'm home, I'm committed to you. But when I go off to work, well, I might fool around a little." *That* would create a rift in your relationship, wouldn't it?

Similarly, if you're living a fragmented faith, you're saying to God, "I'm committed to you in certain areas of my life. But you need to know that when I'm at work, I've got a mistress called my career." Doesn't it make sense that this would stymie your relationship with him?

"No one can serve two masters," cautioned Jesus. "You cannot serve both God and Money." [11] People *think* they can, but when push comes to shove, one of them is inevitably unveiled as the true master of their life.

That's what happened to the successful first-century business executive who thought that he had been juggling those two masters fairly well. But to unmask his real master, Jesus tested him by saying, "Go, sell everything you have and give to the poor, and you will have treasure in heaven. Then come, follow me." [12]

Suddenly the businessman's real priorities were exposed. He walked away in despair, because he realized that his wealth and ambition had a grip on his soul that he didn't have the courage to relinquish.

When we try to serve two masters, our relationship with God always falls short of its potential. We need to be clear that our career is not our master but God is. In other words, the rat race isn't the most important race we're running.

As the apostle Paul said, "I have fought the good fight, I have finished the race, I have kept the faith. Now there is in store for me the crown of righteousness, which the Lord, the righteous Judge, will award to me on that day—and not only to me, but also to all who have longed for his appearing."[13] That's the kind of priceless benefit we receive in eternity when we keep our spiritual priorities in order.

What's more, the very act of living an ethical lifestyle actually draws us closer to God. We're knit together with him when we depend on him for day-to-day guidance on how to grapple with the often-confusing ethical dilemmas that face us in the marketplace.

Rather than giving us the Bible, God could have provided us with a big, fat book of detailed regulations like the U.S. Tax Code, containing concrete answers to every conceivable ethical situation. But that would have caused us to rely on rules instead of a relationship.

Instead, the Bible offers broader moral principles that encourage us to seek out God with our specific ethical questions, to wrestle through our problems with him, and to ask for his guidance when we're not sure which way to go. This dependence and interaction enrich our relationship with him. God, says the Bible, "is intimate with the upright."[14]

WEIGHING THE COSTS AND BENEFITS

There's really no contest between the costs and benefits of exercising our faith in the business world. Yes, there may be some financial losses or relational stress. We have to acknowledge those downsides and be prepared to cope with them.

But just take a look at the benefit side of the ledger. To enjoy the clear conscience that comes from having a character without a price tag dangling from it, to be a trustworthy model in raising our kids, to contribute to raising the community's ethical temperature for the sake of everyone, to be tied closer to God, to achieve his promise of eternal rewards, to live an integrated life that pleases him and that he has every right to expect from his followers—these benefits far outweigh any short-term costs we might face.

Besides, the apostle Peter tells us, "If you endure suffering even when you have done right"—that is, even when you do incur costs because you exercised biblical ethics in the business world—"God will bless you for it."[15]

How about *that* for a promise? This is our ultimate assurance that there really is no way we can lose when we make the daily choice to do business by the Book.

TENSIONS BETWEEN BUSINESS AND FAITH

So how do we make God-honoring decisions when we're trying to resolve marketplace dilemmas? When it comes to selecting from among various choices, comedian Paul Reiser has a unique perspective:

> Here's the thing with decisions. I can *make* them. I just don't feel sure about them afterward. A friend of mine said, "Always go with your gut." Then another friend said to me, "You know what? You should listen to your heart." So now I have one *more* choice to make. Do I go with my heart or my gut? I can't decide. I gotta do an entire autopsy. My heart says *yes*, my gut says *no*, my colon is iffy—I just don't know who to listen to.[16]

Although there is no fill-in-the-blank, one-approach-fits-all answer to ethical choices in the working world, there are some steps we can take to help us make decisions that are consistent with biblical principles.

However, one prerequisite is that we must acknowledge that there are certain tensions between faith and commerce that may never be fully resolved. Laura Nash came to this conclusion after her in-depth study of how the faith of Christians influences their corporate leadership.

Nash, formerly on the faculty of Harvard Business School, interviewed the type of leader who "genuinely wrestles with his Christian conscience and business responsibilities in order to seek out as compatible a response as possible, even though he knows that the concept of being a 'perfect' Christian doing the perfect Christian deed is beyond any human's comprehension."[17]

In her outstanding book *Believers in Business*, Nash outlines seven points of tension faced by authentic Christians in the marketplace:

- The love for God and the pursuit of profit
- Love and the competitive drive
- People needs and profit obligations
- Humility and the ego of success
- Family and work
- Charity and wealth
- Faithful witness in the secular city [18]

She found that when Christians don't shy away from these tensions but instead thoroughly grapple with them, they came up with unexpected, creative, and workable solutions to what seemed at first blush to be insurmountable moral quagmires.

She gives an example of a struggling arts center that hired a printer to produce leaflets for a performance that would benefit AIDS patients at a hospice. Just before delivery, the printer, who is a Christian, discovered that the show would include a gay chorus. Seeing a conflict with his faith, he declined to turn over the leaflets. It was too late for the center to hire another printer. The performance, lacking publicity, lost money and the hospice got nothing.

The printer saw this as an easy, black-and-white decision to oppose homosexuality. But was it really? What about Christian compassion toward the hospice patients? And what about violating his original promise to print the leaflets? When you go deeper, you encounter tension between legitimate values that compete with each other.

Another printer, also a Christian, handled a similar situation differently. After praying and thinking through the various values, he couldn't find a solution that would perfectly satisfy all the biblical perspectives. He concluded he should uphold the commitment he had made to print the leaflets, but said he could not in good conscience make a profit on the job. So he didn't charge his customer, and he told her that he would not print any future promotions for similar performances.[19]

Which choice was "right"? Sometimes it's not as clear-cut as it first appears. But as a general rule, if we pretend these underlying tensions don't exist, we often end up making shallow and short-sighted decisions, yet if we pray and work through those clashing values, we're frequently surprised at the quality of our ultimate choices.

GUARDING AGAINST ETHICAL EROSION

Over the years I've noticed that Christians who are particularly adept at ethically navigating the business world tend to share certain characteristics. For example, prayer is an especially important part of their lives, and their Bible is their most prized resource. King David said, "Your word is a lamp to my feet and a light for my path"[20]—imagery that took on a special meaning for me in 1987 when I was visiting rural India.

One dark night several of us were walking from one village to another, led by a local resident who carried a lantern to light the narrow dirt path. Frustrated at his slow pace and figuring I could find the way myself by the dim moonlight, I stepped off the path to overtake him. Unfortunately, that was the place where the path became a bridge. I couldn't see where I was going and ended up tumbling into a dry creek bed!

And I've found that when I think I can maneuver my way through ethical issues by the dim light of my own instincts, I inevitably take a fall. But when I let the wisdom, principles, and commands of Scripture shine into the situation, my options are much better illuminated.

Also, ethical people are proactive, taking time in advance to identify potential "hot spots" in their business where their integrity is likely to be challenged. By pinpointing and then carefully monitoring possible trouble areas, these Christians are poised to quickly intercept ethical erosion.

In addition, they carefully watch what others are doing—*usually so they can do the exact opposite*! "Do not conform any longer to the pattern of this world, but be transformed by the renewing of your mind," said the apostle Paul. "Then you will be able to test and approve what God's will is—his good, pleasing and perfect will."[21] Explains Doug Sherman and William Hendricks,

> In ambiguous situations, it's a good bet that the crowd will generally stick together—and be wrong.... So in matters of moral ambiguity, if everyone at work seems to head together in a general direction, don't automatically start running with the pack. Sure, they all claim to be "doing their own thing," but it's remarkable how often that ends up as doing the same thing—the wrong thing. You should be the one marching to a different drumbeat.[22]

Finally, Christians who are serious about integrating their faith and their careers seek out relationships with discerning and like-minded people in the same profession for frequent discussion, accountability, mutual prayer, and savvy but godly advice in dealing with the ongoing tension between conscience and commerce.

Ironically, as I was writing this section I got a long-distance call from a journalist who wanted my advice as a former reporter and editor. It seems her news organization was thinking of appointing her religion correspondent, but in her spare time she was becoming more and more involved as a volunteer in an increasingly influential Christian ministry. Was this a conflict of interest? If so, how could it be handled ethically?

We chatted about this for about half an hour, examining the question from a lot of different angles. Finally she said, "Well, Lee, I know what I should do. Thanks for your input." As I hung up the phone, the biblical image of iron sharpening iron came to mind—we keep each other's ethical edge finely honed when we open ourselves to Christian counsel.[23]

There's no way around it: if we want to survive the rat race without becoming rats, we need confidants who love us enough to tell us the truth. Equally important, we need to have a teachable spirit that keeps us open to doing the right thing—even when the wrong thing seems so attractive.

NOW, ABOUT THAT FIVE THOUSAND DOLLARS . . .

Hmmmm. Five thousand dollars in cash, tax free. All I would have to do is violate my journalistic ethics. What would you do in my place?

Since I mentioned the lawyer's bribe attempt at the outset of this chapter, it's only fair that I tell you what I ended up doing. I'll admit I felt tempted. The first thought that flashed through my mind was, "Can I really get away with it?" I started picturing what I could do with the cash. Then I started to rationalize to myself:

"If I'm the only person who can provide these memos so a grieving family might get its day in court, maybe I should do it."

But even though I wasn't yet a Christian, I intuitively went through my own cost-benefit analysis. Sure, I'd be five thousand dollars richer, but how could I look myself in the mirror? How would I live with the anxiety of possibly being discovered? And what would happen if the bribe was ever disclosed? I'd be humiliated, I'd forfeit my career, I'd lose the respect of my family, I'd face prison for tax fraud. Besides, if my character were for sale for just five thousand dollars, it wasn't really worth very much in the first place.

So I turned down the payoff. And many months later I happened to see an article about that lawyer's case. As it turned out, the family did get its day in court and was compensated for its loss—without my illicit assistance.

But don't give me too much credit. The truth is that although I did the right thing, I didn't do it for the right reasons. I didn't snub the bribe because I loved God and wanted to be an imitator of Jesus.

However, even as an atheist, I saw the obvious: the ethics of Christianity make sense in the marketplace. More sense than winning the rat race but becoming a rat.

YOU CAN MAKE A DIFFERENCE THAT WILL LAST FOR ETERNITY

Cartoon buffoon Homer Simpson hadn't seen his born-again neighbor Maude Flanders for a while.

Frankly, I'm not so sure he missed her. The incessantly sunny demeanor of Maude and her husband, Ned, clearly annoyed him. The sugarcoated perkiness of their kids only accentuated the devilish delinquency of Homer's own infamous spike-haired son, Bart. And the Flanderses platitude-spouting faith seemed hopelessly irrelevant to the Simpson clan, which is barely muddling through the daunting realities of everyday life.

Even so, when Homer saw Maude in her backyard, he greeted her warmly. "I haven't seen you around in a couple of weeks," he said. "Where have you been?"

"Oh," Maude replied cheerily, "I've been away at a Bible camp — learning how to be more judgmental."

Zing!

I could imagine millions of viewers around the country erupting in laughter and whispering under their breath, "Amen!"

Because unfortunately, that's what a lot of people think about Christians these days. When Bible-thumpers are portrayed on *The Simpsons*, they exhibit a faith that's rigid and superficial, pushy and moralistic, saccharine and out of sync with reality. And when I was a spiritual skeptic, that was the way I used to stereotype Christians, too. As Sheldon Vanauken said, "The best argument *for* Christianity is Christians: their joy, their certainty, their completeness. But the strongest argument *against* Christianity is also Christians—when they are somber and joyless, when they are self-righteous and smug in complacent consecration, when they are narrow and repressive, then Christianity dies a thousand deaths."

Annie Dillard is equally blunt. "What a pity," she said, "that so hard on the heels of Christ come the Christians." Then there's William Hart, who ranked Jesus third (after Muhammad and Sir Isaac Newton) in his book on the top one hundred most influential people in history, saying, "On his own merits Jesus would definitely be the most influential person ever. The problem is his followers. They have done a relatively very poor job of carrying out his message."

Jesus must have known what was going to happen. And yet that didn't stop him from declaring one of his most outrageous claims of all.

GOD'S MARKETING CHALLENGE

It happened on a hillside outside Capernaum. Jesus had just amazed a crowd by announcing mind-boggling news: the very people who thought they would never be eligible to get into God's kingdom are invited in—not because of *their* goodness but on the basis of *his*.

And Jesus wanted this life-transforming and eternity-altering message to be communicated around the globe and down through history. But how? What was his approach going to be?

That's when Jesus unveiled his strategic—and seemingly out-rageous—plan. In effect, he said to his followers, "*You* are my marketing strategy. *You* are the means by which my message will be spread in your family, your neighborhood, your workplace, and your school. You'll do it by being salt and light. *That's* Plan A. And friends, this had better work, because there is no Plan B."

Clearly, Jesus was using the metaphors of salt and light in a positive sense. He was telling people to be like salt by living a life that causes others to thirst for God, that spices up the world, and that retards the moral decay of society. And just as light exposes and attracts, Jesus was saying, "I want you to live the kind of life that illuminates my truth for people, that shines my compassion into dark places of hopelessness and despair, and that draws people toward me—because I, ultimately, am the light of life."

What an outlandish idea—that frail and fallible, timid and tongue-tied, insecure and inconsistent people like you and me would be the main purveyors of the monumental news that can change people's eternal destinations. It was a high-stakes strat-egy. And the results have been ... well, let's admit it: a bit mixed. Because even though Jesus used the images of salt and light posi-tively, some Christians have managed to turn them into negative metaphors.

SALT THAT STINGS, LIGHT THAT GLARES

If you've ever gotten salt in a wound, you know how much it hurts. If you put too much salt on your food, you quickly spit it out. And excessive light can be bad as well, like when you're driving down a two-lane highway and the glare from an oncoming car's high beams causes you to recoil and avert your eyes.

In a similar way, the problem with some Christians is that even though they have good intentions, they inadvertently repel people from God's kingdom instead of attracting them. At least, I found that to be true when I was an atheist.

Basically, there were four kinds of Christians that caused me to recoil from the faith. If you're a spiritual seeker, see if you can relate to any of these. And if you're a Christian, ask yourself honestly whether you might fit into one of these categories.

First, there were *in-your-face Christians*. An example was a guy I used to pass on a street corner as I walked to my office at the *Chicago Tribune*. He would shout into a bullhorn that distorted his words so much that I couldn't even tell what he was saying. But he was angrily waving a Bible in the air, so I got the basic idea. And I would say to myself, "If *that's* Christianity, count me out!"

Recently I came across a manual of detailed instructions on how Christians can hook up a loudspeaker to their car so they can take their preaching on the road. You've heard of drive-by shootings? Well, these are drive-by *shoutings*!

The guide offered such helpful advice as this: "The faster your car's speed, the shorter your sermon should be." It even provided sample lines to use. For example, if you see a car stopped at a traffic light, you're supposed to declare, "Pull over right now and ask Jesus to save your soul!"

When an in-your-face Christian would shove propaganda into my hand as I walked down the street, I would cram it into the next trash bin. When a Bible-toting couple rang my doorbell, I'd pretend I wasn't home.

These people were always anxious to launch into a spiritual discussion at the most inopportune times. For instance, I could imagine myself squeezing between the rows at a crowded movie theater, looking for an empty seat. "Is that seat saved?" I'd ask the person next to it.

"No, it's not," he'd bellow as he pointed menacingly at me. "But the real question is, Are *you* saved?"

I'll tell you what: I'd scurry for a seat on the other side of the place! The bottom line is that I resented strangers who would try to push themselves, uninvited, into something as personal as my spiritual beliefs.

I also was repulsed by *greeting-card Christians*, whose understanding of their faith was so shallow that they could only talk about it in the kind of simpleminded clichés you find on Christmas cards. I'd ask them a million-dollar question about Christianity, and they'd give me a twenty-five-cent answer—or no response at all. To them, Christianity was emotional, not rational. That would put me off, because I'd think, "How can they believe something that they've obviously never thought through?"

In addition, *holier-than-thou Christians* repelled me. Smug and self-righteous, they painted themselves as being much better than they really were, and tarred people like me as being much worse than we really were, as if every social problem in America stemmed from the fact that everyone didn't agree with them one hundred percent. That angered me.

These Christians had an us-versus-them mentality. The believers were the good guys, and they were supposed to stay away from bad guys like me. I got the idea that if I were to venture into one of their churches, people would frantically whisper behind my back, "Look out! It's one of those hell-bound pagans! Quick, lock up the valuables! Gather the children! Protect the women!" *That's* a turnoff.

The other folks who chased me away from the faith were *cosmetic Christians*. They had a skin-deep spirituality that looked pretty good on the outside but didn't penetrate deep enough to change their behaviors and attitudes.

Like the journalist who was one of the most unscrupulous reporters in Chicago but who let everybody know what a church-going family man he was. Or the politician who proudly publicized his church affiliation during election years but who was a vicious back-stabber behind closed doors. Or the police officer who was the most racist individual I knew but who never missed a Sunday service. Frankly, I don't think anything repulses people like the hypocrisy of cosmetic Christians.

Fortunately, these four kinds of Christians weren't the only ones I encountered during my years as a skeptic. I also met Christ followers named Ron, David, Linda, and Jerry, whose saltiness made me thirsty to learn about the Jesus they seemed to know so well.

What did they do differently? How did they embody Jesus' metaphors of salt and light in twentieth-century terms? Let me answer those questions by telling you the stories about how the Holy Spirit used their characters and attitudes to pull me—gently but powerfully—toward Jesus.

A COSTLY CHRISTIANITY

Ron was salt and light to me for this reason: he lived out his faith, even when it cost him.

I met Ron while I was a *Tribune* reporter covering the criminal courts building, a squat, gloomy facility adjacent to the Cook County Jail, on Chicago's West Side. Day after day I watched a steady stream of defendants—most of them clearly guilty—desperately trying to exploit every loophole to avoid the punishment they deserved. Everybody was looking to cut a deal, to hoodwink the jury, to fool the judge, to beat the rap—anything but take responsibility for what they had done.

Then in walked Ron, who turned everything upside down. Let me give you some background about him.

When he was eight years old, Ron threw a hammer at somebody's head and ended up in juvenile court. That was his first of many encounters with the law. Later he dropped out of school, got mixed up with drugs, and rose to second-in-command of the Belaires, a vicious street gang that terrorized parts of Chicago in the 1960s and 1970s.

He got into big-time trouble when he was twenty-one. A rival gang called the Palmer Street Gaylords brutally assaulted one of Ron's friends, and Ron vowed revenge. He borrowed a gun and went hunting for Bob, who had led the Gaylord attack.

It didn't take long for Ron to track down half a dozen Gaylords as they were emerging from a tavern. Although Bob wasn't among them, his brother Gary was. A plot quickly formed in Ron's depraved mind: he decided to murder Gary, and then when Bob showed up at his brother's funeral, Ron would ambush him too. That way he'd kill *two* Gaylords.

So Ron jumped out of hiding, thrust the gun into Gary's chest, shouted, "Belaires!"—and pulled the trigger.

Click.

The gun misfired. Now Ron was standing in front of six *very* angry Gaylords. As they began to come after him, Ron pointed the gun in the air and pulled the trigger again. This time it went off, sending the Gaylords scattering.

Ron started chasing Gary down the sidewalk, shooting at him as they ran. Finally one of the bullets found its mark, tearing into Gary's back and lodging next to his liver. Gary collapsed face-first on the pavement.

Ron came up to him and flipped him over. "Don't shoot me, man!" Gary pleaded. "Don't shoot me again! Don't kill me!"

But without an ounce of compassion or a moment of hesitation, Ron shoved the gun in Gary's face and pulled the trigger.

Click!

This time the gun was empty.

A siren wailed in the distance. Ron escaped the police, but they promptly issued a warrant for his arrest on a charge of attempted murder. With Ron's extensive criminal record, a conviction would undoubtedly mean twenty years in the penitentiary.

Ron couldn't stomach that. He and his girlfriend fled to Canada, then migrated west and ended up in Portland, Oregon, where Ron got his first legitimate job, working in a metal shop. By divine coincidence, his coworkers were Christians, and through their influence Ron became a committed follower of Jesus.

Over time, Ron's values and character began to change. His girlfriend became a Christian, too, and they got married. They had a little girl named Olivia. Ron became a model employee, an active church participant, and a well-respected member of the community.

But something kept gnawing at him. Even though he had been reconciled with God, he hadn't been reconciled with society. There was still a warrant out for his arrest. And although the police had stopped looking for him and he probably could have spent the rest of his life in Oregon without getting caught, he felt that the only honest thing to do would be to give himself up and face the possibility of twenty years in prison, away from his family.

Otherwise, he said, he'd be living a lie. And as a Christian, he decided that simply wasn't an option.

I was there when Ron appeared in criminal court. Amazingly, unlike the other defendants, who were trying to wiggle off the hook, Ron looked into the judge's eyes and said, "I'm guilty. I did it. I'm responsible. If I need to go to prison, that's okay. But I've become a Christian, and the right thing to do is to admit what I've done and to ask for forgiveness. What I did was wrong, plain and simple, and I'm sorry. I really am."

I was blown away! This was *not* cosmetic Christianity. When somebody takes a costly step like that, you know it must be prompted by a faith that has radically transformed him or her from deep inside.

And that attracted me toward Christianity. Why? Because we are living in wishy-washy times, when the national motto might as well be, "Take the easy way out." So when people say, "I'm going to do something not because it's convenient or easy but because it's right," that intrigues and even inspires others. It causes people to respect them for the depth of their faith. We used to call those kind of people "heroes."

I was so intrigued by what Ron did that he didn't have to approach me to talk about his faith. *I* asked *him* about it. And when he told me how Jesus had changed him from a street gang leader into a Christ follower, he had my complete attention, and he had a special kind of credibility. Both his example and his words made a lasting impression on me.

So if you want to know what it means to be salt and light, here's one answer: *live out your faith even when you have to pay a price.* Because when you take your faith *that* seriously, others who are watching will begin to take it seriously, too.

That means different things for different people. For some, it might mean paying a professional price by refusing to cut ethical corners the way your boss or client wants you to. It might mean paying a social price by speaking up about your faith in the midst of a group that's belittling Christianity. It might mean giving up some of your all-too-rare free time to reach out to a hurting neighbor. It might mean sacrificing your pride by asking someone for forgiveness.

It might mean forfeiting a valued possession because someone needs it more than you do. It might mean forgoing some profitability in your business to live a more balanced family life, which will send a message about your priorities to those around you. It might mean admitting to your boss that you've taken work supplies for personal use and saying you'd like to pay restitution.

Those are salty steps because they're costly steps.

As for Ron, he fully expected to pay a hefty price by spending two decades behind bars. But ironically, the judge said he was so impressed by the way that God had changed Ron's life that he didn't think it was necessary to send him to prison. Instead, he concluded that Ron was no longer a danger to society and gave him probation. "Go home and be with your family," he said.

The ruling amazed me! After court was adjourned, I rushed into the hallway to interview Ron. "What's your reaction to what the judge did?" I asked.

Ron faced me squarely and looked deep into my eyes. "What that judge did was show me grace—sort of like Jesus did," Ron replied. "And Lee, can I tell you something? *If you let him, God will show you grace, too.* Don't forget that." Coming from a guy like Ron, that carried a lot of weight.

In the end, Ron walked out of my life as quickly as he had entered. But our brief encounter in that dingy courthouse eventually turned out to be a defining moment that helped make an eternal difference in my life.

A COMPASSIONATE CHRISTIANITY

Another Christian also gave me a glimpse of what Jesus is like. His name was David, and he didn't just tell me that God loves me, but he demonstrated it through his actions..

Almost thirty years ago my wife, Leslie, gave birth to our first child, a daughter we named Alison Joy. Like all new parents, we were caught up in all the excitement and euphoria of the long-anticipated event.

I remember calling relatives from the recovery room at the hospital. "You know how most newborn babies are all wrinkled and ugly?" I would say. "Well, Alison's not like that! She's absolutely beautiful!"

Then, the following day, Leslie and I were waiting in her room for the nurses to bring Alison for her 1:00 p.m. feeding. But they didn't come. Finally, just before we were going to see what was holding them up, there was a knock at the door. A contingent of glum-faced physicians filed in to give us news that made our hearts jump into our throats.

Something was terribly wrong with Alison. They weren't sure what it was, but it was serious. She had already been transferred to the intensive care unit. They needed our signatures on legal documents to authorize an immediate spinal tap and other tests. We were told to prepare for the worst.

We burst into tears, sobbing from fear and sorrow. *Why her? Why us?* The next several days were a stomach-churning blur. It was agonizing to see our tiny daughter hooked up to machines, with an intravenous needle in her ankle and monitors whirring around her. It was especially bad for us, because when you don't believe in God, there's really nowhere to turn.

But in the midst of that horror, I remember very distinctly receiving a call on a hallway phone at the hospital late one afternoon. It was from David, a man I had known years earlier but hadn't seen in a long time.

I'm not proud to say it, but the truth is that in the course of interacting with David over the years, I had lied to him, I had misled him, I had made fun of him, I had broken promises to him, and I had ruthlessly criticized his church and everything it stood for. But David was a serious Christian, and that's why he was on the phone that day.

"I heard what's going on with your little girl," he said. "What can I do for you? Can I come down there and be with you for a while? Would you like to talk? Can I bring you anything? Can I run some errands for you? Lee, just give the word and I'll be there as soon as I can. In the meantime I'll be praying for your daughter, and so will my friends at our church."

I was thinking, "This is incredible! I can't believe he's willing to drop everything and travel sixty miles just to comfort me and serve me in this crisis. I can't believe he's going to spend time on his knees interceding with his God for my little girl. There's no way in the world that I deserve that—especially from him."

Nearly three decades later I could take you to the precise spot where I received that call. That's how deeply it's seared into my memory. And that's the kind of impact that Christians have when they're willing to go beyond mere words and put the love of Christ into action.

Jesus knew that, which is why he said, "Let your light shine before men, that they may see your good deeds and praise your Father in heaven."[1] That's what being light is all about.

Christians forget that from time to time, but then periodically there's a reminder. For instance, I was reading a book in which author Terry Muck described a letter written by a man who used to have absolutely no interest in spiritual matters.

He lived next door to a Christian, and they had a casual relationship—talks over the back fence, borrowing lawnmowers, stuff like that. Then the non-Christian's wife was stricken with cancer, and she died three months later. Here's part of a letter he wrote afterward:

> I was in total despair. I went through the funeral preparations and the service like I was in a trance. And after the service I went to the path along the river and walked all night. *But I did not walk alone.* My neighbor—afraid for me, I guess—stayed with me all night.
>
> He did not speak; he did not even walk beside me. He just followed me. When the sun finally came up over the river, he came over to me and said, "Let's go get some breakfast."
>
> I go to church now. My neighbor's church. *A religion that can produce the kind of caring and love my neighbor showed me is something I want to find out more about.* I want to be like that. I want to love and be loved like that for the rest of my life.[2]

If you want to be salt and light as Jesus envisioned, here's how: extend his compassion to a neighbor or colleague or friend or stranger who's in need. Instead of being frozen into inaction, just ask yourself, "What would Jesus do?"

Words evaporate quickly, but people remember a gentle act of servanthood forever. Few things are as salt savory or as gently illuminating as a simple act of kindness performed in the name of Jesus.

I can attest to that, because I'll never forget David.

A CONSISTENT CHRISTIANITY

Of all the people who influenced me in my spiritual journey, Linda and Jerry were perhaps the most significant. They were salt and light to me in this way: they were real, even when they didn't know they were being watched.

Years ago Linda and Jerry lived in the same condominium building as Leslie and I, and so we got to know each other pretty well. In fact, our daughter, Alison (who, incidentally, recovered fully from her still-mysterious illness at birth), became best friends with their daughter, Sara.

But what Linda and Jerry didn't realize was how much we were scrutinizing their lifestyle at the time. They were up-front about the fact that they were Christians, and we were curious to see whether they were *real*. Do you know what I mean by that?

We wanted to see whether we could detect a holier-than-thou attitude toward those who didn't subscribe to their theology. We wanted to see how they'd handle conflict in their marriage. We wanted to see whether they'd put on a Christian happy face and pretend they never got angry, worried, or frustrated.

We wanted to see whether they'd be truth tellers and whether they'd ask for forgiveness when they made a mistake. We wanted to see whether they'd hold a grudge if we did something to hurt them. We wanted to see if they were honest about the little things in life. We wanted to hear the comments they would make about people who weren't around.

We watched over a long period of time, and guess what we found? We discovered that they weren't perfect. But then again, they never claimed to be.

Primarily what we saw was a gentle spirit of acceptance toward us, a lot more humility than pride, a willingness to admit when they were wrong, an anxiousness to reconcile when there was conflict, a readiness to acknowledge the rough edges of their character and a sincere effort to smooth them out, a refusal to playact by pretending that the Christian life is always happy, an admission that they struggled with their faith from time to time, but most of all, undergirding everything, we saw an honest desire to become a little more like Jesus, bit by bit, as time went by.

In short, they were *real*. They were salt and light—and Leslie and I became citizens of God's kingdom largely through their example.

Now I don't want to make you paranoid, but if you're a Christ follower you need to know this: *you are being watched*. Your friends, neighbors, and acquaintances are scanning your life with their hypocrisy radar, because they want to know whether you're authentic. And what they observe will either stymie or propel them in their spiritual journey.

So let me come straight out and ask you a question: *What are they going to detect?* Come on, be truthful. Can you honestly say that they will see someone who approaches life with integrity, like Linda and Jerry?

"YOU REPRESENT JESUS TO ME"

Maggie was an example of someone whose perspective on faith had been poisoned by inauthentic Christians. I met her after she ventured, very tentatively, into Willow Creek Community Church, her first visit to any religious institution since childhood. Slowly she became a spiritual seeker, and she wrote me this troubling letter about her earlier experiences with Christians:

> The Christianity I grew up with was so confusing to me even as a child. People said one thing but did another. They appeared very spiritual in public but were abusive in private. What they said and what they did never fit. There was such a discrepancy that I came to hate Christianity, and I did not want to be associated with a church.

Can you see how cosmetic Christians had derailed her journey toward God? But she went on to explain that she had met some Christians at our church and even got involved in a small group of seekers that was led by a Christian couple. She wrote,

> So when I came to Willow Creek and to my small group, I needed gentleness. I needed to be able to ask any question. I needed to have my questions taken seriously. I needed to be treated with respect and validated.
>
> Most of all, I needed to see people whose actions match what they say. I am not looking for perfect, but I am looking for real. *Integrity* is the word that comes to mind. I need to hear real people talk about real life, and I need to know if God is—or can be—a part of real life.
>
> Does he care about the wounds I have? Does he care that I need a place to live? Can I ever be a whole and healthy person? I have asked questions like these. And I have not been laughed at or ignored or invalidated. I have not been pushed or pressured in any way.

Then she added this:

> I don't understand the caring I've received. I don't understand that the leaders don't seem afraid of questions. They don't say things like "You just have to have faith" or "You need to pray more." They don't seem to be afraid to tell who they are. *They seem genuine.*

This young woman ended her letter with a beautiful poem she had written. It contains the heartfelt sentiments of a spiritual seeker toward those of us who are Christians. Read these words carefully, and as you do, imagine that this precious person is speaking directly to you. Because she is.

> *Do you know*
> *do you understand*
> *that you represent*
> *Jesus to me?*

Do you know
do you understand
that when you treat me with gentleness,
it raises the question in my mind
that maybe He is gentle, too.
Maybe He isn't someone
who laughs when I am hurt.

Do you know
do you understand
that when you listen to my questions
and you don't laugh,
I think, "What if Jesus is interested in me, too?"

Do you know
do you understand
that when I hear you talk about arguments
and conflict and scars from your past,
I think, "Maybe I am just a regular person
instead of a bad, no-good little girl
who deserves abuse."

If you care,
I think maybe He cares—
and then there's this flame of hope
that burns inside of me
and for a while
I am afraid to breathe
because it might go out.

Do you know
do you understand
that your words are His words?
Your face, His face
to someone like me?

Please, be who you say you are.
Please, God, don't let this be another trick.
Please let this be real.
Please.

Do you know
do you understand
that you represent
Jesus to me?

Tears pooled in my eyes as I read that poem for the first time. I felt the sting of regret over times when I know spiritual seekers had looked at my life and not seen Jesus. I grieved for the times when my callousness, smugness, or indifference may have slowed someone in their spiritual journey. And I resolved once more just to be *genuine*—with God and with others.

I felt that Maggie's words were so powerful that I wanted to read them to our entire congregation. So I called her one evening to get her permission.

"Maggie, I loved your poem," I told her. "Would it be all right if I read it at the services this weekend?"

"Oh, Lee," she said, "haven't you heard?"

My heart sank. What had happened now? Had she encountered someone who had been like salt that stung or light that glared? Had someone's hypocrisy chased this young woman away from God once again?

"No, Maggie," I replied with trepidation in my voice. "I haven't heard. Tell me what happened."

"No, you don't understand—it's good news," she said. "A few nights ago I gave my life to Jesus!"

I almost jumped out of my chair. "Maggie, that's terrific!" I exclaimed. "That's the best news I've had in a long time. Tell me—what piece of evidence convinced you that the Bible is true? What fact did you uncover that finally established for you that the Resurrection was real?" After all, those were the kind of intellectual issues that played a big role in leading me to faith.

"No, it wasn't like that for me," she replied. *"You see, I just met a whole bunch of people who were like Jesus to me."* She paused as if to shrug. "That's all it took," she said.

I sighed. What a lesson for someone like me, whose first instinct is to try to argue people into God's kingdom with evidence and data and history and logic.

In fact, what a lesson for every Christian: all it took was some people who were salt and light to her—just as Jesus intended in his outrageous strategy that is still managing, after two thousand years, to change the world one life at a time.

GOD CAN GIVE
YOU POWER
AS POWER IS
NEEDED

Ever since I was old enough to read, I wanted to become a newspaper reporter. So when I turned sixteen, I decided to get my first summer job in the industry and begin working my way up the journalistic ladder.

Armed with a directory that listed every daily and weekly periodical in northern Illinois, I stayed home from school one day and started phoning newspapers, in alphabetical order, to see if they wanted to hire an inexperienced teenager.

I called editors in Addison, Antioch, Arlington Heights, and Barrington—sorry, no interest.

I tried Crystal Lake, Dundee, Elgin, Glencoe, Joliet—and one by one the editors turned me down.

After spending most of the day wincing at rejection after rejection, I was getting precariously close to the end of the alphabet. With only a few possibilities left, I called the *Daily Sentinel* in Woodstock, even though I didn't know where the town was located.

I braced myself for another gruff turndown, but instead the editor said, "I might be interested. Come on out and let's talk."

Woodstock turned out to be thirty miles from my house. Since I didn't have a car, I took the train out there, interviewed for the job, and I got it! I was ecstatic—until I found out that the *Sentinel* was an afternoon paper. That meant work began at 6:00 a.m., before any trains were available to shuttle me there.

My only recourse was to go to my parents. "You know how much I want to work on a newspaper," I said, "and now I've got a chance. But I've got to move away from home to do it. I'll be making seventy dollars a week, and I've found a boardinghouse that charges fifteen dollars a week, so I can support myself. How about it? I know I'm only sixteen, but will you let me leave home to follow my dream?"

There are lots of different kinds of parents in the world. Some keep their children on a tight rein, which might be appropriate for some kids, but there's always the danger of inadvertently stifling them.

My parents, though, were the empowering type. They wanted to enable and equip me in a responsible way to have opportunities to grow, learn, and develop. So my mom and dad granted me the permission, and after my sophomore year of high school I moved away from home to work on the Woodstock newspaper. In fact, I ended up working there for three summers, and before I knew it I was climbing the ladder that eventually led to the *Chicago Tribune*.

Here's my point: my parents had virtually complete power over my life, but they didn't use their authority to suppress me. Instead, because they cared deeply about my development and future, they gave me their blessing to become all that I could be.

And that leads me to another one of God's outrageous claims: although he is undeniably powerful, he also chooses to be a *power-sharing* God. He cares enough about us to be willing to infuse us with his strength — *if* we tap into it appropriately. In short, he can give us power as power is needed.

Let me illustrate this with a passage of Scripture that is not only magnificent in its descriptive force but also contains one of the Bible's most encouraging surprise endings.

THE POWER OF A DESERT STORM

In trying to creatively capture the extent of God's incredible strength, King David harkened back to his days as a shepherd, when he would watch awesome storms rumble through the desert with frightening intensity. He wrote what we call Psalm 29, which includes this colorful language extolling God's omnipotence:

> The voice of the LORD is over the waters;

Apparently, this storm was roaring in from the Mediterranean.

> the God of glory thunders,
> the LORD thunders over the mighty waters.
> The voice of the LORD is powerful;
> the voice of the LORD is majestic.
> The voice of the LORD breaks the cedars;
> the LORD breaks in pieces the cedars of Lebanon.

Do you know how big the cedars get in Lebanon? They can grow up to thirty feet in diameter and rise as high as a twelve-story building. But David was saying that a mere whisper from God is enough to spontaneously splinter those towering trees into instant kindling. That's powerful!

> He makes Lebanon skip like a calf,
> Sirion like a young wild ox.

Sirion is a nine-thousand-foot mountain. In other words, God's voice is like a mighty earthquake that makes the plains and mountain ranges shake and quiver and undulate and dance.

> The voice of the LORD strikes
> with flashes of lightning.

Think about the incredible power released by the forty million lightning bolts that strike the United States each year. In a fraction of a second, each lightning flash discharges one hundred million volts of electricity and thirteen thousand million horsepower, at a temperature five times hotter than the surface of the sun! Yet a single utterance from the lips of the Lord is far more potent than all of the lightning in the eighteen hundred thunderstorms taking place at any given moment around the planet.

> The voice of the LORD shakes the desert;
> the LORD shakes the Desert of Kadesh.

Kadesh is in the south; Sirion is in the north — what this means is that God's tremendous power flows across the entire land. Nobody can flee from it.

> The voice of the LORD twists the oaks
> and strips the forests bare.

Remember seeing photographs after Mount St. Helens erupted? In a blast with the explosive force of five hundred atomic bombs, giant trees were toppled like matchsticks and stripped clean of their bark over a total of 230 square miles — millions and millions of trees, enough to construct three hundred thousand houses. Yet that is child's play compared with the power of God. It would only take a murmur from him to flatten the entire 815 million acres of the Amazon Rainforest.

So what's our natural response to a God whose strength is so immense that it completely dwarfs the incredible energy released in a desert storm?

> And in his temple all cry, "Glory!"
> The LORD sits enthroned over the flood;
> the LORD is enthroned as King forever.

What other reaction can we have but to worship him for being such a mighty and breathtakingly awesome God who richly deserves to reign over all of his creation?

But then David's poem takes a critically important turn. After describing God's power, the psalm comes to a sudden conclusion with a totally unexpected twist:

> The LORD gives strength to his people;
> the LORD blesses his people with peace.

Here's the point: our omnipotent God doesn't simply hoard his power. Instead, he is an empowering Deity who offers to share his strength with those he created. And that's a good thing, because the result is that we can find peace when we're panicky, endurance when we're empty, and courage when we're cowardly. "For God did not give us a spirit of timidity," said the apostle Paul, "but a spirit of power, of love and of self-discipline."[1]

What an outrageous claim from an outlandishly strong God!

Who doesn't need power like that in their life? Who wouldn't want to be on the receiving end of God's generous offer to infuse us with his supernatural strength? There are lots of areas in which we could benefit from tapping into his might, but I'm going to focus on three of our most common needs: power when there's pain, power when we're tempted, and power to do the right thing.

POWER WHEN A ROGUE WIND THREATENS

For instance, we need God's power to get us through the times of pain that we simply don't believe we can get through on our own. Let me give you an example.

I was having lunch one Saturday afternoon in August when the kitchen phone rang. The caller identified himself as an emergency room physician, and he said a friend of mine named Bob urgently needed to talk to me. My first thought was, "Uh-oh. Knowing Bob and how intense he is, I bet he's had a heart attack."

The doctor handed the phone to Bob, but the noise that came through the receiver didn't sound human—it was an anguished and heartrending wail.

"Bob," I said, "calm down, calm down. Tell me what's wrong."

It took a few moments for Bob to catch his breath and gather his composure as best he could. "It's my daughter," he managed to say before bursting into sobs again. "She's been hit by a drunk driver. They're saying she's brain-dead! Please, Lee—come to the hospital!"

I arrived in the intensive care unit in a matter of minutes. There she was, the side of her head shaven from emergency brain surgery, her eyes swollen shut, her face bruised and battered, a machine breathing for her. It was a horrendous sight.

I took Bob's hand and I took hers, which was limp and cold, and I prayed for both of them. And as I was praying, I couldn't help thinking about my only daughter and how I once felt so powerless as an atheist while I stood beside her crib in the hospital's neonatal care unit and watched her fight for her young life.

Let me tell you something very sobering: what happened to my friend Bob is going to happen to you. It may not be the same sort of tragedy, but it's inevitable that you—someday, somehow—will experience the kind of soul-piercing heartbreak that comes from a loss too painful to bear. You're not immune and neither am I.

Jesus said as much: "These things I have spoken to you, that in Me you may have peace. In the world, you have tribulation, but take courage; I have overcome the world."[2] He was saying with clarity that we live in a place that has been distorted and corrupted by sin, and we will have to suffer the consequences during the time that we're here.

But in that verse Jesus also offers hope. He says that we can receive the very two things we need the most when a rogue wind threatens to capsize our life—peace and courage. And where do they come from? From a God who gives us the strength to get through the pain that we thought we could never get through on our own.

Today if you were to sit down with my friend Bob over a cup of coffee, he would tell you in no uncertain terms that his daughter's death was the deepest and darkest valley he's ever trudged through. But he would also tell you with conviction that if God hadn't walked with him and empowered him and strengthened him, he never would have made it out the other side. No, not in one piece.

When the day comes that you need to access that kind of strength, how will you get it? That's the big question, isn't it? *How*. Well, hold on for a few moments, and then I'll deal with that issue as clearly as I can.

POWER WHEN TEMPTATIONS BECKON

Not only do we desperately need the strength of God when tragedy stalks us, but we also need his power to avoid doing what we know we shouldn't do.

Temptations lure us every day. I once saw a bumper sticker that said, "Lead me not into temptation; I'm perfectly capable of finding it on my own." C. S. Lewis put it this way: "A silly idea is current that good people do not know what temptation means. This is an obvious lie. Only those who try to resist temptation know how strong it is."

Temptations are those unethical or immoral shortcuts that inevitably lead us down a dead-end road:

- Should you shade the truth on your résumé? *Hey, nobody ever checks those things.*
- Should you make a move on that new person at work? *If you're discreet, your spouse will never suspect.*

- Should you rent that X-rated movie? *What's the harm; you're an adult.*
- Should you take credit for your assistant's ideas? *If you do it right, he'll never find out and you'll reap the rewards.*
- Should you report that side income to the IRS? *Certainly not, they don't have any way of tracking it.*
- Should you go way out to the end of an already shaky financial limb and buy that expensive car? *You deserve some fun, don't you?*

Before I became a Christian, I had two criteria for determining which temptations I would indulge in. First, how much pleasure would it bring me? And second, what were the odds I'd get in trouble? As a result, I ended up giving in to short-term pleasures that inevitably yielded long-term headaches.

After I became a follower of Jesus, I found that temptations didn't stop. To make matters worse, my initial viewpoint of God's attitude toward temptations was all wrong. I pictured God as if he had a choke collar on me, like the one I put on my giant dog, Nick, when I was a kid. Every time Nick would threaten to wander where he thought he could have some fun—maybe to get to know that cute little poodle down the block—I gave that collar a quick pull and he was yanked back into line. I pictured God holding my leash, just daring me to succumb to a temptation so he could angrily jerk me back by the neck. So I felt intimidated and alone.

But as I read the Bible, I found out that's not God's attitude at all. He isn't arbitrarily trying to spoil my fun; he lovingly wants to protect me from the emotional, physical, relational, and spiritual downside that can come when we indulge ourselves in temptations.

Actually, he's in my corner. "For we do not have a high priest who is unable to sympathize with our weaknesses," says the Bible, "but we have one who has been tempted in every way, just as we are—yet was without sin."[3]

It's always easier to talk about dealing with temptation with someone who's been there. So now when I talk to Jesus about the pressures I'm under to compromise my morality or take ethical shortcuts, I don't imagine him saying, "Tsk, tsk! Shame on you for even having those thoughts!" Instead, I picture him saying, "I know, I know. Believe me, I understand. Here—let me help you."

And he does help. "God is faithful; he will not let you be tempted beyond what you can bear," the apostle Paul assured us. "But when you are tempted, he will also provide a way out so that you can stand up under it."[4]

But again the real question is *how*. Practically speaking, how can we access that strength? Well, hang on a little longer and we'll explore that.

POWER TO LIVE RIGHT

God says he can help us avoid those harmful activities that we know we shouldn't get entangled in. But what about the flip side of that? The truth is, we also need God's help to do what we know we *should* do but what we lack the power to do on our own.

If you've read the Bible, you know it contains a lot of teaching about how we should live if we want to be men and women of godly character. But I'm willing to confess that without God's help, I just can't do a lot of it.

- Serve others? Sorry, but I'd rather put my own needs first.
- Be humble? Everybody knows that the way to get ahead these days is to be your own biggest cheerleader.
- Be generous? My inclination is to cling to my possessions.
- Be patient? Not likely when you're stuck in rush hour traffic through a construction zone or behind someone with thirty items in the express lane at the grocery store.

- Forgive those who've hurt me? Hey, I come from Chicago, where the credo is, "Don't get mad—get even!"

As Christians, our objective in life should be that "Christ is formed" in us.[5] That involves going down an often-arduous path of submission, growth, and maturity that, frankly, I simply can't walk by myself. I need God's power if I'm going to make progress—but again comes the question of *how*. Isn't that the key? We all *want* God's power, but how do we *get* it? I don't want to skirt that issue any longer.

Accessing the power of God isn't a matter of pushing the right buttons, chanting the right words, and then suddenly being transformed into a Christian version of the Mighty Morphin Power Rangers. However, there are some biblical steps we can take when we're feeling overwhelmed by tragedy, vulnerable to temptation, or too weak to grow in character—or for that matter, when we feel timid, defeated, or fragile in our faith.

I call them the "five A's" to make them easier for me to remember. I discovered them while searching the pages of the Bible, and as I've applied them in my own life through the years, I've invariably found that they are a tremendous help. As you read them, consider how they can position you to tap into the power of our omnipotent God.

Step #1: Admit That You're Weak Without God

My first reaction in a crisis is to try to get through it by myself, because I don't like to depend on anyone else. But here's the thing: *we can't be filled with the power of God until we first empty ourselves of the pretense that we can get by on our own.*

We need to admit that we can't get through this tragedy, we can't resist this temptation, we can't mold our character, without some outside intervention. So often in Scripture—from Moses to Paul—we see people humbly admitting their weakness first and then God filling them with his power.

In fact, Paul said at one point, "But [the Lord] said to me, 'My grace is sufficient for you, for my power is made perfect in weakness.' Therefore I will boast all the more gladly about my weaknesses, so that Christ's power may rest on me."[6]

The longer we stubbornly resist the obvious — that we're ultimately powerless by ourselves — the deeper we sink into the mire. After all, we can't reach out and cling to God's strength if we're too busy straining to clutch our own self-sufficiency.

"Nothing so furthers our prayer life as the feeling of our own helplessness," Ole Hallesby wrote in his classic book *Prayer*. "It is only when we are helpless that we really open our hearts to God."

Step #2: Affirm God's Power and Presence

Once we come face-to-face with the reality of our own weakness, we need to remind ourselves that we follow an all-powerful God who all throughout history has an uncanny track record of infusing his followers with strength.

The Bible says we need to keep that truth at the forefront of our mind: "Look to the LORD and his strength; seek his face always. Remember the wonders he has done, his miracles, and the judgments he pronounced."[7]

In other words, let yourself dwell on how he empowered Moses, strengthened David, undergirded Daniel, emboldened Peter, and supported Paul. Remember how time after time God has proven himself to be trustworthy.

A while ago I met with a young woman who had a very fragile and doubt-plagued faith. As we talked, the reason became apparent: she had never really read the Bible. She wasn't familiar with the great history of how God has repeatedly come through for his followers. So I picked up a pad of paper and wrote a simple prescription: "Read the Bible." Don't just consume Christian books and tapes. Study the real thing.

In addition to acknowledging God's power, we also should affirm his willingness to be present in our lives.

Alison was once in a high school chorus that sang "From a Distance," the song Bette Midler made popular. When they came to the lyrics that said, "God is watching us from a distance," I wanted to stand up and shout, "Hey, that's not true!"

Out of sympathy for Alison, I restrained myself. But I wanted to let everybody know that God doesn't just see us from afar. He's here. He's close. He's accessible. The Lord told Joshua, "Be strong and courageous. Do not be terrified; do not be discouraged, for the LORD your God will be with you wherever you go."[8]

Just affirming this truth can make a big difference. Our confidence, courage, and strength are bolstered when we remember that the same God who has empowered his people throughout the ages is the very same God who's willing to be present in our life today—right now, in the midst of our crisis, temptation, or character crossroads.

Step #3: Align Yourself with God's Will

Remember the country-western song with the plaintive refrain, "Looking for love in all the wrong places"? The truth is that sometimes we're looking for God's strength for all the wrong reasons. However, God's power isn't contained in some electrical outlet that we can plug into for any purpose we want.

"I am the vine; you are the branches," Jesus said.[9] That means you and I need to be intimately connected with God and his purposes. He goes on to say, "If a man remains in me and I in him, he will bear much fruit." In other words, it's when we're working in concert and harmony with God that he's willing to give us the power to accomplish great things. The verse concludes with this stark but appropriate reminder: "Apart from me you can do nothing." When we're independently pursuing our own agenda, we shouldn't have the expectation that God will necessarily contribute to it.

Think about it. It wouldn't make sense for God to supernaturally renew our strength so we could pursue a pet project that runs contrary to his own plan for our life. We need to make sure we're traveling the road he wants for us before we seek his help in moving down it. Look at it this way: if he wants what's best for us, wouldn't it make sense for us to get in sync with him?

Aligning ourselves with God's will begins when we initially put our trust in Jesus Christ as the forgiver of our sins and the leader of our life. And it's an ongoing process as we continue to grow in our relationship with him and increasingly submit to his agenda for our life.

As we mature in our faith, we become more and more adept at discerning his will. We grow familiar with his voice. We immerse ourselves in his Book and consistently test everything against it. We receive guidance from the indwelling Holy Spirit. We seek wise counsel from other Christians. And we develop confidence that as we head in God's direction, we're going the right way—and he will be available to encourage and empower us.

Step #4: Ask God for the Power You Need

When I was in high school, my brother Ray bought a gleaming new Corvette convertible. Of course, I always wanted to borrow it, but I was too intimidated to come right out and ask. So I would beat around the bush by dropping not-so-subtle hints.

"I guess the car's just going to sit there all night, huh?" I'd say casually. "All alone. All by itself. Sort of a shame. It looks like it might need some exercise...." I'd go on and on until Ray would finally exclaim, "Look, Lee, if you want to borrow the car, just *ask*!"

Too often we desperately want God's intervention in our lives, but we beat around the bush. The Bible says simply, "You do not have, because you do not ask God."[10] We need to come right out and express to him the desire of our heart.

Having admitted our inability to handle the matter ourselves, having affirmed God's power and presence in our life, and having aligned ourselves with God by wanting what he wants for us, we should forthrightly and specifically ask him for his supernatural help.

Sometimes I've done that and—*wow!*—I've experienced a flood of boldness, courage, and effectiveness that I can only attribute to the work of God in my life. For instance, I can think of times when I've been cowering in fear before getting up to speak to a crowd. I would be absolutely convinced of both their disinterest and my inability to say anything worthwhile. But after going through these first four steps, I would find myself in the middle of my talk and think, "Where did *this* come from? Why am I able to clearly articulate thoughts that seemed so muddled just an hour ago? Why do I feel confidence instead of cowardice?" And I would know without a doubt that the source was God.

But I'll be honest—it doesn't always happen that way. There are times when I've gone through those first four steps and I don't feel any different. I'm still scared and weak. Has that ever happened to you? If so, what should you do? I've found that the best strategy is to move to the final step.

Step #5: Act Out of Obedience to God

My friend Bill Hybels pointed out to me a pattern in Scripture that teaches this: *even when we don't feel empowered, if we nevertheless take action by obediently proceeding down the road that God wants us to walk, he will give us power as power is needed.*

As an example, Bill pointed to Jesus in the Garden of Gethsemane. He was overwhelmed with emotion over his impending death. He felt weak and fearful, but after praying and ensuring that he was aligned with his Father's will, he obediently walked out of that garden, into the arms of his betrayer, and down the road toward death. God gave him strength as strength was needed.

He was able to endure the whipping, the beating, the mocking, the crown of thorns, the searing nails in his hands and feet, and the crushing weight of the world's sins on his shoulders. He got through all of it until he declared, "It is finished,"[11] having paid the price to redeem the world. God the Father made sure his Son had the exact amount of strength he needed to carry out his all-important redemptive mission in the world.

And when you and I walk down the road of obedience to God even when we're not feeling empowered, what we're doing is demonstrating *faith*. Faith isn't just believing something—it's belief *and* behavior. It's believing something and taking action in accordance with what we believe. Someone once defined faith as "belief gone courageous."

The Bible says, "Without faith it is impossible to please God."[12] But it's also true that *with* faith—that is, by being obedient and by trusting that God will come through for us—we'll receive power as power is needed.

I've seen this demonstrated in my own life time after time. For example, a while ago I knew I should reconcile with someone I had mistreated, but I felt too intimidated and embarrassed to do it. It was going to be hard for me to admit fault. I was afraid he might rage at me. I wasn't even sure how I would bring up the subject without being awkward about it.

So I admitted that I needed God's strength. I affirmed that he's powerful and that he's with me. I knew I was aligned with his will, because the Bible tells me, "If it is possible, as far as it depends on you, live at peace with everyone."[13] And I prayed, asking God for the courage to follow through.

Instead of feeling electrified with power, I still felt apprehensive and inadequate. Even so, I made the conscious decision to take the fifth step. That meant I had to *act* by doing what I knew God wanted me to do.

I went over to the phone and forced myself to dial the man's number, knowing that if I walked down the road of obedience, God would give me power as power was needed. And sure enough, as the conversation unfolded that night, God emboldened me and strengthened me through that very difficult talk, and today I'm reconciled with that friend.

So if you need power in your life, *take action*. If you're overwhelmed by a personal tragedy, put one foot in front of the other and go to your church to seek help, trusting that God will give you strength as strength is needed.

If temptation has its tentacles wrapped around you, *take action*. Pick up the phone to tell the off-limits person you've been flirting with that this must stop. Pack up the X-rated videos and throw them out. Open your closet and begin packing so you can move out from the live-in arrangement with your boyfriend or girlfriend. Yes, these are difficult steps to take, but when you move in the direction you know God wants you to go, you can trust that he will give you power as power is needed.

If character shortcomings are keeping you from doing what you know is right, *take action*. Go to the phone and dial a trusted Christian friend. Tell him about it and ask him to lovingly hold you accountable and help you grow in this area. And expect that God will give you power as power is needed.

Brother Andrew can testify to the effectiveness of this step. He has gained the nickname God's Smuggler for creatively sneaking millions of Bibles into closed countries throughout the world, including societies so hostile to Christianity that nobody thought anybody could penetrate them. How was he able to do it?

Once he sensed God was leading him to bring Christian materials into a nation, Brother Andrew took concrete action in obedience, even when the door of entry seemed securely shut at first. Somehow as he approached the border with his books, God would always empower him to fulfill his mission. Brother Andrew described it this way:

The door may seem closed, but it's only closed the way a super-market door is closed. It stays shut when you remain at a distance, but as you deliberately move toward it, a magic eye above it sees you coming, and the door opens. God is waiting for us to walk forward in obedience so he can open the door for us to serve him.[14]

What you'll find is that when you demonstrate faith by taking specific steps of obedience to God, he is more than willing to inter-vene supernaturally in your life. Through it all, just hold on to the words of King David: "Commit your way to the LORD, trust also in him *and he will do it.* And he will bring forth your righteousness as the light, and your judgment as the noonday."[15]

POWER TO REACH YOUR POTENTIAL

Chances are, you need God's strength for some area of your life. We all do, and God already knows that. In fact, as God looks at you right now, sitting there reading this book, what does he see?

Does he see someone who's timid, fearful, and paralyzed? Someone who's buckling under the weight of life? Someone who routinely caves in to temptations? Someone who's unable to sum-mon the courage to do what's right or who feels too weak to stop from doing what's wrong? Someone whose faith gauge is register-ing dangerously near empty? What does God see when he looks at you?

Hold on a second—don't answer too fast.

First let me tell you a story. It's about someone who was the weakest member of a faithless family living on the wrong side of the tracks. He had a tentative and doubt-filled personality. And when we encounter him in the Bible, he's cowering out of fear that some marauding outlaws might murder him.

His name was Gideon. One day an angel appeared to him, and guess how he greeted this quivering coward?

He could have called out, "Hey, you yellow-bellied chicken!" or "Hey, you with the flimsy spine!" But instead, the angel said something entirely unexpected. He declared, "Hey, Gideon, *you mighty warrior!*"

Why did he call him that? Because God was able to see Gideon not only for what he was but for what he could become—*if* he accessed the power of God. With that God knew Gideon had the potential to develop into a difference maker who acted out of courage and boldness.

In the end Gideon did receive God's strength. Even though he stumbled occasionally, he went on to achieve great things for God. And his name has lived through the centuries to this very day.[16]

So let me rephrase my question: *As God looks at you sitting there right now, what might he call out to you?*

How about "Hey, you difference maker!" or "Hey, you kingdom builder!" or "Hey, you great man of character!" or "Hey, you wonderful woman of integrity!" or "Hey, you tremendous parent!" or "Hey, you with the inspiring faith!" or "Hey, you pillar of strength!" or "Hey, you model of virtue!" or "Hey, you modern-day Gideon!"

Think for a moment. Imagine what you might become if you lean on the strength of God instead of your own. Go ahead—consider the possibilities.

You can be sure of this: God already has.

YOU GAIN
WHEN YOU GIVE
YOURSELF AWAY

His name is George, but that's not what the bullies called him at his junior high school near Chicago. Day after day they pelted him with names like "stupid," "moron," and "weird." They taunted him, pushed him, punched him, and tried to goad him into fighting—all because George is a little different.

In the end they won a bitter victory. Because of the incessant harassment and the inability of teachers to curtail it, George's parents decided to pull him out of school and teach him at home.

Unfortunately, bullies are a way of life. They are the people who are stronger than we are—physically, economically, or whatever—and who take great pleasure in pushing us around just so we don't forget it. Statistics indicate that three out of four people have been victimized by a bully at one time in their life. Said one expert, "Bullying is all about power."

In the preceding chapter, we talked about the phenomenal power of God. And if the old adage is true—that power corrupts and absolute power corrupts absolutely—it would be understandable if God were a cosmic bully, throwing his weight around, belittling and intimidating us, and smugly rubbing our noses in the fact that in the grand scheme of things he's the boss and we are nothing but puny and weak.

But that's not what God is like.

Look at what happened as Jesus ate with his followers one day, as recorded in John 13. The third and fourth verses of that chapter constitute one of the most outrageous individual sentences in the entire Bible. It's like a non sequitur, in which two thoughts just don't seem to go together, because they're fundamentally at odds.

The first part of the sentence says, "Jesus knew that the Father had put all things under his power, and that he had come from God and was returning to God; so ..." In other words, Jesus was fully aware that he was God, that he was all-powerful, that he could do whatever he wanted, that he had existed from eternity as part of the Trinity and would soon return to his hallowed and exalted stature in heaven.

But then there's that seemingly insignificant word *so*. So ... knowing all that heady, ego-inflating stuff, what does Jesus do? Does he use his superiority to bully the disciples? Does he arrogantly demand that they pamper and cater to him?

Here's the incongruous conclusion to the sentence: "So he got up from the meal, took off his outer clothing, and wrapped a towel around his waist." Unexpectedly, amazingly, Jesus took on the demeanor of a servant, getting ready to wash his disciples' dirty, grimy, smelly feet and gently pat them dry with a towel. The all-powerful, all-knowing Jesus was choosing to perform a distasteful task that was so demeaning that none of the disciples had been willing to stoop to do it themselves. What an incredible, humble display of pure servanthood—from the one who could have rightfully demanded to be served himself!

Who can fathom this great and wonderful mystery, that Jesus "did not come to be served, but to serve, and to give his life as a ransom for many"?[1]

PASSING THE TOWEL TO YOU

Even though the concepts of raw power and lowly servanthood appear to contradict each other, both qualities unquestionably reside in God. Ultimately, God is a servant because God is love, and love by its very nature involves the giving of oneself. In fact, that's the essence of Christ's life as described in Philippians 2:6–8, which Eugene Peterson renders so masterfully in *The Message*:

> [Jesus] had equal status with God but didn't think so much of himself that he had to cling to the advantages of that status no matter what. Not at all. When the time came, he set aside the privileges of deity and took on the status of a slave, became *human*! Having become human, he stayed human. It was an incredibly humbling process. He didn't claim special privileges. Instead, he lived a selfless, obedient life and then died a selfless, obedient death—and the worst kind of death at that: a crucifixion.[2]

That's what we commemorate on Good Friday—that Jesus served as our substitute to pay the death penalty we deserve for the wrongdoing we've committed. This Jesus who by all rights could have been a bully, instead became a suffering servant for you and me, even though our rebellion and wrongdoing warrant nothing less than eternal condemnation.

Outrageous? Absolutely! And yet that's just the beginning of the story, because Jesus then asks you and me to do something outlandish, too. Having towel-dried the last of his disciples' feet, Jesus turned to those assembled and uttered these remarkable words: "I have set you an example that you should do as I have done for you."[3]

And here's the point I want to make: it's understandable that we would want to worship God for his willingness to be a servant so we could be forgiven and reconciled with him. But as counterintuitive as it sounds, we also ought to be thanking him for inviting us into a servant lifestyle. Because in the end that's where we'll find the kind of soul satisfaction that we would otherwise miss if we merely lived to indulge ourselves.

The Influence of Towel Bearers

Fresh out of journalism school, having worked as a reporter at the *Chicago Tribune* for only five months, I was given the intimidating assignment of writing a thirty-part series on the poor of Chicago. The concept was for me to profile a different needy family each day, telling their story in a human interest feature that would encourage people to give to the Neediest Kids Fund, a joint effort of the Chicago media to help underprivileged children at Christmas.

As I delved into this assignment, roaming the city in search of appropriate families to write about, I stumbled across something that I had never really thought about before. For the first time, my eyes were opened to the vast, informal network of Christians who were sacrificially serving the poor. I came upon food pantries, homeless shelters, clothing centers, job-training institutes, nursing homes, drug rehabilitation programs, sports ministries for kids—all operated by Christian charities.

I was especially inspired by an emergency shelter for homeless families that was operated by the Salvation Army on Chicago's North Side. During my research I became a regular in that facility, hanging around to talk with displaced families but also quietly observing the volunteers who poured their lives into selflessly serving these otherwise forgotten people. For me personally, the *Tribune* assignment faded into the background as I began focusing on the much larger story of what was motivating these Christians to give so much of their time, energy, and money to helping others. As an atheist, it just didn't make sense to me. I wanted to know *why*.

These volunteers weren't serving reluctantly or out of compulsion. On the contrary, it energized them. It seemed to bring them great excitement and contentment. It appeared to flow naturally out of their lives. Over and over I got the sense that they simply couldn't *not* serve. It was woven into the fabric of who they were.

And their impact, though rarely written about, was mind-boggling. They founded hospitals, ran schools, provided food, donated clothing, performed counseling, rehabilitated buildings, cared for the elderly, served unwed mothers, weaned addicts off drugs, trained the unemployed, built homes, and offered encouragement. What's more, they gave huge amounts of their money. One study showed that churches and synagogues contribute more than any other nongovernmental institution to America's social services. Donations top nineteen billion dollars a year, with another six billion dollars' worth of volunteer effort being offered annually.[4]

I learned that these "towel bearers," who reach out to care for people much as Jesus washed the feet of his followers, are primarily motivated by gratitude for the way Christ served them with his death. And they have found that as a supernatural by-product of their servanthood, God has a tendency to flow satisfaction into their lives as well. Fulfillment isn't their goal, but in the end it's what they receive.

While I was doing some research into the very different lives of Mother Teresa and the rock star Madonna, I came across an unexpected contrast. Here was Madonna, who has focused all her energies on trying to please herself, saying she doesn't even *know* anybody who's happy. But Mother Teresa devoted her entire life to serving God and others, and she said she was incredibly satisfied.

I wanted to know, *What's the origin of that kind of fulfillment?* And through the years—first as a skeptic, then as a Christian myself—I've noticed six specific sources for it. Walk with me through these next few pages, and we'll explore them together.

TOWEL BEARERS FIND FULFILLMENT IN BEING OBEDIENT TO GOD

John Newton callously dealt in the commodity of human flesh as a slave trader before Christ transformed his life. He's best remembered for writing the song "Amazing Grace," but one of his most enduring insights was a comment about servanthood. He said that if two angels in heaven were given assignments by God at the same instant, one of them to go and rule over the greatest nation on earth and the other to go sweep the streets of the dirtiest village, *each angel would be completely indifferent as to which one got which assignment.*

It simply wouldn't matter to them. Why? Because the real joy lies in being obedient to God. *For a Christ follower, the important thing isn't what God has us doing; the important thing is that we're doing what God wants us to do.*

When we're obedient to God's direction for our life, the Holy Spirit gives us a quiet sense of affirmation, sort of like a celestial pat on the back. And I'll tell you what: towel bearers live for God's smile of approval on their lives. It fires them up like nothing else.

TOWEL BEARERS FIND FULFILLMENT IN USING THEIR SPIRITUAL GIFTS

When I traveled to a Christian-run orphanage in south India in 1987, I brought along an instant camera because I knew the children had never seen a photograph of themselves. I would snap a picture of them, one at a time, and then watch the expression on their faces while the photo slowly developed in front of their eyes. As it gained greater and greater clarity, their eyes would get wider and wider, and they'd break into a broad smile. Then they'd giggle and laugh. They were absolutely fascinated to see what they looked like on film.

An analogous process happens to Christians when they go through a training course to discover their spiritual gift, that divine enablement that God gives each of his followers so they can serve him and others. The Bible lists such gifts as teaching, administration, evangelism, leadership, mercy, helping, shepherding, encouragement, and others.

As the course unfolds, the participants begin to see themselves as they never have before. They identify their gifts, explore their temperament and personality type, and discover that they are uniquely wired up to accomplish something significant for the kingdom of God. As they get greater and greater clarity about their potential to be a difference maker, it's as if they're seeing themselves in a completely new light.

I remember when I first discovered that my primary spiritual gift is evangelism, or helping others understand what it means to become a follower of Jesus. It happened out of nowhere one day when my boss at the newspaper asked me why I was a Christian. I had never explained that to anybody before, but I closed his office door and talked for forty-five minutes about the difference Christ was making in my life.

When I emerged from his office, it was as if my entire life up until that meeting had been a movie shot in very grainy black-and-white film with scratchy sound—but this forty-five minutes had been in bright, vivid Technicolor with rich Dolby stereo! Instantly I knew I wanted to develop and deploy my evangelism gift in any way I could from that day forward.

There's a unique sense of fulfillment that comes when we submit our gifts to God's use and ask him to energize them in a supernatural way—and then step back to watch what he does. It can be the difference between merely existing in black and white and living a life in full, brilliant color.

TOWEL BEARERS FIND FULFILLMENT IN COSTLY SACRIFICES

Fulfillment and *fun* aren't necessarily synonyms. Lots of times, serving others is physically taxing, emotionally draining, financially expensive, or downright dangerous. Yet amazingly, those are the very times when God seems to delight in bringing an extra dose of grace into the lives of towel bearers.

A hard-nosed British journalist saw this for himself when he traveled to India to see Mother Teresa's ministry in Calcutta. After watching the volunteers serving with her, he wrote, "Their life is tough and austere by worldly standards, but I have never in my life met such delightful, happy servants, or seen such an atmosphere of absolute joy as they create." Even in the midst of costly sacrifice, God was flowing a refreshing river of satisfaction into their lives.

I once read a moving story that David Jeremiah wrote about the founder of World Vision, the international Christian relief agency. Bob Pierce had advanced leukemia, but he went to visit a colleague in Indonesia before he died. As they were walking through a small village, they came upon a young girl lying on a bamboo mat next to a river. She was dying of cancer and had only a short time to live.

Bob was indignant. He demanded to know why she wasn't in a clinic. But his friend explained that she was from the jungle and wished to spend her last days next to the river, where it was cool and familiar.

As Bob gazed at her, he felt such compassion that he got down on his knees in the mud, took her hand, and began stroking it. Although she didn't understand him, he prayed for her. Afterward she looked up and said something. "What did she say?" Bob asked his friend.

His friend replied, "She said, 'If I could only sleep again, if I could only sleep again.'" It seemed that her pain was too great to allow her the relief of rest.

Bob began to weep. Then he reached into his pocket and took out his own sleeping pills, the ones his doctor had given him because the pain from his leukemia was too great for him to sleep at night.

He handed the bottle to his friend. "You make sure this young lady gets a good night's sleep," he said, "as long as these pills last."

Bob was ten days away from where he could get his prescription refilled. That meant ten painful and restless nights. That day his servanthood cost him greatly. But even in the midst of his suffering, God infused him with a supernatural sense of satisfaction that he had done the right thing.[5]

I'm not saying that servants should constantly abuse themselves or merely become passive doormats. But I am saying that towel bearing inevitably carries costs, and even when the cost is high, God can nevertheless be counted upon to bring fulfillment to his followers.

TOWEL BEARERS FIND FULFILLMENT WHEN GOD TURNS THEIR PAIN TO GAIN

Some towel bearers are wounded servants. Having themselves faced tragedy or sorrow, illness or loss, they are then able to turn around and uniquely help people who are facing similar circumstances. They find particular pleasure—almost a kind of spiritual revenge against the injustice of a sin-corrupted world—as they witness how God takes their afflictions and draws something positive from them.

Yolanda Lugo is an example. Four years before I first talked with her, she had developed Hodgkin's disease, which is cancer of the lymph system. For a twenty-year-old woman just beginning to enjoy life, it was a devastating diagnosis, especially since physicians warned her that the disease was already spreading rather extensively through her body.

Yolanda told me how she had asked God to give her the strength to battle her illness, and he did. He gave her courage and fortitude as she underwent chemotherapy, radiation treatment, and surgery. Eventually her cancer went into remission.

Despite her suffering, Yolanda kept alive her dream of becoming a New York City police officer. She persevered because of her desire "to serve and protect," and finally, at age twenty-four, she was selected to join the department. It was a personal triumph for her—but she never foresaw how God would choose to use her illness to accomplish something that nobody else could have done.

The drama unfolded one day when Yolanda was driving home on the Verrazano Narrows Bridge, which connects Staten Island and Brooklyn. Suddenly a man jumped from his car and clambered to the top of a bridge abutment that was two hundred feet above the water.

Yolanda slammed on her brakes and ran over. "What are you doing?" she shouted.

"Get away from me!" came the reply. "I'm going to jump! I'm going to kill myself!"

Yolanda had never faced anything like this before. She wasn't sure what to do, so she just tried talking to him. He responded by cutting her off. "Look, get out of here!" he shouted. "I know you don't care about me!"

"Hey, I'm off duty. I didn't have to stop. I don't have to be here. I don't have to talk to you," Yolanda said. "But I want to. I want to help."

The man paused. "Well, then," he said. "Come on up."

Yolanda wasn't fond of heights, and this abutment overlooked a twenty-story drop to the icy water below. But she only hesitated for a moment. Then Yolanda—who weighed all of ninety-nine pounds—climbed up. When she managed to get close enough to the man, she tried to talk him down again, but every time, he would turn hostile and threaten once more to jump.

"You don't care about me!" he said. "Nobody does. My wife has left me; I've got all kinds of family problems. I'm going to end it all right now—"

He was poised to leap. Yolanda had only a split second to respond. But when she spoke, her words stopped him cold. "I know about problems," she said softly.

The man was taken off guard. Again he paused. "What do you mean?" he asked, sounding genuinely curious. "How can a person like you know about problems?"

Yolanda told him, "I've got cancer."

"Really? Where do you have cancer?"

Yolanda started describing her illness to him. She talked about her own fears and uncertainties. She spoke about the pain she had endured. And she explained how God had helped her cope with her circumstances.

"I got help," she said. *"Please—let me help you."*

Several tense moments passed. "Maybe I need a friend," he said quietly.

Yolanda smiled. "Then I'll be your friend."

I don't know if any psychiatrist could have talked that desperate man out of suicide. He was right on the edge of leaping into oblivion. But I know this: he connected with Yolanda because of the pain and problems she had gone through. God used her own pain to reach that man in the unique way that he needed to be helped.

In the end he climbed down with her, and she accompanied him as he went to receive counseling and spiritual help. The following day the newspapers hailed Yolanda as a hero. But she would be the first to tell you that it was God who turned her illness—her liability—into an asset to save another life.

He does that all the time, usually in less spectacular ways. For those with physical or emotional scars, for those who have been beaten up by life or have endured relational wounds, God can open up opportunities to influence others who are going through a similar ordeal. And when he does that, it's an inspiring sight to behold and a satisfying mission to fulfill.

TOWEL BEARERS FIND FULFILLMENT IN POINTING PEOPLE TOWARD CHRIST

Bill Perkins told me the story about a little British orphan staring longingly through the window of a donut shop right after World War II. The scent had his mouth watering, but he didn't have any money. He was quietly praying for something good to eat.

An American soldier happened by. "You want some?" he asked, gesturing toward the bakery. The boy nodded eagerly, so the American went inside, bought a dozen donuts, and silently handed the bag to the youngster.

The kid looked down at the bag, then up into the soldier's face. "Mister," he said with a voice of innocent wonder, *"are you God?"*

In a way, towel bearers represent Christ to those they serve. "Let your light shine before men," said Jesus, "that they may see your good deeds and praise your Father in heaven."[6]

One of the more exhilarating thrills for a towel bearer is when their love for Jesus shines through their servanthood so much that somebody opens up to God for the first time. Then the towel bearer gets to watch the amazing spectacle of God revolutionizing another human life—to see their values transformed, their relationships renewed, their character overhauled, and their priorities rearranged.

A while ago I had a chance to serve a friend who was going through some tough personal circumstances. I spent a week counseling him, and in the end he made the decision to follow Jesus. Now his life is beginning to change. In fact, here's a note he wrote to me a few weeks later:

Lee,

I've been reading the Bible *every* night. I'm nearly through Matthew. It's an *amazing* book! The first time I read it, twenty-four years ago, it meant little to me. Now nearly every sentence has a profound message and impacts my life. I had never read the Psalms before. Their intensity is almost overwhelming....

I suspect there are going to be some extremely difficult times ahead, especially in the next few weeks and months. I'm trying to let Jesus guide me, rather than trying to handle it all by myself. I've found that when things get tough, the most comforting thing I can say is, "Jesus loves me."

Thanks.

Just try to pry that note from me! Out of all the experiences I've ever had, nothing is more satisfying than having a front-row seat to watch Jesus revolutionize the life of another human being.

Some Christians, though, will never know the impact they've had until they reach heaven. I remember when Willow Creek Community Church held a memorial service for a husband and wife killed in a car accident. They had been veteran servants in the church's tape ministry, in which they reproduced tens of thousands of teaching tapes that went out to people around the world. They may never have met those people personally, but because those tapes carried the redemptive message of Christ, they will meet some of them in heaven.

And they'll celebrate together for eternity.

TOWEL BEARERS FIND FULFILLMENT IN GOD'S PROMISE TO REWARD THEM

Imagine this: our omniscient God sees every act of service motivated by his love, every instance of giving to build his kingdom, every sacrifice in his name, and he solemnly promises to reward us in eternity. "God is not unjust," says the writer of Hebrews. "He will not forget your work and the love you have shown him as you have helped his people and continue to help them."[7]

He even remembers our acts of kindness that we ourselves have forgotten! Let me give you an example. Choose a day at random from the past. For instance, let's suppose we were to rewind the tape of history to the last Saturday of April 1989. What were you doing on that day? Can you remember? Maybe you spent part of that day with a towel over your arm, serving people in the name of Christ, and you can't even recall it. But God remembers.

In fact, let's zero in on only one congregation—Willow Creek Community Church in South Barrington, Illinois. As God looks back to that cool April day many years ago, what does he remember?

At 8:30 that morning, Kim Rasmussen, a leader in the junior high ministry, was impacting the lives of half a dozen eighth-grade girls while they volunteered to clean a park as a gesture of kindness to the community. *And God remembers.* He clearly recalls how Kim's influence on a girl named Julie helped awaken her to God's love.

At 10:15 a.m. that day, Dale Nusbaum and his five-year-old son Tyler were vacuuming and cleaning offices at the church, getting them ready for another week of ministry. Meanwhile, downstairs a corporate president named Jack Mains was meticulously cleaning windows in preparation for that evening's church service for spiritual seekers. *And God remembers.*

Also that morning, a group of single adults was turning a dilapidated building in Chicago's Logan Square neighborhood into a recreation center and oasis of safety for inner-city kids. The volunteer foreman, Bill Kolker, arrived early that day and watched some teenagers playing basketball in the partially completed facility. "I was in tears," he said. "I receive my reward by seeing these kids." *And God remembers.*

At 1:45 in the afternoon, Carolyn Schuldt was sitting next to the bed of Elaine Ducay, who was dying of cancer in a hospital near the church. Carolyn held her hand, whispered calming words of encouragement, prayed with her, and tried to be Jesus to her. *And God remembers*. As it turned out, Elaine never got to leave the hospital. But less than a month later she did go Home.

At 2:00 p.m., a Sunday school leader named Karen Smiskol was hosting a picnic next to the church pond for some fifth-grade girls, to let them know that they matter to God and they matter to her. "I like the joy of giving my friendship to them," Karen said. *And God remembers*.

At 3:00 in the afternoon, Robert Green, who's terribly afraid of heights, was precariously perched atop a ladder while he aimed lights for the upcoming service, so people could see the stage where the message of Christ would be explained. *And God remembers*.

At 3:30 p.m., Fred Turner was teaching a five-year-old boy named Chris how to fly a kite for the first time in his life. Chris was from a single-parent home, and Fred was giving his time as a sort of surrogate dad, playing baseball with Chris, hammering nails with him, and talking about Jesus to him. *And God remembers*.

At 3:45 in the afternoon, a distraught woman was sitting in the church's food pantry. Her husband had just left her and their two children, and she was trembling from fear and frustration. A volunteer named Sue Blacker knelt down next to her and listened to her story. "You are really courageous," Sue told her. "We're glad we can help you through this and stand by you. You know, you matter to God. It's easy to forget that in your situation, but you do. You truly matter to God." *And he won't forget that*.

At 6:35 p.m., a twenty-seven-year-old chemist named Chris Scorzo—or "Mr. Chris," as the kids call him—was in Sunday school, helping eighty-seven children, ages four and five, understand that there *is* a God and that he loves them. The kids will never forget that, and neither will God.

SMOOTH OR CALLUSED HANDS?

Those are just a few examples from one day in one church in one community many years ago. Acts of servanthood go on in churches and Christian ministries around the clock and around the world—and every single sacrificial moment is imprinted in God's memory, to be recalled someday when eternal rewards are given.

And the question is, What will he remember about you? Will he recall how you humbly picked up a towel, draped it over your arm, and stooped to serve others who were in need?

"Christian spirituality is the spirituality of the Poor Man of Nazareth who took upon himself the form of a servant," wrote Kenneth Leech. "To follow the way of the Kingdom is therefore to follow him who fed the hungry, healed the sick, befriended the outcast, and blessed the peacemakers."[8]

Willow Creek's senior pastor, Bill Hybels, put it this way: "I would never want to reach out someday with a soft, uncallused hand—a hand never dirtied by serving—and shake the nail-pierced hand of Jesus."

With that sobering perspective, let me ask again, *What will God remember about you?*

A Dose of Doubt May Strengthen Your Faith

Lee, I need your help. I see so many people around the church who have such a strong faith that I feel like I don't fit in. I would like *to feel confident, I* wish *I didn't have doubts, but I've got more questions than answers. Now I'm beginning to doubt whether I'm a Christian at all. Can you relate to any of this? What should I do? Could you get back to me right away?*

I recognized the signature: this was a bright and sincere business executive whom I was considering for a future leadership role in the church.

But his letter didn't alarm me. Actually, I found it encouraging that he was refusing to hide his skepticism and ride on the spiritual coattails of others. Besides, I *have* gone through times when I could relate to what he was saying. And maybe the same is true of you.

Perhaps you've questioned whether God has really forgiven you. Or you've wondered whether the Bible can be completely trusted. Or you can't reconcile the world's suffering with a loving God. Or you've read an article by a scientist or liberal theologian that kicked the legs of your faith right out from under you.

The truth is that a spiritual virus has been going around Christian circles for centuries, and it's called doubt. If you haven't caught it yet, you will. In fact, we could divide Christians into three groups. The first would consist of those who have doubted. The second would be those who haven't doubted yet but who will. The third group would be those who are brain-dead.

Because if you're a thinking person at all—if you seriously contemplate your faith and what it means to follow Jesus—the chances are that every once in a while you're going to come down with some questions, issues, concerns, uncertainties, hesitations, or doubts.

And by the way, that's not just a Christian phenomenon. I can personally attest that atheists also doubt their position from time to time. As C. S. Lewis wrote, "Now that I am a Christian I do have moods in which the whole thing looks very improbable; but when I was an atheist I had moods in which Christianity looked terribly probable."[1]

So the issue isn't whether you will catch the doubt virus; we're all carriers to some degree. The big question is, How can we prevent that virus from turning into a virulent disease that ultimately ravages our faith?

But God's outrageous claim is that you can survive your bouts with doubt—and not only that but your faith could very well emerge even stronger as a result. As incredible as it sounds, doubting may turn out to be the healthiest thing you've ever done!

STAGGERING BETWEEN YES AND NO

There's no doubt about it: doubt scares many Christians. They stare into the darkness at night, pestered by vague uncertainties and persistent questions that make them feel anxious and vulnerable, almost as if they were experiencing spiritual vertigo.

And to make matters worse, most Christians are reluctant to breathe a word about this, because they don't want to be embarrassed. "I was so glad to hear you say that doubt is common, because I thought I was the only one," a woman told me after I spoke on this topic. "I was afraid to admit I had questions. I didn't want everybody around here to think I was some kind of wimp!"

When we keep our doubts suppressed inside, we unwittingly give them more and more power over us. On the other hand, when we finally let them emerge and face them squarely, it's amazing how often their potency disappears.

So let's put the doubt virus under the microscope where we can expose it to scrutiny and destroy some of our misconceptions that give it undue strength. And believe me, there are *plenty* of misunderstandings about it.

For instance, most Christians think that doubt is the opposite of faith, but it isn't. The opposite of faith is unbelief, and that's an extremely important distinction to understand. Said Os Guinness in his classic book *In Two Minds*, "Doubt comes from a word meaning 'two.' To believe is to be 'in one mind' about accepting something as true; to disbelieve is to be 'in one mind' about rejecting it. To doubt is to waver between the two, to believe and disbelieve at once and so to be 'in two minds.'"[2]

Guinness pointed out that in the Bible, unbelief refers to a willful refusal to believe or a deliberate decision to disobey God. But to doubt is something different. When we doubt, we're being indecisive or ambivalent over an issue. We haven't come down squarely on the side of disbelief, but we're up in the air over some questions or concerns. "Doubt does not mean denial or negation," wrote Karl Barth. "Doubt only means swaying and staggering between Yes and No."[3]

Lynn Anderson, whose book *If I Really Believe, Why Do I Have These Doubts?* candidly describes his struggles with faith, said nonbelievers are people "who have made a conscious or unconscious choice not to have faith." In contrast, doubters may be uncertain whether they have real faith or may not know exactly what to believe, but "they still want to have faith."[4]

Let me offer some words of encouragement: *you can have a strong faith and still have some doubts.* You can be heaven-bound and nevertheless express uncertainty over some theological issues. You can be a full-fledged Christian without absolutely settling every single question of life once and for all. In fact, it has been said that struggling with God over the issues of life doesn't show a *lack* of faith — that *is* faith. If you don't believe me, just peruse the Psalms!

"True believers can experience doubt," said Gary Habermas, a scholar who has extensively researched this topic. "In both the Old and New Testaments, believers clearly express wide ranges of questioning, especially on such topics as pain and evil, God's personal dealing with his people, and the issue of evidence for one's belief. On each of those subjects, doubt is clearly expressed by prominent believers."[5]

Go ahead — breathe a sigh of relief. Those words might be just what you needed to hear to begin neutralizing the anxiety that the doubt virus has been generating inside you.

SLIPPING FROM CERTAINTY TO DOUBT

Not only is doubt different from disbelief but, contrary to popular opinion, doubt isn't unforgivable, either. God doesn't condemn us when we question him. In discussing this subject with me, Habermas offered a persuasive illustration involving John the Baptist.

If anybody should have been immune to the doubt virus, Habermas said, it would be John. He had given his entire life to paving the way for Jesus. He was the one who confidently pointed to Jesus and declared, "Look, the Lamb of God, who takes away the sin of the world!"[6] He baptized Jesus and then personally witnessed the heavens opening up and God proclaiming, "You are my Son, whom I love; with you I am well pleased."[7] This is the person who said about Jesus, "I have seen and I testify that this is the Son of God."[8]

But when he was wallowing in prison, awaiting execution, questions began swirling in John's mind. Suddenly he wasn't so sure anymore. The historian Luke describes how John sent two of his friends to track down Jesus and ask him point-blank, "Are you the one who was to come, or should we expect someone else?"[9] That was John's way of saying, "I used to be convinced you were the Messiah, but now .... well, I'm wondering."

How does Jesus react? Not by slam-dunking John. Not by shaming him. Instead, he tells John's disciples, "Go back and report to John what you have seen and heard: The blind receive sight, the lame walk, those who have leprosy are cured, the deaf hear, the dead are raised, and the good news is preached to the poor."[10]

That is, he instructs them to provide John with all the evidence they have seen for themselves that confirms that Jesus is indeed the Messiah. Then, Jesus suggests, John's plague of doubt will be healed.

And guess how this affects the way Jesus views John. Instead of concluding that his questions have rendered him useless or disqualified him from any role in the kingdom, Jesus declares, "I tell you, among those born of women there is no one greater than John."[11]

Think about that—Jesus uttered those words about John the Doubter! And in the midst of your sincere questions and concerns, while you're wrestling with your honest hesitations and uncertainties, Jesus won't slam-dunk you either.

Don't you think God would rather have you be honest with him about your doubts than have you profess a phony faith? He knows what's going on inside us anyway; it's absurd to think we can mask our doubts from him. An authentic relationship means telling the truth about how we feel—and that's the kind of relationship God wants with us.

THE UPSIDE OF DOUBT

Another common misconception is that the doubt virus is always damaging to our spiritual health. However, the outrageous truth is that God can use our doubts to produce some extremely positive side effects.

To maintain our medical analogy, this is like getting an immunization. To help your body fight off a future disease, doctors inject you with a small amount of the very same illness so you will build up antibodies that will battle off that sickness if it ever threatens you. Your body is actually healthier for the experience. Similarly, when you're infected with the doubt virus and it propels you to seek answers to your questions, you emerge stronger than ever, because your faith has been confirmed once more. You emerge with new confidence in dealing with doubt in the future.

That's what happened to me when I was a fairly new Christian and volunteered to respond to cards submitted by church attenders who had questions. One Sunday a twelve-year-old girl turned in a card that simply said she wanted to know more about Jesus. "Could you and your wife come have dinner with me and my dad so we could talk?" she asked in a subsequent phone conversation.

"Of course!" I replied enthusiastically. I couldn't imagine a better way to spend an evening than telling a child and her father about Jesus.

But when Leslie and I arrived at their house, I glanced at the coffee table and saw a stack of scholarly books written by critics of Christianity. It turned out that the girl's father was a scientist who had been studying critiques of the faith for a long time.

Over pizza and soft drinks, he peppered me with questions until midnight, and many of his challenges caught me completely off guard. Frankly, a few sent tremors through my faith. I finally said, "I can't answer all of your questions, but I don't think that after two thousand years you'll be the first person to destroy the foundation of Christianity. So let me do some research and get back to you."

This doubt-generating experience prompted me to delve into new areas of research—in which I soon found satisfying answers that boosted my confidence in Christianity to even greater heights. Today I'm better equipped to handle these kinds of questions when they arise, and I'm less likely to let tough questions generate doubts. In short, my faith is healthier for the experience.

Author Mark Littleton agrees that this kind of experience can be a tremendous benefit. "Through doubt we can learn more than through naive trust," he said. "Truth can be tested. Doubt is the fire through which it passes. But when it has been tried it will come forth as gold."[12]

Francis Bacon said it well nearly four hundred years ago: "If a man will begin with certainties, he shall end in doubts; but if he will be content to begin with doubts, he shall end in certainties."

DISCOVERING GOD'S FOOTPRINTS

That's not the only positive outcome we can experience when we work through our doubts. Sometimes when we're afflicted with uncertainties, we get the feeling that God is absent from our life, yet Henri Nouwen said this can actually turn out to be a blessing in disguise. We can only plumb the mystery of God's presence, he said, when we experience a deep awareness of his absence. When this absence creates a deeper and deeper longing inside us for God, that's when we "discover his footprints":

> Just as the love of a mother for her son can grow deeper when he is far away, just as children can learn to appreciate their parents more when they have left home, just as lovers can rediscover each other during long periods of absence, so our intimate relationship

with God can become deeper and more mature by the purifying experience of his absence.[13]

How ironic—when our doubts distance us from God, we can develop a fresh new hunger for his presence in our life and thus emerge with a faith that's healthier than ever. What an amazing testimony to God's willingness to grow our faith if we resolve to take a step toward him even while our own uncertainties threaten to push us away.

And there's yet another way that doubt can be healthy for us: it can save us from the consequences of our own gullibility. For instance, what if David Koresh's followers had questioned his bizarre biblical teachings before they were led to their destruction at Waco? What if residents of Jonestown had doubted the teachings of Jim Jones before he lured them into the trap of mass suicide? Sometimes we experience doubt because we sense we're being led astray—and heeding that caution can be the best step we can take.

"Test everything," cautioned the apostle Paul. "Hold on to the good."[14] When we're receiving teaching that doesn't square with Scripture, it's time to question the teacher—and let our doubts lead us away from harm. Godly teachers encourage questions; those with something to hide are the ones who demand unthinking obedience.

The doubt virus, then, can serve us well in certain circumstances —if we seek prompt and thorough treatment for the infection. Instead of eating away at our faith, it might actually leave us stronger than before. At the turn of the century, Quaker pastor Rufus Jones put it this way: "A rebuilt faith is superior to an inherited faith that has never stood the strain of a great testing storm. If you have not clung to a broken piece of your old ship in the dark night of the soul, your faith may not have the sustaining power to carry you through to the end of the journey."[15]

When you're feeling dizzy and disoriented because of doubt, remember that observation. As you emerge from your uncertainties, you may very well possess a heartier faith, a deeper faith, a more resilient and enduring faith than before it was put to the test.

In *The Gift of Doubt*, Gary E. Parker acknowledges that some people may be uncomfortable with this idea that doubt can strengthen a person of faith. But he believes it's true: "If faith never encounters doubt, if truth never struggles with error, if good never battles with evil, how can faith know its own power? In my own pilgrimage, if I have to choose between a faith that has stared doubt in the eye and made it blink, or a naive faith that has never known the firing line of faith, I will choose the former every time."[16]

And as someone who has personally experienced how doubt can purify faith, I would make the same choice—no doubt about it.

Despite its potential upside, though, it's not a good idea to go out of our way to find doubt. And when we do experience uncertainties, we should always be working positively to resolve them. That's because if we passively allow the doubt virus to ravage our beliefs, it might ultimately decimate our faith. But to determine the right prescription for combating the virus, we need to understand the various ways that doubt can infect us—through our mind, our emotions, and our will.

THINKING IT OVER

One place doubt often gains entry to our lives is through our intellectual concerns about the faith. For instance, we start to wonder whether angels, demons, heaven, hell, miracles, and the Resurrection are really rational to believe in. We're especially vulnerable to the doubt virus if we don't know *why* we believe what we believe.

It might start with a conversation in which an acquaintance asks, "So you believe Jesus is God?"

"Sure," you say. "Of course."

"Well, why do you believe that?" he asks.

You take out your Bible and are about to show him all the passages demonstrating that Jesus is God, but he cuts you off. "Wait a second—you don't expect me to believe anything in *that* book, do you?"

You're taken aback. "Well, why not?"

"Everyone knows it's full of contradictions, mythology, superstition, and bad science. C'mon, this is the twenty-first century! Why in the world would you believe that book is the Word of God?"

"Uh ... well," you stammer, "I just do, that's all!"

This is when germs of doubt appear. Maybe he's right. Maybe you've swallowed the Jesus story hook, line, and sinker, without asking the right questions. How *do* you know that the Bible is reliable?

It's been said that Christians should *believe simply*—that is, have the pure faith of a child—but they shouldn't just *simply believe*. That's because the chances are that someone, sometime, somewhere is going to challenge your faith. Not knowing why you believe what you believe makes you especially susceptible to the doubt virus.

And so does not knowing *what* you believe. If you have a distorted or imbalanced view of God, this can set you up for unwarranted disappointments that are a breeding ground for the doubt virus. For instance, if you know all about God's love but nothing about his justice, holiness, and righteousness, you're going to develop doubts about why he does what he does and why he doesn't do what you think he ought to do.

Or if you think God has promised to promptly answer every single one of your prayers, you're going to develop doubts when he doesn't seem to be coming through for you. Or if you believe he guarantees health and wealth to those who just exercise enough faith, you're going to begin questioning your faith when finances and healing don't automatically come. Or if you think your faith offers blanket protection from life's turbulence, you're going to develop uncertainties when difficulties continue to beset you.

The problem isn't with God. He never promised these things in the first place. The problem is that when we have an inaccurate view of his promises and character, it creates unrealistic expectations. The result: an infection of doubt.

THE CONGENITAL DOUBTER

Not only can our mind be a breeding ground for doubt but so can our emotions. For some, faith is built entirely on feelings. They had a euphoric experience when they gave their life to Christ and were emotionally pumped up for a while, but eventually that spiritual high began to wear off—and they started to panic out of fear that their faith was disappearing or that they never were a *real* Christian in the first place.

Essentially, they've misunderstood the role of emotions and faith. Faith isn't fundamentally a feeling; it's a decision of the will to follow Jesus Christ, and it doesn't ebb and flow depending on how emotionally charged we feel.

Personality can be a factor, too. Just as certain people are more susceptible to particular diseases, some temperaments—especially those that tend to be melancholy or contemplative—are more vulnerable to questions and doubts. For instance, Lynn Anderson describes himself as a "congenital doubter":

> We are the adults who are haunted by "existential angst"—a fundamental sense of uncertainty about the basics of existence—and tend to be plagued with troubling questions that we can't sweep under the rug. We don't mean to be obnoxious, and we do not want to be rebellious or irreverent. Many of us, in fact, long to be doubt free.... Experts may disagree on where these doubts come from, but it *feels* like we were born with them![17]

Author and educator Daniel Taylor uses the term "reflective Christian" to describe the person who is "first, and foremost, a question asker—one who finds in every experience and assertion something that requires further investigation. He or she is a stone turner, attracted to the creepy-crawly things that live under the rocks and behind human pronouncements."[18]

He cites the author of Ecclesiastes as such a person: "So I turned my mind to understand, to investigate and to search out wisdom and the scheme of things."[19]

Doubt also tends to develop among those who have been emotionally scarred from an experience in their past. If they suffered parental abuse as a child, if they were abandoned by their parents or spouse, if they've felt unloved by those most important to them, they may develop chronic uncertainties about God. Deep down inside they may be waiting for God to let them down the way people in their past have.

Interestingly, many of the all-time biggest unbelievers—such atheists as Karl Marx, Sigmund Freud, Bertrand Russell, Jean Paul Sartre, Friedrich Nietzsche, and Albert Camus, among others— had their father die or abandon them when they were young, or had serious conflict with him.[20]

While most victims of parental abandonment don't resort to the extreme of atheism, it is true that they sometimes find themselves having difficulty trusting their heavenly Father. And where there's a lack of trust, doubt soon follows.

CHOICES THAT LEAD TO DOUBT

In addition to our mind and emotions, doubt can also enter our lives through our will, or the part of us that makes choices. For example, doubts can multiply when a Christian makes the deliberate decision not to turn away from a pattern of wrongdoing in his life.

Sin, of course, creates a lack of peace, and a sense of being separated from God. So when the person can't find peace, he questions why God isn't comforting him. When he feels God is distant, he begins to question whether God's there at all—while the whole time, the underlying cause of his doubt is his own willful choice to cling to sin.

A stubborn sense of pride can be a contributing factor as well. "The proud man *needs* to doubt because the sense of his own importance demands it," Guinness said. "It is not in his nature to bow to anyone."[21] Consequently, he goes out of his way to invite doubt in order to justify his decision not to allow God full access to his life. Theologian Alister McGrath agrees that our lack of humility can invite doubt, but for a different reason. "All of us are tempted to believe that, because we haven't got the answers to the hard questions of faith, there aren't any answers to those questions," he said.[22]

And there's no question that doubt will sweep through you like wildfire if you've never actually made the decision to commit your life to Christ. Maybe you're living on a hand-me-down faith from your parents or believe that you're a Christian because you were baptized as a child, attend church, or are in general agreement with Christian doctrine.

But the Bible is clear that we need to make a choice to receive the free gift of forgiveness and eternal life that Christ is offering. When we do that, we're adopted into God's family and begin a relationship with him that will draw us closer and closer to him over time. In addition, the Holy Spirit will quietly assure us that we belong to God.

Apart from that life-changing and eternity-altering decision, it's no wonder that a person would feel that God is distant and detached—and it's no wonder that doubts would continue to multiply as a result.

Finally, let me acknowledge the role that Satan plays in spreading the doubt virus wherever he can and encouraging it to grow out of control. Jesus called him "the father of lies"[23] because of the way he whispers distortions in our ear to create mistrust and confusion.

We shouldn't fall into the trap of ignoring the threat he poses, but we also shouldn't get entangled in a second trap: becoming fixated on him. As the apostle John reminded Christ followers, "You, dear children, are from God …. the one who is in you is greater than the one who is in the world."[24]

WALKING TOWARD CERTAINTY

Those are a few of the ways we can get infected with doubt. Once we're afflicted, it's imperative that we do something to regain our spiritual health. And often that's not easy.

I don't want to mislead you into thinking that there's some spiritual elixir that will cure your questions. Some people end up living with a frustrating low-grade infection of doubt over long periods. At the same time, however, there *is* hope.

"When does doubt become unbelief?" asked Alister McGrath. "Answer: when you let it."[25] *So don't let it.* By taking action, you can prevent questions, concerns, or doubts from multiplying out of control into full-fledged disbelief.

As I've dealt with people through the years—ranging from those who were merely pestered by pesky questions to some who would qualify as "congenital doubters"—I've found that there are five steps that can help in battling the doubt virus. To make them easy to remember, I've taken the word *faith* and used each letter as the beginning of each step.

Step #1: Find the Root of Your Doubt

This is the diagnostic phase, the time when you delve into what's behind your particular strain of doubt. I've just gone over several examples of how doubt can infect us through our mind, our emotion, and our will, and maybe as you were reading, you concluded, "Hey, that's me!" If I didn't mention your own species of doubt, do some self-examination and research so you can pinpoint it.

Tom is an example of someone who was chronically beset by intellectual doubts but couldn't figure out why. As I was helping him through this first step, I finally came to the conclusion that his doubts were rooted in his misunderstanding of what faith is all about.

He was demanding absolute proof concerning God, and no matter how much evidence he unearthed, it always fell short of perfect certainty. That's where his doubts came in.

Once we diagnosed the cause of his doubt, I was able to help him understand that the existence of God can neither be completely proved nor disproved. There is plenty of evidence that points convincingly in the direction of God—but ultimately we need to take a step of faith in that same direction by putting our trust in him.

With the concept of faith clarified, Tom was able to deal constructively with his doubts and feel confident that his trust in God was well placed.

Step #2: Ask God and Others for Help

Be as honest with God as the father whose son was gripped by evil. "I do believe," he said to Jesus. "Help me overcome my unbelief!"[26] Actually, he wasn't suffering from unbelief but was afflicted with doubt—remember, there's a difference. But the key is this: *he asked Jesus to help him—and Jesus did.* He healed his son.

Turn to God for help—not as a last resort but as a top priority. Ask him to lead you to answers, to provide you with insight, to give you wisdom, and to bolster your confidence. Tell him of your desire for a strong and vibrant faith.

Then turn to Christians in your life. This is why it's so important to be part of a small circle of friends in which authenticity is encouraged and spiritual growth is promoted. James said we should honestly admit our struggles and shortcomings to each other and pray for one another. Why? So, James said, that we may be healed.[27]

I've found it's particularly helpful to seek out people who have a strong faith themselves. I suppose this goes back to a childhood experience. When we were kids, my younger sister, Lorena, came down with the mumps, and I was jealous over all the gifts she received as a result. So I hung around her until I came down with the disease myself—and I reaped a harvest of goodies, too.

While faith isn't literally contagious, we can benefit from hanging around with people who have deep and abiding beliefs. They tend to anchor and reassure us, and we can always learn from the spiritual practices that they have integrated into their life to help them build a doubt-resistant faith.

Step #3: Implement a Course of Treatment

Once you've found the root cause of your doubt and sought wisdom from both God and godly advisors, then you're in a better position to identify and implement a strategy for fighting the doubt virus.

For instance, instead of just concluding that you've got some vague intellectual concerns about Christianity, take the time to write down the specific questions you have. This discipline will help you zero in on exactly what's troubling you. You'll be surprised by how many resources are readily available to help you pursue satisfying answers.

Or perhaps you've determined that emotional issues are creating germs of doubt. Maybe an appropriate course of action would be to discuss them with a pastor or Christian counselor who can assist you in resolving them.

Or if it's a matter of the will, ask yourself specifically where you're holding back from God. After all, the choice is yours: you can let willful disobedience or pride plague you with doubt for the rest of your life, or you can submit your whole self to God and really experience the adventure of Christianity.

And if you're not certain that you have ever really given your life to Christ, make sure once and for all—pray to receive Christ as your forgiver and leader. It's all right if this turns out to be a re-commitment. But once you've done it with sincerity, put the issue to rest. The Bible assures us that when we humbly receive Christ's gift of eternal life, we're adopted into his family forever. We don't have to doubt our salvation anymore.

Diagnosing the root of your doubt, seeking counsel, and implementing a course of action will put you on the road to recovery, although you may have to deal with some relapses along the way. The next step is important in warding off infections in the future.

Step #4: Take Scrupulous Care of Your Spiritual Health

A body is less susceptible to viruses when it's healthy because it can fight off minor infections before they become serious. In a similar way, a strong faith is better able to fight off the doubt virus before it gains a foothold and threatens to overwhelm your defenses. Just as a body is strengthened through good nourishment and exercise, your faith becomes stronger through both knowledge and action.

By knowledge, I mean getting serious about learning more about God and why he's trustworthy. That involves not only reading books *about* the Bible but studying the Bible itself in a consistent and systematic way. For a good grounding in how to do that meaningfully, I often recommend *Living by the Book*, by Howard and William Hendricks, as a helpful introduction to personal Bible study.[28]

And through your day-to-day actions, build up your faith by exercising it. We learn best by doing, and we learn best about the trustworthiness of God when we make the daily decision to submit our lives to him and enthusiastically press the envelope of our faith. As King David said, taste and see for yourself that the Lord is good.[29]

When you do these things, this is what happens: whenever you're threatened by doubt, it's much easier to look back on your knowledge about God, and your personal experience with him, and say, "I may not know the answer to this particular question yet, but I've got plenty of evidence that God is real, that the Bible is reliable, and that God cares about me. All of that gives me confidence that God has an answer for this question. So I'm not going to panic or toss my faith out the window. I'm not going to get mired in despair or fall into disillusionment. Instead, I'll keep relying on God, because he has shown me over and over that my trust in him is well founded."

That's how we develop a shield that will deflect doubt when we're exposed to it.

Step #5: Hold Your Remaining Questions in Tension

God's thoughts and ways are higher than ours. We're limited people with limited minds, so we can't expect to understand everything about our unlimited God. Consequently, there are bound to be some mysteries that won't be resolved for the time being.

In some cases we'll get a better glimpse of an answer as we mature in our faith through the years. But in many instances we'll have to wait for eternity, when we can raise our hand and say, "Jesus, I've got a question that's been bothering me for a while now. Exactly how does predestination fit in with free will? Precisely how does this Trinity thing work? Why didn't I seem to hear from you that time when I was hurting so bad? Why is it, as a little boy once wrote, 'I prayed for a puppy but got a little brother instead'?"

I'll tell you what: my arm is going to be in the air. I'm sure yours will be, too, and that's okay. God will answer. After all, we've got forever to satisfy our curiosity!

Until then we can say, "I may not have answers to every single one of my peripheral questions, but the answers I do have point me unmistakably toward God as being real, as being dependable, and as being a Father who loves me. Because of that, my faith can stay intact even while I hold some issues in abeyance."

That's not an irrational faith. Instead, that's dealing with our doubts responsibly by making an informed decision to suspend judgment for a while. It's concluding, from all the available evidence, that God can be trusted and that therefore it's permissible to take a wait-and-see attitude toward a particular issue. Actually, if we had one hundred percent of the answers to one hundred percent of our questions, there wouldn't be any room for faith at all.

So as you deal with your doubts, remember this: we may feel perplexed by mysteries, but there is no mystery to God. He understands all. As Gary Parker put it, "I may not have the answer to many questions, but I know the One who does."[30]

The apostle Paul also knew that one. And Paul understood how little he himself knew. When you're fighting off a doubt virus, try transforming Paul's words into a personal prayer: "Lord, I can see and understand only a little about you now, as if I were peering at your reflection in a poor mirror, but someday I am going to see you in your completeness, face-to-face. Now all that I know is hazy and blurred, but then I will see everything clearly, just as clearly as you see into my heart right now."[31]

God Has a Cure
for Your
Secret Loneliness

Celebrities don't blush anymore when news breaks that they're pregnant outside of marriage. Using recreational drugs doesn't have the stigma it once had in Hollywood. Divorce? Arrests? Movie stars bear their souls five nights a week on *Entertainment Tonight*. And checking into the Betty Ford Clinic has almost become a rite of passage for those in the public spotlight.

But there's one admission that people are loathe to make, whether they're a star on television or someone who fixes televisions in a repair shop. It's just too embarrassing. It penetrates too deeply to the core of who they are. And when writer Marla Paul reluctantly confessed it in a newspaper column, she was secretly hoping no one would read it.

Her admission: *she was lonely.*

Loneliness is such a humiliating malady that it ought to have its own politically correct euphemism: "relationally challenged." Or its own telethon. Anything to make it safer to confess. Because right now it's a taboo, an affliction of loners and misfits. And—to be honest—of respectable people like you and me.

"The loneliness saddens me," Marla wrote. "How did it happen that I could be forty-two years old and not have enough friends?"

She said some changes in her life—including moving to a different state and deciding to work at home—ruptured her circle of relationships and "it seems as if every woman's friendship quota has been filled and she is no longer accepting new applicants."

She finally asked her husband, "Is it me?" She was starting to wonder. Or were people just too busy for new friends? Were they so enmeshed in existing relationships that they were closed off to any new acquaintances? "Or," she added, "am I just imagining that everyone else has this tight coterie of fellowship except me?"

She ended her column this way:

> I think there are women out there who don't know how lonely they are. It's easy enough to fill up the day with work and family. But no matter how much I enjoy my job and love my husband and child, they are not enough.
>
> I recently read my daughter Hans Christian Andersen's *The Ugly Duckling*. I felt an immediate kinship with this bird who flies from place to place looking for the creatures with whom he belongs. He eventually finds them.
>
> I hope I do too.[1]

FEELING LIKE A WARTHOG

Then something surprising happened.

The day after Marla's column appeared, the telephone started ringing. People stopped her on the street and at her daughter's school. Letters poured in from housewives, executives, and university professors. The column generated seven times more mail than usual.

"They wanted to share their frustration and estrangement," Marla said. "All were tremendously relieved to discover they weren't the only ones."

Wrote one working mother of two, from a prestigious Chicago suburb, "The column helped ease my growing paranoia that I was becoming a social outcast for no reason that I could fathom." Added a woman from a rural community, "Now I know it's not because I have red hair and a pug nose. You start to look for what's wrong with you." Other letters had similar themes:

- "I feel like a mutant warthog—why else are people so disinterested in returning my friendship overtures?"
- "I need friends. I want friends. I wonder exactly what is going on. Why don't other people have a need to make friends?"
- "I try to focus on the people who I am friends with and not the ones who don't want anything to do with me. But it's hard."

"Yes, it is," Marla summed up. "Sometimes it seems easier to give up and accept this disconnectedness as a dark and unshakable companion. But it's not the companion I want. I want friends. And so I, too, persevere."[2]

"AND HE SHALL STAND ALONE"

None of this, of course, is unique to women. Men are notorious for having acquaintances, teammates, business associates, customers, golfing buddies, and fishing pals—all relationships that go about as deep as the thin layer of ice atop a frozen pond.

"The American male is lonely and friendless, but he tries to maintain his macho image at all costs, even if it means isolation from people," observed Jim Conway, who writes on men's issues.[3]

In his helpful book *Men Without Friends*, David W. Smith summarizes several factors that hinder men from making and maintaining relationships with other men, including the fact that as youngsters, most are encouraged to suppress their emotions, to be competitive, to keep their personal needs and longings deep inside, and to look up to role models who are independent and impersonal.[4]

In fact, Smith said so many men consider social isolation to be normal that when a writer surveyed males on whether they had any close friends, the very question perplexed many of them. A typical response was, "No, why? Should I?"

In *Men: A Book for Women*, James Wagenvoord wrote this tongue-in-cheek creed for "real men," based on the way males are brought up in this culture. As you read it, think about how each of these attitudes works against formation of intimate relationships.

He shall not cry.

He shall not display weakness.

He shall not need affection or gentleness or warmth.

He shall comfort, but not desire comforting.

He shall be needed, but not need.

He shall touch, but not be touched.

He shall be steel, not flesh.

He shall be inviolate in his manhood.

And he shall stand alone.[5]

How's that for a formula for relational disaster? Fueled by this kind of social conditioning and the increasing rootlessness of our society, loneliness is becoming a national disease. Said psychologist Richard Farson, "Millions of people in America have never had one minute in their whole lifetime where they could 'let down' and share with another person their deeper feelings." What a remarkable—and depressing—observation!

Not surprisingly, there's a cost to all of this. Dr. James Lynch, in *The Broken Heart*, cites statistics showing that adults without deep relationships have a death rate that's twice as high as those who enjoy regular caring interaction with others.

Ironically, we live in a culture in which many people scrupulously monitor their cholesterol intake and calorie consumption but at the same time blithely ignore their relational life, which, according to scientists, has just as much impact on their physical health as obesity, smoking, high blood pressure, and lack of exercise.[6]

RISKS AND REWARDS OF COMMUNITY

Okay, I'll admit it: there have been times in my life when I've been profoundly lonely. Despite a flourishing career, lots of good acquaintances, and a fulfilling marriage, I've slogged through eras when I've ached for a friend to whom I could bare my soul.

I can personally attest to the biblical truth that human beings were not designed to live relationally disconnected lives. As outrageous as it may sound, we will never feel whole until we experience community, first with God and then with other people. Without that we will inevitably sense something deeply awry in the depths of our soul.

After all, we were created in the image of a God who has reveled for all of eternity in a mysterious form of interrelationship among the Father, Son, and Holy Spirit. So this concept of community has its origin in the Godhead. It's appropriate, then, that shortly after God created the first person, he concluded, "It is not good for the man to be alone."[7] Man needed someone to share his life with.

As for Jesus, he garnered a large following of people, but in both his divinity and humanness he also desired the companionship of a small cadre of disciples. Yet even that wasn't enough.

He then developed a richer relationship among Peter, James, and John, who formed his inner sphere of confidants. And among those intimate friends, he was closer to John than anyone else. In this way, Jesus was modeling a relationally healthy life.

Here's the encouraging news: you don't have to suffer the incessant anguish of loneliness. God has equipped us with both the capacity and desire to go deep with other human beings, to jointly experience life's joys and sorrows, to encourage one another, to celebrate each other, to serve each other: to "do life" together. It's a treasure God wants you to have.

Yes, it will require some risk taking to claim it. But the biggest risk comes in *not* seeking community. As C. S. Lewis said,

> Love anything, and your heart will certainly be wrung and possibly broken. If you want to make sure of keeping it intact, you must give your heart to no one.... Wrap it carefully round with hobbies and little luxuries: avoid all entanglements; lock it up safe in the casket or coffin of your selfishness. But in that casket—safe, dark, motionless, airless—it will change. It will not be broken: instead, it will become unbreakable, impenetrable, irredeemable.[8]

In short, the upside is too great and the downside too scary not to pursue authentic relationships. But how do we begin? Casual friendships are easy, but deeper relationships can be much more challenging to initiate and cultivate. On top of that, a lot of people have let their friendship-building skills atrophy over time, if they ever possessed them at all.

So let's start here and now. Let's stop waiting for friendships to just happen. The time has come to shelve our loneliness and, as outlandish as it sounds, get extremely intentional about building some relationships. With the Bible providing our guidance, let's get back to basics.

What are the ingredients in a friendship that's rich and real, caring and enduring, intimate and mutually fulfilling? I've found that there are at least five that are essential in developing ongoing, secure, and satisfying friendships: affinity, acceptance, authenticity, assistance, and affirmation.

INGREDIENT #1: AFFINITY—
CELEBRATING WHAT WE HOLD IN COMMON

Chemists use the term *affinity* to describe the attraction that causes atoms to bond with each other. In friendships, affinity at its most basic level is an attraction between two people. You *like* the other person. The Old Testament describes the first time a low-status shepherd named David met the king's firstborn son, named Jonathan. From the start they just plain enjoyed each other. They hit it off.

It's easy to test whether you have affinity with another person: imagine him or her walking into a room where you're doing some work. What's your immediate reaction? If they light up your mood, if a smile comes to your face, if you happily take a break from your project to engage them, then there's definitely affinity between you.

But there's more to affinity than just liking someone. Affinity also refers to the common ground that people share. For instance, "surface-level affinity" is when we share some interest or activity with the other individual.

Maybe we both like to play golf or tennis. Maybe we do some business together. Maybe our kids are the same age and we're both on the same PTA committee. We enjoy getting together and working on a common activity or toward a joint goal, but our conversation generally revolves around the task at hand. Mostly we talk about safe subjects.

Our lives are full of these relationships. Studies show that the average person can have several hundred of these acquaintances, and there's nothing wrong with them. But we shouldn't fool ourselves into thinking that they are more significant than they really are, because these fragile friendships inevitably fracture under stress.

"A man of many companions may come to ruin," the Bible cautions, "but there is a friend who sticks closer than a brother."[9] Here the writer is contrasting our numerous surface-level relationships with our fewer but closer friendships, and he's warning us that quantity doesn't equal quality.

Just ask Lee Iacocca. He said the biggest surprise of his career wasn't when he was fired as president of Ford Motor Company; it was what happened afterward. "I was hurting pretty bad," he said in his autobiography. "I could have used a phone call from someone who said, 'Let's have coffee.' But most of my friends deserted me. It was the greatest shock of my life."[10]

Those relationships were apparently based on the surface-level affinity of merely having a common workplace and sharing corporate goals, so when stress came—*snap!*—the friendships fragmented.

But "the friend who sticks closer than a brother" is one with whom we share "deep-level affinity." In these cases, the common ground isn't just an activity, it's common values. We have a consensus concerning our core beliefs. We don't just talk about a task we're doing together; we share emotions and personal experiences. We connect on a much more profound level.

Hearts Beating in Unison

The Bible says that "the soul of Jonathan was knit to the soul of David."[11] In his book *Quality Friendship*, Gary Inrig points out, "The word *knit* is helpful because it reminds us that you knit together things that are of the same nature. Jonathan and David were men who had much in common."[12] Their souls were entwined because they shared a deeply held love for God. That was the basis of their friendship.

The point, said Inrig, is this: *"The quality of a friendship is nearly always determined by the quality of that which unites us."* [13] That means that if our common bond is an activity, sport, or business venture, surface-level affinity will probably result. But if the common bond consists of deeply felt values, there's at least the possibility of much closer bonding. We may only have a few of these friendships, but they are the ones that bring the richest rewards.

I've had all kinds of friendships in my life, but by far the most fulfilling have been those in which our commonality was Christ. It's those in which we shared the substance of our souls, we had a joint allegiance to Jesus, we prayed together and gave each other godly counsel and encouragement, and our hearts beat in unison for kingdom objectives.

So take a moment to run through your mental database of relationships. In each instance ask yourself, "What's our common ground? If you took away the activity we share, would our relationship wither? Or do we have the potential of going much deeper, because we share common values?"

And if you're looking for a new relationship in hopes of sinking deep roots, try looking among those who have the same core beliefs. That's why a vibrant, authentic, and loving church provides an excellent environment for finding a soul mate.

Not only will you start with a commonly held set of values but the very nature of Christianity encourages the honesty, encouragement, sincerity, and caring that combine to yield meaningful friendships.

INGREDIENT #2: ACCEPTANCE— RELATING ON AN "AS IS" BASIS

"Accept one another, then," urged the apostle Paul, "just as Christ accepted you."[14] How did he do that? *Unconditionally*.

"We must decide to develop friendships in which we demand nothing in return. Love, in order to work, must be unconditional," said Ted Engstrom in *The Fine Art of Friendship*. "Just as God accepts us on an 'as is' basis, so, too, must we enter into friendships based on taking the other person unconditionally into the relationship."[15]

Gary Inrig, who has written extensively on friendship, tells the tale of some parents on the East Coast who got a telephone call from their son during the Korean War. They were thrilled, because they hadn't heard from him for many months. He said he was in San Francisco on his way home.

"Mom, I just wanted to let you know that I'm bringing a buddy home with me," he said. "He got hurt pretty bad, and he only has one eye, one arm, and one leg. I'd sure like him to live with us."

"Sure, son," his mother replied. "He sounds like a brave man. We can find room for him for a while."

"Mom, you don't understand. I want him to come live with us."

"Well, okay," she finally said. "We could try it for six months or so."

"No, Mom, I want him to stay always. He needs us. He's only got one eye, one arm, and one leg. He's really in bad shape."

By now his mother had lost her patience. "Son, you're being unrealistic about this. You're emotional because you've been in a war. That boy will be a drag on you and a constant problem for all of us. Be reasonable."

The phone clicked dead. The next day, the parents got a telegram: their son had committed suicide. A week later the parents received the body. They looked down with unspeakable sorrow on the corpse of their son—who had one eye, one arm, and one leg.[16]

Even with our disabilities, character flaws, shortcomings, insecurities, and immaturity, don't all of us just want to be accepted for who we are? Don't we need to know that somebody accepts us because they want to, not because they have to for some reason?

David W. Smith describes a plaque that defines friendship this way: "A friend is one who knows you as you are, understands where you've been, accepts who you've become, and still gently invites you to grow."[17]

But our natural inclination isn't to accept people. We tend to be like the religious leaders of Jesus' day, who were quick to judge, criticize, and ostracize others. Like them, we want other people to conform to us, so we set up little tests to see whether they measure up.

Yet Proverbs says, "A friend loves at all times."[18] That doesn't mean we condone our friends' moral lapses or approve of their character flaws. Instead, it means we follow Christ's example of cherishing people themselves while extending them grace.

One night I was dining with an out-of-town friend I hadn't seen for quite a while. During our conversation, he confessed to me that he had cheated on his wife. He felt devastated by it, and we discussed the matter at length. At the end he made a very revealing comment: "Lee, don't tell anybody about this. Not even Leslie. I wouldn't want her to think less of me."

I found it fascinating that he wasn't worried that *I* would think less of him. The reason was that we were friends, and within the context of our relationship he could feel safe and accepted because in the past I had confessed my failures to him and he still accepted me.

"Even if a man is caught in any trespass," says the Bible, "you who are spiritual, restore such a one in a spirit of gentleness, *each one* looking to yourself, lest you too be tempted."[19]

The truth is that we're better able to accept others if we stay in touch with our own mistakes, deficiencies, and blunders. It's easier to extend the hand of acceptance to a friend if we imagine our other hand simultaneously reaching out to receive acceptance and forgiveness from Christ for our own sins.

When you're evaluating your relational life, ask yourself what attitude you bring into your friendships—critical and judgmental or accepting and gracious? Do you try to get other people to conform to all of your opinions, or do you celebrate the way they're different from you?

"As we ask the Holy Spirit to replace our cautious, critical attitude, which tends to evaluate and reject people, with his love, which yearns to accept them, we will experience a new and liberating way of relating to people," said Inrig.[20]

INGREDIENT #3: AUTHENTICITY— FEELING SAFE ENOUGH TO BE REAL

At some point, if a relationship is going to involve more than snorkeling on the surface, you've both got to dive deep into each other's lives. Authentic relationships are characterized by self-disclosure, transparency, honesty, and vulnerability. There's an increasing consistency between what we're like on the inside and how we act in each other's presence.

Jesus exhibited authenticity in his relationship with his disciples. For example, think of how vulnerable the all-powerful Son of God was being when he conceded to his closest friends in the Garden of Gethsemene, "My soul is overwhelmed with sorrow to the point of death."[21]

Authenticity begins when one person in the relationship sends up a relational trial balloon by disclosing part of his real self and then cautiously watches to see how the other individual reacts. If there's affirmation, encouragement, and personal disclosure from the other person, he's apt to continue down the path toward a deeper friendship. If not, he will retreat to safer but superficial grounds.

Years ago I was part of a group of guys who got together for breakfast every Saturday morning. We liked to think that we had some deep relationships going, but if you were to listen to our conversations, you'd see we were mostly talking about "da Bears," "da Bulls," "da Cubs," and "da Hawks." (Hey, this was Chicago!)

One day one of the guys was quiet. We routinely asked him how things were going, expecting a smile and a simple, "Fine, how 'bout you?" Instead, he blurted out, "Guys, my marriage is falling apart and I don't know what to do!" I was so shocked that I almost dropped my toast. With one outburst he had shattered our group's veneer.

Suddenly we found ourselves rallying around him, praying for him, and revealing things about ourselves that we had suppressed in the past. The experience drew us together like we had never been before, and it changed the dynamics of our group forever. One person's risk taking had revolutionized our relationships.

Going deep requires disclosure. Transparency should be appropriate, equal, and gradual, and it should come after trust and confidentiality have been established, but at some point it has to come, or the relationship will remain shallow and ultimately unfulfilling.

Being Too Opaque

However, it's important to be aware that there are dangers with disclosure on both ends of the transparency continuum. On one extreme are those who are scared to death over being authentic with their friends. Often these people are great at slapping backs and engaging in clever banter, but they intentionally slide over opportunities to go the next step deeper.

Fear is usually the cause. They fear that people will find out they're not as spiritual as they've pretended to be. There's fear of embarrassment, of rejection, of disclosing something that might be used against them later, and of a phenomenon called the "reverse halo effect."

The "halo effect" is when a person demonstrates competency in one area of life and people assume—often with no real basis—that he or she is equally competent in other areas. For instance, people might give extra weight to the political opinions of an actor just because he has achieved status in the movies. Somehow the ability to star in a show makes people assume he must know something about foreign policy.

According to Gerard Egan, the "reverse halo effect" is when people learn about a flaw in a person and assume—again, perhaps with no real basis—that the person is similarly flawed in other areas of life. So people perceive that an attorney who admits some marital shortcomings might also lack competence in his law practice. Intuitive fear of this phenomenon can cause people to hold back from fully disclosing the problems they're struggling with.[22]

Some people live their whole lives on this opaque end of the transparency continuum. Author Judson Swihart describes their life:

> Some people are like medieval castles. Their high walls keep them safe from being hurt. They protect themselves emotionally by permitting no exchange of feelings with others. No one can enter. They are secure from attack. However, inspection of the occupant finds him or her lonely, rattling around the castle alone. The castle-dweller is a self-made prisoner. He or she needs to feel loved by someone, but the walls are so high that it is difficult to reach out or for anyone else to reach in.[23]

You can rescue yourself from this self-imposed isolation, but it means taking a risk by launching a relational trial balloon—and if you take that scary step, you may get burned. Some of your worst fears may be realized. That's reality. Yet it's necessary to move down the continuum toward greater transparency, if you ever want to reap the benefits of being in true community with others.

Being Too Transparent

On the other hand, some people are way over on the opposite extreme of the transparency continuum. They are relational voyeurs. They tell you too much, too early in your friendship. In fact, they can't seem to stop telling you about their past, their secrets, their feelings, their wounds, and their inner conflicts.

Pretty soon, instead of a friendship you've got therapy going on, which can be frustrating to you if you don't feel qualified to help, and frustrating to the other person because they're not getting the professional input they need.

Inappropriate transparency can erode relationships, and it's often a sign that the person needs an experienced and godly counselor in addition to a friend. Here are some indicators that you're too far over on this end of the continuum:

- Your level of disclosure is consistently disproportionate to the other person's.
- Your conversations chronically center on your long-ago hurts instead of the present and future.
- Your transparency is pushing the other person away instead of drawing him or her closer to you.

It's in the middle of the transparency continuum that we find the healthiest and best-balanced relationships. So how can you begin to achieve authenticity equilibrium? I've found that straightforward honesty is the best policy.

If you have a surface-level relationship that you think it's time to deepen, have a frank conversation in which you say, "I've really appreciated our friendship. We've gotten to know each other and developed trust over the months. But now I think it's time that we go beneath the surface. I'm willing to promise confidentiality, to accept you for who you are, to stick by you, and to be honest about who I am. So what would you say about us really opening up our lives to each other—for the sake of us both?"

If there's agreement, begin to risk vulnerability a step at a time. And when your friend reciprocates, listen intently, empathize, and offer encouragement. Evaluate as you go. Work together to gradually develop a safe place where each of you feels the freedom to be honest about your emotions, your struggles, your doubts, your fears, and your aspirations.

Again think through your database of relationships. Identify some of your most promising friendships. Is it possible that a surface-level acquaintance of yours may be secretly waiting for you to make the first move on the journey toward a more authentic relationship? If so, take a risk. Make a call. Get together.

Go ahead—make a break from your castle.

INGREDIENT #4: ASSISTANCE—
PUTTING OUR FRIENDS FIRST

Friends help friends grow, mature, develop, and become all they can be. They draw the best out of each other. They serve each other. "Be devoted to one another in brotherly love," said the apostle Paul. "Honor one another above yourselves."[24]

Too many times people enter relationships with a solely selfish agenda. Someone once said that if Galileo were a baby boomer, he would have concluded that the sun revolves around himself—and unfortunately we all share that egocentric attitude to some degree. But when we enter into a friendship with the explicit goal of getting our own emotional and psychological needs met, we invariably end up disappointed.

Yet here's the irony: when our goal at the outset is to meet the *other* person's needs—to build up, serve, and support our friend—then we nearly always end up benefiting in the long run. Booker T. Washington said, "You cannot hold a man down without staying down with him." And the flip side of that is true, too: if you lift someone else up, you'll find yourself lifted up as well.

"You are allowed to keep only that which you consciously give away," commented Ted Engstrom. "Give away your friendship, and you will receive friendship in return. Give away your self, and your 'better' self will return to you many times over."[25]

So a great approach to deepening a friendship is to have a candid conversation in which you ask, "What can I do to be a better friend to you? How can I serve you better? How can I help you fulfill the potential that God has implanted in you?"

Speaking the Truth in Love

One way we can assist our friends is through accountability. There's a proverb that says, "As iron sharpens iron, so one man sharpens another."[26] Friends keep friends on the cutting edge of personal growth, by monitoring their progress and being willing to speak the truth to them in love, even when it means a confrontation.

This is how I handle it: during conversations with my closest friends, each of us shares the areas of life in which we're most likely to be tempted and those where we most want to develop. Then from time to time we ask each other how we're doing in those particular areas. We take time to listen and probe.

Scientists have studied factories and found that when workers are aware they're being watched, the quality and quantity of their output goes up. If I've been honest with my friends about the areas I need to beware of and grow in, and if I know that the next time we meet they're going to look me in the eye and ask me how I'm doing with them, I'm going to be motivated to avoid what I need to avoid and to develop what I need to develop. I need that in my life, and so do my friends.

Chuck Swindoll defined accountability this way: "[It] includes being willing to explain one's actions; being open, unguarded, and nondefensive about one's motives; answering for one's life; supplying the reasons why."

All of this needs to be done in the context of a supportive and caring environment. Otherwise accountability can become a legalistic and controlling intrusion. And accountability, to be effective, should be invited, never imposed.

There are times when I've had a friend sternly confront me when I've been in danger of straying off course. I've been receptive to that kind of correction and even thankful for it. Why? Because I've been confident that he's had my best interest at heart. I know he cares for my well-being and wants the best for me and my family. With that kind of attitude, a friend can tell me anything I need to hear.

But here's a caveat: if you actually find yourself enjoying the process of confronting your friend, then stop and do a heart check.

You might be speaking the truth to him, but are you really doing it in love?

INGREDIENT #5: *AFFIRMATION*—CHEERLEADING YOUR FRIEND

Another way to assist a friend is through affirmation. "People have a way of becoming what you encourage them to be," said D. L. Moody, "not what you nag them to be."

As a friend, you are strategically positioned in the other person's life to enthusiastically cheer him or her on. In fact, one of the reasons my close friend Mark Mittelberg and I get along so well is that we're each other's biggest boosters. I have more confidence in him than he has in himself, and that's how he feels about me. That makes for a terrific combination!

"Affirmation becomes a process of encouragement which moves your friend to use all of his resources to arrive at the highest level of productivity and creativity," Jim Conway said.[27]

But, he added, sometimes there are subterranean factors that hinder us from affirming others. Maybe your life experiences haven't equipped you to encourage others spontaneously, perhaps you have an unwillingness to forgive them for some past hurt, or it could be that you feel competitive with them and have a subconscious desire to cut them down. Ironically, the person who's lousy at affirming others is often insecure himself, because *he* needs to be affirmed![28]

But if you're specific with your affirmation and offer it consistently, accentuating the positive and dealing constructively with the negative, you can infuse your friends with the confidence and courage to go the next step in their endeavors.

So when is the last time you told your closest friends how important they are to you? How long has it been since you've painted a compelling vision for them of what you believe God could accomplish through their unique talents, personalities, and temperaments? When's the last time you were their most vocal and unabashed cheerleader?

When We Fail to Say the Words

The absence of affirmation can cut deep. I know that from personal experience. As a youngster, I ached to hear my dad tell me that I mattered to him. I hungered to hear him say, "Lee, I'm proud of you. You're really special to me. Son, I really like who you are."

In retrospect, I suspect he was trying to communicate those feelings to me in other ways, but I needed to *hear* it from him, and I didn't. It created a wound in me that I eventually tried to heal through workaholism as I strived to earn the respect that I needed so much from him.

My dad died in 1979 while I was away at law school. I flew back for the wake, sitting by myself next to a wall. And that's when an amazing thing happened.

One by one a steady stream of my dad's friends, none of whom I knew, stopped by to greet me. What astonished me was what they said: "Are you Wally's son? Oh, he was so proud of you. He used to brag about you all the time. When you went off to Yale Law School, he was just thrilled. When you'd have a byline in the *Tribune*, he was always showing it to everybody. He couldn't stop talking about you! You were such an important part of his life."

I sat there stunned. I had no idea my dad felt that way. He hadn't told me. I had to wait until he was dead to find out. And I wondered what it would have done to our relationship if he had told me himself while we still had time together.

The lesson is this: whatever you do, never assume that your friend—or your spouse and children, for that matter—know how you feel about them. Everyone needs to be told from time to time. *So tell them.* If you do nothing else as a result of this chapter, *tell them*. Write them a letter, give them a call, invite them out for coffee. Please, don't put it off until you end up regretting your procrastination.

Affinity, acceptance, authenticity, and assistance are all important ingredients in the recipe for rich relationships, but affirmation—well, I'll tell you what: that's the spice. You don't want to do without that.

TWO CHOICES, TWO OUTCOMES

At 8:23 on the evening of March 24, 1992, an acquaintance of mine named Bill was teaching a class in marketing at Harper College in Palatine, Illinois, when his upper aorta spontaneously ruptured.

Pain clenched him. Color drained from his face. A student called the paramedics, and Bill was rushed to the hospital, then immediately transferred to another facility for seven hours of emergency surgery. There was only one chance in fifty that he'd come out alive.

Before the surgery even started, his friends began arriving at the hospital. First one, then two, then five, and finally fifteen of them huddled together for hours of intense prayer. They comforted his wife and children. And that night, all fifteen of them camped in and around his room so they could be close to him and his family during their crisis.

Miraculously Bill survived. And he emerged with an even greater appreciation for friendships. Through the years, Bill has devoted himself to cultivating close and authentic relationships with other Christians. These friends have brought rich texture and enjoyment to his life, as he has to theirs. In his time of need he was glad he had made the investment.

What a contrast to a relative of his. He was a Christian, too, but he had never opened his life to others in a meaningful way. He never reached out to "do life" in community. He stayed on the opaque end of the transparency continuum, spending his time rattling around alone in his castle, safe and secure, unbloodied by conflict but also untouched by the transforming grace of deep and abiding friendships.

After he died there was a brief service at his graveside. Bill and his wife attended, but what struck them was this: in the vast expanse of the cemetery, they were the only ones who had shown up for him. It was the legacy of a friendless life.

To put it bluntly, you have a choice. God has given you the desire and capacity to enter into community with others and thereby drive a stake through the loneliness that would otherwise darken your life. It's scary, it's risky, it's time-consuming, it's messy, it's frustrating. And it's worth it.

Just ask Bill.

GOD'S RULES ON SEX
CAN LIBERATE US

In the 1950s America was rocked by scandal when actress Ingrid Bergman conceived a child out of wedlock. So hot was the firestorm of indignation that she was chased out of Hollywood.

Fast forward forty years.

Actress Connie Seleca and John Tesh, then host of *Entertainment Tonight*, announced their engagement—and casually mentioned that they *weren't* going to engage in sex before their wedding day.

The reaction: Hollywood was aghast. *People* magazine slapped the story on its cover, with the headline, "TV Star Weds *ET* Host After a Year of Romance—But No Sex." When Tesh appeared on Maury Povich's talk show, Povich was unable to conceal his incredulity.

"John!" he declared. "In this day and age, you didn't consummate your marriage beforehand?"

Tesh shook his head. "Isn't that a comment on our society," he replied, "that not having sex before marriage would be seen as being such a big deal?"

Attitudes toward sex have been flipped upside down in recent decades. But the reason is not that people have lost clarity on what the Bible teaches, which is that sexual expression should be reserved for men and women who are married to each other. For the most part, people are well aware that this is the biblical stand.

Instead, people increasingly believe that while God may be omniscient and omnipotent, that while he's certainly holy and merciful, the truth of the matter is that when it comes to sex, we really know better than he does. Few people would actually come right out and *say* that, but they behave as if this were their belief.

They think to themselves, "The Bible's certainly outdated and outmoded when it comes to sex, isn't it? It's sure narrow and repressive and, worse yet, politically incorrect. Those kinds of strict rules may have worked a few thousand years ago when people were primitive, but today—well, we're more educated and enlightened. And I think I'm smart enough to figure out what's best for me."

We can see this unstated opinion played out in a number of arenas—especially Hollywood.

LIGHTS, CAMERA, ACTION!

When the movie *Endless Love* caused a stir because of the way it portrayed the sexual awakening—and subsequent obsession—of two teenagers, the director strongly defended his work. "I'm not encouraging fifteen-year-olds to make love," he insisted. "They do that anyway. *I'm just telling them it's quite normal.*"[1]

From soap operas to motion pictures, from cable TV to MTV, the entertainment industry fuels a popular culture in which the attitude is that sex outside of marriage is positive, not negative. For the most part, Hollywood portrays casual sex as nothing more than a natural—and expected—progression in a relationship.

Few in the audience seemed to raise an eyebrow when the widowed commander-in-chief quickly bedded a perky political consultant in the movie *The American President*. Reviewers focused on the romance—certainly not the immorality—of a lonely Iowa housewife's adulterous fling with a visiting photographer in *The*

Bridges of Madison County. Audiences thought *My Big Fat Greek Wedding* was cute and inspiring—overlooking the fact that the two main characters gleefully went to bed together before solemnly walking the aisle together.

In fact, studies have shown that over 90 percent of all sexual encounters on television and in the movies are between unmarried people. Before the average American turns eighteen, he or she has witnessed more than seventy thousand images of sex or suggested sexual intercourse between people who aren't wed to each other.

Yet Hollywood remains a fantasyland in more ways than one. Rarely does television show any consequences from the choice to become sexually active outside of marriage. Few get pregnant, few catch a disease, few suffer emotional trauma.

And when an unwed character *does* get pregnant—for example, fictional journalist Murphy Brown—her life barely skips a beat. Somehow Brown's baby got cared for by her housepainter or friends. Somehow the infant rarely kept her up at night or complicated her life. Somehow the child grew from infancy to toddler with blinding speed and a minimum of hassles.

What kind of impact does all of this have on viewers? There's no question that television plays a major role in shaping attitudes, which is why advertisers and politicians are willing to invest billions of dollars a year in commercials.

And parents can testify firsthand to the influence television has on their children. For instance, there's the story of the mother who asked her six-year-old son what time he would like his afternoon snack. He replied, "Four o'clock eastern, three o'clock central!"

Amazingly, a Lou Harris and Associates poll disclosed that nearly half of American teenagers believe that television portrays an accurate picture of the consequences of premarital sex! When they're making their own decisions about whether to become sexually active, they often look to TV for their cues—and they see nothing but bright green lights.

WHAT YOU SEE CAN HURT YOU

Not only does Hollywood think it knows more about sex than God, but so do those who consume pornography. The unease and embarrassment they feel when purchasing "adult" material suggests that they're at least generally aware that pornography doesn't come with God's seal of approval.

But their attitude seems to be, "There's nothing really wrong with some erotic magazines or X-rated videos. They can spice up my sex life and encourage a healthy hunger for sexual relations. Besides, God created the human body, didn't he? All I'm doing is admiring it!"

So today there are more hard-core pornographic shops than McDonald's restaurants. Video stores import into our neighborhoods, cable TV pumps into our living rooms, and the Internet overflows with the kind of material that used to come only in a brown paper wrapper.

According to a 1994 study, nearly half of American men and one out of six women bought erotic materials in the preceding year. Then, as the Internet came online, it became possible to access pornography anonymously—and Christians who would never have walked into an "adult" bookstore found themselves dabbling in it. For many, the attitude is "I can handle this. I know what I'm doing. What you see can't hurt you."

People who choose to have sex before marriage are also saying that they know better than God. It's certainly no secret that premarital sex is coloring outside God's moral boundaries, but many people sincerely believe that they know what's best.

Their reasoning goes this way: "Doesn't it make sense to try out a relationship before you commit to another person for a lifetime? You wouldn't invest twenty thousand dollars in a car without test-driving it first, would you? So why not take your potential spouse out for a spin? It seems logical that you're more likely to have a better marriage in the future if you try out each other sexually in the present."

How widespread are those attitudes? Only seven out of one hundred women born between 1933 and 1942 lived with a boyfriend prior to getting married; by the end of the century, almost two-thirds of adults had a cohabiting relationship before marriage. Today, it's almost becoming the norm.

What's more, religious conservatism doesn't render people immune from sexual experimentation beyond the marriage bed. According to a study, nearly 20 percent of conservative Protestants had two or more lovers in the last year, a percentage slightly higher than for Catholics and mainline Protestants. Thirty-seven percent of conservative Protestants, 40 percent of Catholics, and 43 percent of mainline Protestants have had five or more sex partners since age eighteen.[2]

SEX IS MORE THAN SKIN ON SKIN

The truth is that those who believe they know more about sex than God have bought into a very destructive myth. God's outrageous claim is that our sexuality isn't the result of an evolutionary accident but was intentionally and lovingly created by God himself—and that yes, Maury Povich, even in this day and age, Father still knows best.

As outlandish as it may sound to some, real sexual liberation and true intimacy are found within the moral boundaries that God has compassionately designed for us. In fact, as this chapter will show, the latest research by social scientists is confirming over and over again that God's way is the best way. It's one more remarkable bit of affirmation that his wisdom really works.

Unfortunately, the intersection of the sacred and the sensual has been a fertile breeding ground for misconceptions through the ages. Christians have acquired the reputation of being sexually repressed and prudish—a reputation somewhat justified by misguided attempts in centuries past to declare sex a necessary evil. But if we use the Bible as our source, we find that God intended sex to be a wonderful and important part of the bonding process between husbands and wives. He designed it not just for procreation but for pleasure as well.

The Bible says that sexual intercourse allows two people to experience a unique oneness.[3] When our sexuality is expressed in the context of the loving, secure, trust-filled, long-lasting, and safe environment of marriage, it's a mysterious method of mathematics in which one plus one equals one.

In his Bible paraphrase, Eugene Peterson renders 1 Corinthians 6:16, a passage echoing that concept, this way:

> There's more to sex than mere skin on skin. Sex is as much spiritual mystery as physical fact. As written in Scripture, "The two become one." Since we want to become spiritually one with the Master, we must not pursue the kind of sex that avoids commitment and intimacy, leaving us more lonely than ever—the kind of sex that can never "become one."[4]

God's design is for husbands and wives to enjoy a vital, regular, and mutually satisfying physical relationship. Scripture tells husbands and wives that their bodies belong not just to themselves but to their spouses as well. Then the Bible adds, "Do not deprive each other except by mutual consent and for a time, so that you may devote yourselves to prayer."[5]

Knowing the allure of sex and its potential for abuse, God in his compassion also drew appropriate boundaries as a way of protecting us from pain. We transgress those lines of morality at our own risk—and there has been a proliferation of empirical evidence in recent years that we, as a society, are increasingly suffering the consequences of ignoring his commands.

THE TRUTH ABOUT CONSEQUENCES

In light of our collective experience during the last few decades, who can doubt anymore that God's approach to sex is better than Hollywood's? The consequences that the entertainment industry irresponsibly overlooks are eroding the moral foundation of our nation—as well as its health—at an alarming pace.

For example, television may not depict the consequences of the fifty-seven types of sexually transmitted diseases, but scientists report that they are at an epidemic level. Every day, another 41,000 Americans contract one of these pernicious illnesses. Two-thirds of all sexually transmitted diseases occur in people twenty-five years of age or younger. Some of these illnesses, like herpes, are incurable; others cause infertility; AIDS can carry a death sentence.

Another often-deadly disease—cervical cancer—also is being spread by unfaithful husbands. In 1996 researchers established that women are five to eleven times more likely to develop this disease if their spouses have multiple sexual partners. This is because cervical cancer is directly linked to a virus that is spread by sexual intercourse. "In effect, the husband takes cancer home to his wife," said a scientist at Johns Hopkins University School of Medicine.

The World Health Organization estimates that there are a third of a *billion* cases of sexually transmitted diseases around the planet, and at least thirty-eight million people worldwide already carry the HIV virus, which causes AIDS. In 2003 alone, an estimated five million people contracted HIV—more than in any single year since the epidemic began. More than twenty *million* people have already died of AIDS. Dr. David Pence, an expert on AIDS, declared, "We are indeed at war with a virus quite capable of destroying our civilization."[6]

Television also overlooks how these consequences get passed down through the generations. You've heard about the horrific polio epidemic of the 1950s? In 1996 alone, more babies were born with birth defects from sexually transmitted diseases than all of the children afflicted with polio during that entire ten-year epidemic. In 2003, 630,000 children under the age of fifteen acquired HIV — 90 percent of them becoming infected through their mothers. For children between the ages of one and four, AIDS is already the ninth leading cause of death — and before long it's expected to become one of the top five killers.

In addition, television seldom shows the consequences of the inadvertent pregnancies that occur in premarital sex. At the middle-class suburban high school down the road from where I'm writing this, one hundred girls get pregnant each year. That's about average. Nationwide, a teenager gets pregnant every thirty seconds around the clock, for a total of one million per year. The price tag for society: an estimated one hundred *billion* dollars in medical, welfare, and other costs over the next two decades.

Around the country, 1.2 million babies are born without fathers each year, and these children face terrible disadvantages in virtually every area of life — socially, financially, emotionally, behaviorally, academically, and even physically. They lose across the board — and society is reeling as a result. Even so, the pace of unwed pregnancies is accelerating. Two out of three children born in 1996 will end up living in a single-parent household before their eighteenth birthday.

Further, television doesn't show the trauma suffered by the 1.2 million American women — including four hundred thousand teenagers — who end their pregnancies with abortions each year.

One study showed they are more likely to attempt suicide than other women; in other research, psychiatrists reported negative psychiatric manifestations in 55 percent of women who had undergone legal abortions; and in another study, "even those women who were strongly supportive of the right to abort reacted to their own abortions with regret, anger, embarrassment, fear of disapproval, and even shame."[7]

Many live with an aching regret they cannot seem to resolve. Said a Washington, D.C., psychiatrist and obstetrician who has performed thousands of abortions,

> I think every woman .... has a trauma at destroying a pregnancy.... A psychological price is paid.... It may be alienation, it may be a pushing away from human warmth, perhaps a hardening of the maternal instinct. Something happens on the deepest levels of a woman's consciousness when she destroys a pregnancy. I know that as a psychiatrist.[8]

Television doesn't show the consequences of sexual addiction, that compulsive behavior that causes thirteen million Americans to engage in risky and self-destructive activities.

Television rarely shows the emotional devastation that occurs when nonmarital intimacy is followed by abandonment. Or the shame, guilt, and crushed self-esteem that can haunt a person after a sexual encounter that burns tantalizingly bright for a short time but then turns ice-cold.

Ask any counselor on a suicide hotline, and he or she will tell you that the most common calls concern shattered relationships, especially those in which sex was involved. One study showed that 85 percent of unmarried women under psychiatric care were sexually active.

Hollywood has led the charge in the sexual revolution, but the casualties are piling up every day. Nearly two thousand years ago the apostle Paul wrote words that still have the ring of truth: "All other sins a man commits are outside his body, but he who sins sexually sins against his own body."[9]

THE HIGH PRICE OF CHEAP THRILLS

There's yet another consequence of sex outside of marriage that television probably will never show: the spiritual costs. However, this can be the most painful of all.

The Bible says that our wrongdoing causes a separation between us and our holy God.[10] Part of the way in which this happens
is that people are aware deep down inside that they're rebelling
against God when they choose their way instead of his.

So if they're engaging in illicit sex, they naturally tend to shy
away from talking with God in prayer, to shrink back from worshiping him and coming to the Communion table, to stop reading
the Bible, and to stop interacting with Christian friends whose
moral lifestyle only accentuates their own sin. They learn to plug
their ears to the promptings of the Holy Spirit as he tries to dis-
suade them from straying.

As a result, their spiritual life shrivels as their heart turns numb
and indifferent toward God. Often what had once been a rich and
thriving relationship with him drains away until they feel spiritually parched.

There's no way to sugarcoat this: people cannot be tightly
related to God at the same time they are knowingly and defi-
antly violating God's boundaries concerning sexuality. You can't
be boldly rebelling against him in any ongoing way and expect
to experience unhindered growth in your relationship with him.
That's a terrible consequence for Christians.

Hollywood may gloss over these costs, but they're real, and
God wants to spare us from them. Please understand this: God
doesn't oppose sexual sin because he doesn't want us to have fun;
he opposes it in the same way parents oppose a car that's careening
toward their child—out of loving concern to avert the impending
harm.

What should we do? One thing's for certain—we can't hide
from the all-pervasive media, but we can be discerning. When a
television show, movie, or music video tries to convince you that
everybody's enjoying sex outside of marriage, that adultery is in
and fidelity is out, that only losers and loners aren't out trolling for
cheap thrills, call it the lie that it is.

Train your children to second-guess the values that the media are peddling, so they don't unwittingly buy into distorted images. Help your kids avoid what happened to one girl who forfeited her virginity and then wrote, "I just couldn't compete with what I saw on television; the bombardment never stopped, and so I said, ['What's the difference?']"[11]

And when temptation is beckoning, when your hormones are pumping and you're being enticed down the path that Hollywood so alluringly portrays, pause for a moment to count the costs — the physical, emotional, psychological, and spiritual consequences. Compare that awful downside with the fleeting and hollow upside of giving in. Let that help you make the choice to stay within the moral framework that God has created for us — because although it sounds outrageous, it's within those restrictions that authentic sexual freedom lies.

THE DANGERS OF VISUAL ADULTERY

What would God say to consumers of "adult" materials who think it's merely a harmless catalyst for pepping up their sex lives? I think he'd simply tell them, "I know better. When I urge you to steer clear of that stuff, it's for your own sake."

The apostle Paul said, "Finally, brothers, whatever is true, whatever is noble, whatever is right, whatever is pure, whatever is lovely, whatever is admirable — if anything is excellent or praiseworthy — think about such things."[12]

It's not that God is embarrassed by the human bodies he created. But he made them to express their sexuality within a relationship that is loving, committed, and monogamous — qualities that pornography defiles at every turn.

Pornography paints a world in which sex is cold, mechanical, transient, degrading, and increasingly violent. Twenty percent of pornographic material depicts acts of sexual assault and rape, and that percentage is increasing rapidly.

Inevitably, these images desensitize those who view them, twisting their thinking, attitudes, and values. Psychology professor Vincent Cline said that the shocking and repulsive soon become commonplace, then legitimized, then acceptable, then attractive.[13]

In one study, a group of average men expressed revulsion toward sexual assaults and extended compassion toward victims who had been molested. But after viewing pornography, their attitudes were transformed. They had become more flippant toward rape, which they saw as something women deserved or wanted.

That's the lie in 97 percent of violent pornography — that women actually want to be assaulted and will come to enjoy it. Another study, by a Canadian researcher, suggests that even nonviolent pornographic images can weaken men's attitudes toward sexual assault.[14]

And for those who wonder whether there's a connection between pornography and the actual commission of violent crimes, take a look at what happened in Pasco County, Florida, where the sheriff conducted a year-long crackdown on "adult" material. At the end of the year, there were 53 percent fewer sexual assaults in that county compared with other areas of Florida.

This was the conclusion of former U.S. Surgeon General C. Everett Koop: "I believe we have enough evidence to implicate pornography .... as a kind of 'accessory' to antisocial actions that produce grave and profoundly harmful outcomes."[15]

Pornography won't spice up your sex life; it will poison it. It introduces false comparisons, it prompts men to act out fantasies that can degrade their spouse instead of affirming and valuing her, and it introduces distrust and selfishness into the relationship. "Pornography makes women and children into objects, pieces of meat on public display," said Chuck Colson. "Pornography reduces these ... creatures to trash. As it does so, it jeers at the God who has conferred human dignity."[16]

In his book *Christians in a Sex-Crazed Culture*, Bill Hybels wrote that God designed sexuality to flow out of a loving and intimate relationship in which there's nurturing, communication, sharing, serving, romancing, and tenderness. When those values are cultivated in a marriage, they arouse sexual interest. But

> the use of pornography short-circuits all of that. It reduces the sexual dimension of marriage to a biologically induced athletic event, and eventually ... there is no longer much emphasis on the loving part of marriage. Once that is drained out of a relationship, the heart and soul of marital sexuality is gone. The woman starts feeling used and abused, and the man starts feeling frustrated and empty. He begins to think that a new position, a new activity or, better yet, a new partner or partners would relieve his frustration and emptiness.[17]

Too often the use of pornography can start men on a descent into more and more bizarre material, like the downhill slide of a drug addict who needs stronger and stronger doses to get the same high. If you don't think pornography can be psychologically addicting, then consider this letter written by a man who attended Hybels' church:

> I am an emotional invalid. I am crippled by my addiction to pornography. It paralyzes my spiritual life, it perverts my view of the world, it distorts my social life, it wreaks havoc in my emotional stability ... and I just can't stop.... Lust eats me up, yet it does not satisfy.... [Pornography] promises me everything, it produces nothing.[18]

God would tell us, "Trust me in this: the images that you allow into your mind inevitably affect who you become, how you act, what you pursue, and how you feel about yourself and others." Again, Father knows best—and as we've seen, the latest research is backing him up.

Don't think that God is mistaken in your case and that somehow you can innocently dabble in pornography while being miraculously impervious to its effects. "So, if you think you are standing firm, be careful that you don't fall," Paul warned.[19]

So clean house. Install an Internet filter that will block obscene material from your computer. Go to that secret stash of magazines or hidden stack of X-rated videos and put them at the curb for the next garbage pickup. Do it before you slide any farther—and before your kids stumble across them.

Consider this ominous statistic: 70 percent of pornography eventually winds up in the hands of children. What's more, the average age of first exposure to Internet pornography is now eleven years. Nearly half of school-aged children receive pornographic spam each and every day, while 80 percent of teenagers between the ages of fifteen and seventeen have experienced multiple exposures to hard-core porn. If obscene images can warp an adult's view of sexuality, think how devastating they can be in twisting your own child's attitudes during the critical time when his or her sexual identity is being formed.

"I got into my brother's pornographic magazines when I was growing up," one forty-five-year-old businessman told me, "and it distorted my view of intimacy so much that to this day I haven't been able to undo it all. I'm still unraveling the ways it has undermined my relationships with women. I feel like I was sabotaged as a kid."

For those who feel a compulsion to consume pornography, it's important to talk to someone about it. If you don't, it will sink its claws deeper and deeper into you. Tell a friend you can trust and ask him to walk you through recovery. Or talk it over with a pastor or Christian counselor who can help you get at the root of this dependency before it damages your relationships.

But first and foremost, talk it over with God. When *Discipleship Journal* asked its readers when they were most likely to succumb to temptation, the greatest number of respondents—more than eight out of ten—said it was when they had not been spending much time with the Lord.

Don't let your embarrassment over pornography continue to create a wedge between you and God. Go to him for help—now.

MYTHS ABOUT "TRIAL MARRIAGES"

For those who sincerely think it's best to test out a relationship by having premarital sex, I believe God would say, "You're putting yourself and your entire future in terrible jeopardy. Believe me, I know what's best for you."

For years people have been scoffing at the Bible's teaching on sex, but again the social research is piling up on God's side. As Ray Short points out in his book *Sex, Love, or Infatuation*:

- If you think that living together is going to make your eventual marriage stronger, think again. Statistics demonstrate that those who live together are twice as likely to get divorced after they do marry.
- Studies have shown that the more premarital sex you have, the *less* likely you'll be happy in your future marriage and the *more* likely that you or your spouse will cheat after you're wed. Most likely to commit adultery: women who had engaged in premarital sex.
- While couples often think that premarital sex will strengthen their eventual sex life when they're married, research shows that the exact opposite is true. Married couples are *less* likely to have a satisfactory sex life if they live together first.[20]

Other research has established that a woman is far more likely to be physically abused by a live-in lover than by a husband and that she's five times more likely to be forced into an unwanted sex act by a boyfriend than a spouse. Those most likely to be pushed into sex against their will are women who are living with a man prior to marriage.

Robert Moeller, who has written extensively about marriage, observed that the very concept of a "trial marriage" is a contradiction in terms. "By definition marriage is an exclusive, lifetime, permanent commitment," he said. "How can something temporary, nonbinding, and open ended be considered a test of something that's just the opposite?" He added that cohabiting creates distrust:

> When couples say, "We just want to see if we're compatible before we get married," what they're really saying is, "We have doubts about each other as future partners. And we want a quick and easy way out of this if we don't like it." Can you see what uncertainty does to sexual intimacy? It hangs a big question mark over the bed. "Is today the last time we'll make love? What if my partner meets someone more interesting? If I don't please or perform up to standards, is this relationship over?" The reason married sex is so superior to "trial sex" is that the questions which plague cohabiting couples have already been settled.[21]

Some of the most startling research on this subject was published in 1994 by researchers at the University of Chicago. They interviewed 3,432 Americans, in an effort to produce the most accurate and comprehensive insights into human sexuality in our country. Their findings were so myth shattering that they captured front-page attention. Among their conclusions:

- Married couples reported being the most physically pleased and emotionally satisfied.
- The lowest rates of satisfaction were among single men and women — the very ones presumed to be having the hottest sex.
- The group having the most sex is not the young and footloose but the married.

- Physical and emotional satisfaction started to decline when people had more than one sex partner.[22]

The scientists admitted being especially surprised when their data revealed that the most consistently sexually satisfied women in the country were conservative Protestants, followed closely by Catholics and mainline Protestants—all of whom had a significantly higher frequency of orgasm than those with no religious affiliation. But after thinking about it, the scientists came up with an explanation: maybe those who follow biblical teachings "firmly believe in the holiness of marriage and of sexuality as an expression of their love for their husbands."[23]

No kidding!

The researchers added that "despite the popular image of the straight-laced conservative Protestants, there is at least circumstantial evidence that the image may be a myth at least as it pertains to sexual intercourse."[24]

Again and again there has been independent confirmation by social scientists that God's plan for our sexuality really does make sense. As ironic as it may sound, the truth is that his boundaries don't bind us, but they liberate us to experience intimacy in its most fulfilling form.

As the University of Chicago researchers said, "Our results could be read to mean that an orthodox view of romance, courtship, and sexuality—your mom's view, perhaps—is the only route to happiness and sexual satisfaction."[25] That, the scientists said, was not what they intended. But clearly that's where the evidence points.

FORGIVENESS AND CLEANSING

When it comes to our sexuality, as in all other areas of our life, God can be trusted. Though our sexual passions may run hot, we can trust that God will empower us to live the kind of life he wants us to lead. Though temptations abound, we can trust that God will help us from falling into self-destructive behavior. Those with sexual stress in their marriage can trust that God will walk them through it. Victims of sexual assault can trust that he will gently bind their emotional wounds.

And though we have all strayed sexually—whether in thought, word, or deed—we can also trust that God's forgiveness is readily available to all who ask for it. Though sexual misconduct can leave an especially stubborn stain of shame, he can scrub us clean when we humbly turn to him and admit our wrongdoing rather than try to rationalize it.

God delights—*he absolutely revels*—in answering the kind of prayer that King David uttered: "Wash away all my iniquity and cleanse me from my sin."[26] When you come to him with a heartfelt request like that, he will forgive you (which is external and restores us in God's sight) and he will cleanse you (which takes place inside us as God over time releases us from our shame).

I know. He's done it for me. I don't like to talk about this, because it's personal and painful, but in my days as an atheist, when my highest goal in life was to experience pleasure, I lived a promiscuous lifestyle and left disillusioned victims in my wake.

I would use whatever tactic it took, from false flattery to manipulative lies, to achieve a conquest. Afterward I would callously walk away, never giving a second thought to the other person. Mission accomplished.

I thought I knew best. I was wrong. Instead of happiness and fulfillment, I found nothing but emptiness. And it's a testimony to the height and breadth of the grace of God that he has forgiven me and eased my burden of regret over the years.

Now I can echo the apostle John's words of joyous amazement: "How great is the love the Father has lavished on us, that we should be called children of God!"[27] Imagine, someone like me—and yes, even a person like you—lovingly adopted into the family of God forever.

But maybe you're still skeptical. Perhaps you think you're the exception, someone outside the range of God's forgiving power. If that's the case, maybe this letter will help. It was sent to the leaders at Willow Creek Community Church by a young woman from the congregation. See what she found about God's willingness to forgive—and consider how you might find release from the transgressions that still haunt you.

> I grew up in a home where guilt was a powerful tool for discipline. I grew up a shy, scared girl, immobilized by guilt and feeling responsible for anything and everything bad that occurred, and mostly feeling unworthy and unlovable to God.
>
> When I was in college, because of lots of bad choices, I found myself pregnant at the end of my junior year. At the time, the only decision I could live with was to have an abortion. I couldn't live with knowing how I disappointed my parents. I couldn't live with nine months of guilt and shame. I couldn't live with being responsible for my actions.
>
> The entire day of the ordeal, I *knew* I was violating a sacred commandment of God's. I was willfully murdering this life. And I believed with all my heart he could never forgive me.
>
> Through a friendship, I began coming to Willow Creek and became immersed in biblical teaching. I heard dozens of messages on forgiveness and repentance and how Jesus died for me to bear my sins. I heard it all—but I never believed it in my heart. I never owned it. *How could God forgive me for killing my baby?*
>
> I finally made a commitment to Jesus Christ in February 1989, and that June I felt I needed to take the step of making my faith public through baptism. During the ceremony, there was a big wooden cross on the stage, and we were to write some of our sins on a piece of paper and pin it to the cross just before we were baptized, as a symbol that we were forgiven by God.
>
> I remember my fear—the most fear I *ever* remember—as I wrote as tiny as I could on a piece of paper the word *abortion*. I was scared someone would open up the paper and read it and find out

it was me. I almost wanted to walk out of the auditorium during the service—the guilt and fear were that strong.

When my turn came, I walked up toward the center of the stage toward the cross, pinned the paper there, and was directed over toward Bill Hybels to be baptized. He looked me straight in the eyes. I thought for sure he was going to read in my eyes the terrible secret I had kept from everybody for so long.

But instead, I felt that God was telling me, "I love you. It's okay. You are forgiven. You are forgiven!" I felt so much love for me—a terrible sinner. That's the first time I've ever really *felt* forgiveness and unconditional love. It was unbelievable, and it was indescribable.

Afterward we all sang "I'm Forever Grateful," and I cried with so much joy and relief. *Relief,* after all these years.

As incredible as it sounds, regardless of how far you have strayed sexually, there is hope, there is cleansing, there is forgiveness, and there is new life available through Jesus. That's the outrageous claim of the gospel.

RANDOM ACTS
OF KINDNESS
AREN'T ENOUGH

Darla took out her crayons and scrawled a letter to her heavenly Father:

Dear Mr. God,

Did you really mean, "Do unto others as they do unto you"?
Because if you did, then I'm going to fix my brother![1]

Little Darla isn't the first person to creatively rewrite the Golden Rule. Politicians in Chicago have their own rendering: "Do unto others *before* they do unto you." And everybody in the business world knows the famous corporate version: "Whoever owns the gold gets to make the rules."

But those, of course, are corruptions of the Golden Rule that Jesus articulated in one of the most widely quoted Bible verses in the world. In what has been called the Mount Everest of ethics, the uppermost peak of the greatest sermon in history, Jesus said in the Sermon on the Mount, "So in everything, do to others what you would have them do to you, for this sums up the Law and the Prophets."[2]

He was explaining that if you want the Cliffs Notes summary of the Bible's entire teaching on how to relate to others, this absolutely outlandish and revolutionary statement is it. What's more, he wasn't saying that we should abide by this rule only when we feel like it, through random acts of kindness expressed on a whim, but that this should become a day-in, day-out lifestyle of compassion and caring.

No other religious leader had ever taught this before, which might surprise you because it's commonly said that virtually every religious system in the world has its own golden rule. While it's true many do, the difference is that every other religion I've seen had a weaker version that was expressed in a negative form. For instance:

- Five hundred years before Jesus was born, someone asked Confucius, "Is there one word that may serve as a rule of practice for all one's life?" Confucius replied, "Is not *reciprocity* such a word? What you do not want done to yourself, do not do to others."

- Four hundred years before Christ, a philosopher in Athens taught, "Whatever angers you when you suffer at the hands of others, do not do to others."

- About three hundred years before Christ, the Stoics had a teaching that said, "What you do not want to be done to you, do not do to anyone else."

- Roughly two hundred years before Christ, the author of *The Tobit*, which is part of the Apocrypha, wrote this particularly succinct version: "What thou thyself hatest, to no man do."

And two decades before Jesus was born, a young student came up to the great Jewish Rabbi Hillel. "I'm ready to convert to Judaism," he said, "on one condition—that you teach me the whole Law while I stand on one leg."

In other words, "Spare me all the complexities and intricacies, the nuances and the details—if you can't boil down to a few words how we should deal with others, then I'm not interested."

So while the student was performing his impromptu flamingo imitation, Hillel replied, "What is hateful to yourself, do to no other; that is the whole Law, and the rest is commentary. Go and learn."

GOLD VERSUS PYRITE

As far as they go, those maxims might be helpful. But there's a big difference between their negative approach and how Jesus intentionally crafted the Golden Rule.

For instance, in some religious traditions the negative version is essentially based on selfish reciprocity—*I won't hurt you because I hope, in return, that you won't hurt me.* That's just protecting your own self-interest, and there's nothing especially admirable about that.

But by contrast the basis of the Golden Rule is selfless generosity. Jesus was telling us to be caring toward others not to get something in return but regardless of whether the other person pays back the favor or not.

And here's another significant difference: under the negative versions, a person could merely live a passive, detached, and uninvolved life by simply not doing harm to others. However, the Golden Rule calls on us to go on the compassion offensive by grabbing the initiative and deliberately choosing a policy of being kind toward other people. As Christian scholar D. A. Carson wrote,

> The negative form would teach behavior like this: If you do not enjoy being robbed, don't rob others. If you do not like being cursed, don't curse others.... If you do not care to be clubbed over the head, don't club others over the head. However, the positive form teaches behavior like this: If you enjoy being loved, love

others. If you like to receive things, give to others. If you like being appreciated, appreciate others. The positive form is thus far more searching than its negative counterpart. Here there is no permission to withdraw into a world where I offend no one, but accomplish no positive good, either.[3]

Someone once explained the difference this way: if you own a car, the negative rule would tell you, "Just don't run anybody over. Don't get drunk and cross the centerline." The Golden Rule would include that admonition but would go even farther by saying, "When people need a ride, offer it to them. If the widow down the block needs to go to the grocery store, make yourself available. If a stranger is trying to get home, give him a lift. Make an effort to go on the lookout for ways you can serve people in a manner that you would want them to serve you."

It's this sweeping and countercultural quality that makes the Golden Rule so incredibly outrageous. In fact, just imagine what the world would be like if everyone were to live by it.

The terror alert would go down to the safe "green" level. We wouldn't have to lock our doors at night. We could send our kids to the park without worrying about them. Sales of automobile anti-theft devices would plummet. We could shake hands on a business deal and feel supremely confident that we wouldn't be double-crossed. There would be no office politics, no hurtful gossip, no racism, no drive-by shootings, no hate crimes, no suicide bombings or beheadings in the Mideast, no starvation or genocide in Africa, no corruption or double-dealing in Washington, D.C. Nobody would cut you off on the expressway, and during the winter all the people who own snowblowers would gladly clear everybody else's driveways. We would live in a world of forgiveness, compassion, peace, goodwill—and even unfailing good manners!

Yet the world isn't like that. And the problem isn't that the Golden Rule is too esoteric or complicated to understand. "We do not do unto others as we would wish them to do unto us, because the whole time we are thinking only about ourselves, and we never transfer our thought to the other person," said theologian D. Martyn Lloyd-Jones.

That's the condition of the world because of sin: we're primarily selfish people who are preoccupied with our own well-being. Whenever most people go out of their way to help someone else, they have mixed motives. They always want to know what they'll get out of the deal.

It's like the story of some children whose cat had recently delivered a litter of kittens. The youngsters peered into the cardboard box and watched in delight as the tiny kittens snuggled together.

"Aw, isn't that cute?" exclaimed a little girl. "They love each other so much that they're trying to keep each other warm."

"Well, not exactly," replied her world-wise mother. "Actually, they're trying to keep *themselves* warm."

In contrast, here's what the Golden Rule is all about: *trying to keep somebody else warm, even if it means that we get cold in the process.*

As idyllic as it would be to live in a world where the Golden Rule was universally followed, we know that's not going to happen. Despite the efforts of some people to promote National Random Acts of Kindness Week (a concept, ironically, championed by a congressman who was later convicted of the unkindly acts of extortion and tax evasion), one study showed that Americans are becoming more cynical and less compassionate.

Some people lose their good intentions in the face of everyday pressures and realities, as did the California motorist whose car had a license plate that included the word "Peace." Police said that after she tailgated a slow-moving pickup truck on a two-lane canyon road, she pulled alongside the other vehicle, swatted at it with an aluminum baseball bat, and then threw a can of air freshener at it as she roared past. "She said she was in a hurry and was getting frustrated," said the state trooper who ticketed her. When he asked about her license plate, "She told me she got it because she thought there was so much violence going on in today's society."

The Bible tells us that people naturally tend to balk at submitting to God's laws and teachings, including the Golden Rule.[4] And yet as Christ followers supernaturally empowered by the Holy Spirit, we can help change a little corner of our world if we put the rule into action.

How do we do that? As I've attempted to implement the Golden Rule in my own day-to-day living—admittedly, not always successfully—I've found that I frequently need to recalibrate my perspective. In a world that all too frequently revolves around me, I've got to purposefully reorient my attitude on a regular basis if I'm ever going to follow this outlandish teaching of Jesus.

SEEING THROUGH HEAVEN'S EYES

I periodically need to remind myself of the value that God places on other human beings, even when I don't know the other person or when he or she is very different from me. But to be honest, that's not natural for me to do.

Every once in a while, though, I get a reminder, like reading about an incident that occurred in North Carolina in 1995. Ten-year-old Lawrence Shields was picking through a bucket of debris in a gemstone mine when a rock piqued his interest. "I just liked the shape of it," he said.

When he knocked off the dirt and grit that were clinging to it, and as he rubbed it on his shirt to polish it up, he saw that this was much more than just a rock. It turned out to be a sapphire. And not just any sapphire—a *1,061-carat* sapphire!

Here's the point: when we look at other people, we tend to focus on the outside, which is soiled by sin. We see the rebellion or failure, the bizarre lifestyle or proud attitude, and we often overlook the real value that's on the inside—where each one of us is a gem of incalculable worth, created in the image of almighty God. We, as individuals, are so valued and loved that God was willing to pay the infinite price of his Son's death to clean away our sin and restore us to himself.

So when you look at someone whose life has been thoroughly corrupted by sin, can you say to yourself, "Their life situation may be *awful*, but the image of God within them is *awesome*!" Can you look at the people you may have devalued because they're different from you or poorer than you or less educated than you, and imagine the ultimate value that God attaches to them despite their circumstances?

It's like one of my favorite songs, "In Heaven's Eyes," in which Phil McHugh pictured people as they appear to God and found no worthless losers and no hopeless causes. When we see people from God's perspective, all of a sudden we have a new inspiration to treat them with the same dignity, respect, and honor that we desire for ourselves.

Does that sound naive? Maybe so. But apart from that divinely altered perception, I don't have a chance of being obedient to Christ's command that I love others as myself. It's simply not going to happen.

That's one reason why a motto of the church where I became a Christian is that people matter to God. *All* people. It's a reminder to all of us that we need to see each other as having untold value in the eyes of Jesus.

CRAWLING INTO SOMEONE'S LIFE

There's another shift in perspective that has to take place. In whatever circumstances we're in, we need to see the situation from the viewpoint of others. This merely means that we're more inclined to treat others as we'd like to be treated when we put ourselves in their shoes and see their predicament from their angle. As the apostle Paul said, "Carry each other's burdens, and in this way you will fulfill the law of Christ."[5] How can we carry another person's burden until we understand the burden as he or she sees it?

I received a lesson along these lines late one Wednesday night when I was a teaching pastor at Willow Creek Community Church. After an exhausting day of work and an evening church service, I was getting ready to go to bed, when the phone rang.

On the other end of the line was a young couple who had been driving about half an hour away from my home when their car broke down. They didn't have any money, there weren't any gas stations open at that hour, and their two kids were bundled in the backseat. Since they were new to town, they didn't know anybody to call for help. But they had been to our church for one of our services a few days earlier and had seen my name in the program. So they looked up my number in the phone book.

"I know this is a terrible imposition," the man said, "but yours is the only name we remembered."

My first exasperated thought was, "We've got nearly a hundred different ministries at the church—don't we have one that picks up people when their cars break down?" My second unspoken reaction was, "Didn't they see Bill Hybels' name in the program? He's the senior pastor! Why couldn't they have called *him*? He lives closer than I do!" My third thought was, "Who can I call to handle this, so I don't have to bother?"

Frankly, I was feeling put-upon and sorry for myself. After all, a warm and cozy bed was beckoning, and I thought I deserved some peace and quiet after logging a long day.

But then I caught myself. I had to shift my perspective. I tried to imagine the situation from their viewpoint. What must it be like to be new in town, not knowing anybody, and be stranded late at night with your kids in the car? When I pictured that, my attitude started to soften. That's when I finally asked myself, "What would I want them to do for me if I were in their situation?"

So I got in my car and drove over to pick them up and drive them to their apartment. Then I promptly forgot about the incident—until three years later.

After I finished speaking at one of our weekend services, that same guy came down to say hello. As it turned out, both he and his wife had gotten deeply involved in the church during the intervening years.

"I just want you to know I've never forgotten how you rescued us that night," he said. "When there have been times that I've been tempted to get disillusioned about the church or Christians, I think about that, and it reminds me that people really do care."

Gulp. I felt embarrassed as I recalled my initial grousing when I got his call. But his gratitude over all those years just demonstrates the power of the Golden Rule. When we follow it even though it's inconvenient, others may be impacted in deep ways. Why? Because living it out is so thoroughly unexpected—so absolutely against the grain—in our every-person-for-himself society.

So is there someone whose life you need to crawl into for a moment to view the world from their perspective? Maybe one of your children or an employee or even your boss? I can tell you from personal experience that this can transform your whole attitude toward them. Suddenly you'll be more willing to help them as you'd want to be helped.

Like the time I was impatiently standing in line at the grocery store on a brutally frigid evening, anxious to get to my warm home for dinner. But the line wasn't moving. I waited and waited. I shifted my weight. I sighed loudly. I muttered under my breath. Still no movement. What was taking so long? Was the cashier a trainee? Was some customer chattering away to her? My blood pressure was rising fast.

Finally I looked at the head of the line to see who was daring to delay me—and I saw a tiny elderly woman slowly and painfully pulling dollar bills out of her wallet in slow motion, her hands red and raw and stiffened by the icy weather. She could barely move her fingers. Apparently she had walked to the store in the subzero weather.

Oh, man. My perspective was instantly readjusted. I glanced heavenward for forgiveness, then walked over to say, "Excuse me, ma'am, you don't know me, but it's cold outside and I've got a car. May I give you a ride home?"

This is what I've found: the Golden Rule becomes the most natural response in the world once you see life from the other person's vantage point.

LOVE FROM BEYOND OURSELVES

The Golden Rule must be fueled by love, because our motivation is not primarily based on what we can get in return. Of course, in a limited way people can tap into their own resources of love and apply the Golden Rule sporadically, here and there, depending on their mood. For instance, people might be willing to spread around some goodwill each February during Random Acts of Kindness Week. That's fine, but to live it out consistently—to make it a day-by-day lifestyle even in really difficult, inconvenient, and sacrificial situations—we need a fuel beyond what comes from within. We need to tap into God's limitless source of love.

Once, someone asked Jesus what God's greatest law is, and he answered in two parts. The first part was to love God with all our heart, soul, mind, and strength; the second part was to love our neighbor as ourselves.[6] Do you see why the order of those two laws is so critically important?

Because when we open up our lives to God, receive his grace, and yield ourselves to him, he begins to shrink our self-centeredness and simultaneously enlarge our capacity to be more caring toward others. When it comes to the Golden Rule, said Lloyd-Jones, "You do not start with your neighbor, you start with God." Loving God is what ultimately enables us to love others.

In fact, when the apostle Paul listed nine qualities that the Holy Spirit increasingly manifests in the lives of those who follow Christ, the very first one he mentions is love.[7]

It's a love fueled by God.

A CONDUIT FOR CHRIST'S CURRENT

Test yourself on this. If you've been a Christian for a long time, think back to the attitude you had toward other people five years *before* you met Jesus. Now think about your attitude toward them five years *after* you appropriated God's grace in your life. You can see a difference, can't you? I hope so!

I started out as an atheist who was in compassion deficit. I viewed other people primarily as tools to be used in my own professional and social advancement. But after I became a Christian and began to increasingly submit my character and values to Christ, my attitude toward others began to change.

In fact, the difference was so pronounced that a few months after I became a Christian, my five-year-old daughter said to my wife, "Mommy, I want God to do for me what he's done for Daddy."

Even at that tender age, she could see that God was already chipping away at the cynicism that had encrusted her father's heart. She was already beginning to notice a marked change in the way I was relating to others.

God not only enlarges our capacity for compassion but also continually empowers us to spread love to others. Trying to live out the Golden Rule without God is like drawing power from a battery. It works for a while, but sooner or later if there isn't an external source to recharge it, the battery's going to sputter and run out of energy.

However, the analogy changes when you're not operating under your own power but you're letting God express his love through your life. This is how Mother Teresa described it: "The wire is you and me; the current is God. We have the power to let the current pass through us, use us, and produce the light of the world—Jesus Christ."

A wire never runs out of power if it's attached to an inexhaustible source, and God's love never runs dry. That's why Mother Teresa would spend time every morning connecting with God in prayer, meditating on the sacrifice he made on her behalf, and drinking in his love from the Bible, so during the day she could merely act as a conduit to channel that compassion to others.

In fact, let me issue a warning: you're inevitably headed for bitter disillusionment if you try to live out the Golden Rule under your own power, without allowing God to expand your heart and work through your life. If the Golden Rule appeals to your altruistic side and you're thinking about pursuing it out of your own secular zeal, forget it.

When people don't reciprocate, when they fail to express gratitude, when they take advantage of your generosity, when nobody seems to care that doing something kind for others is eating up your time, energy, and resources, you're going to start getting cynical and wondering why you're bothering.

But the apostle John wrote this about Christians: "We love because [God] first loved us."[8] He did something *for* us, and then he does something *through* us.

Maybe a story can illustrate how this gets played out. I was flying into Midway Airport in Chicago late at night during a terrible blizzard several years ago. The passenger sitting next to me turned out to be an engineer from India. As we talked I found out he was planning to take a bus to O'Hare Airport and then have his pregnant wife drive down from a distant suburb with his two young children to pick him up. To me, that sounded like a formula for frustration.

"Look, I have a car parked at Midway," I told him. "How about if I give you a lift home?"

He was very grateful, and during our drive he asked why I had been willing to go out of my way for a stranger like him. The question took me a bit off guard, but I tried to explain. "Has anybody ever done something so kind for you that it makes you want to pass a kindness along to someone else?" I asked.

He thought for a moment and then nodded slightly.

"Well, here's the thing," I said. "Jesus Christ has done something incredibly kind for me."

As we talked some more, he understood. And that's just one example of how God's love gets passed along in a love-starved world.

MAKING A CHOICE TO MAKE A DIFFERENCE

Plain and simple, doing for others what you want them to do for you is an act of the will. We have to decide day by day to conscientiously apply ourselves to living it out despite everything that works against us.

Otherwise our busyness can cause life to flash by in such a blur that we won't pause long enough to consider others. Or sometimes we get intimidated into inaction because we see the mountain of needs in the world and we feel that whatever we do just won't make any difference. It's so easy to forget this fundamental truth: *no expression of compassion to another human being is a wasted effort.*

This struck me afresh when I was reading the words of a new volunteer who had gone to serve with Mother Teresa among the poorest of the poor in Calcutta. On their tour of a children's home, Mother Teresa spotted an infant who had been rescued from the streets but who was beyond medical help. The child was surely going to die that day.

So Mother Teresa picked up that baby and handed her to the new volunteer, with these simple instructions: "Don't let this child die without being loved."

This is what the volunteer said later: "I held her in my arms and I loved her until she died at six o'clock in the evening. I spent the hours humming Brahms' Lullaby, and do you know—*I could feel that baby, as tiny and as weak as she was, pressing herself against me.*"[9] Even a dying infant responds to a simple act of human kindness.

You don't have to take it upon yourself to change the world. Face it, you can't anyway. But just in the course of everyday life—from common courtesies to going out of your way to assist those in need—doing to others what you would want them to do to you will make a difference in both their life and your own.

I vividly remember an incident that occurred during the spring when I was in fifth grade. Each day before our morning and afternoon recesses, we would choose sides for kickball.

In the classroom's elaborate but unwritten social structure, there were two boys who were consistently ostracized. Ted was a computer geek back in the days of the slide rule. He wore thick glasses, talked with a high-pitched voice, and wasn't very athletic. The other youngster, Johnny, who was overweight and dull-witted, had failed the fifth grade twice, so he was older than the rest of us. Nobody hung out with either of them. In fact, they weren't even friends with each other!

One day our teacher sent Ted and Johnny out of the class to run an errand. When they were gone, she turned to the class and said, "Twice a day you choose sides for kickball, and every time Ted and Johnny are selected last. I know you're not intending to hurt them, but why not try something different for a change? Why not do for them what you'd want them to do for you?"

The next day, I was captain for one of the kickball teams, which meant I had first pick. I'll tell you what: I don't remember much about fifth grade. I can't recall the books we read or what the classroom looked like or the subjects we studied or most of the other students.

But to this day if I close my eyes, I can still see the look of absolute joyful surprise on Ted's face when I chose him first for my kickball team. And I'll never forget the excited expression on Johnny's face when the other captain selected him as his first choice.

Was this a big thing? No. Did it change the world? Of course not. But it *did* something to me. More than four decades later I remember it. And I'll bet if you were to track down Ted and Johnny and ask them about that warm spring day back in 1963, they'd recall all the details, because I'm sure it did something to them too.

We had merely treated them with dignity and respect, the way all of us wanted to be treated. And that's all we need to decide to do each day as we encounter waiters and cashiers, colleagues and competitors, neighbors and friends, bosses and employees, children and parents, blue-collar laborers and white-collar executives, people in trouble and people who are just muddling through life.

We just need to make the decision to do it. When we do, people will be impacted.

And so will we.

THE GOLDEN TOUCH

My friend Mark Mittelberg can attest to the power of a single act of kindness. When he was living in North Dakota, he ducked inside a grocery store one afternoon to pick up a few things. While there he decided to buy a bouquet of flowers for his wife, Heidi. As he was standing in line at the cash register, an elderly woman ahead of him noticed the flowers.

"Is it your wife's birthday?" she asked.

"No," Mark said. "I just wanted to surprise her."

The woman sighed. "My late husband used to do that for me," she said wistfully. "It was his way of saying, 'I love you.' But that was many, many years ago." She smiled weakly. "Many years."

When her turn came at the cashier, the woman paid for her groceries, turned and said good-bye, and walked away, pushing a small cart. Suddenly an idea struck Mark. He quickly paid for his flowers and food items — and then dashed into the parking lot to find the woman.

"Here," he said as he held out the bouquet for her. "Your husband isn't here to do this, so I'd like to give you these."

The woman was so moved by this gesture that she invited Mark to visit her nearby apartment for a cup of tea. While they sipped their refreshments, she brought out old pictures of her husband and reminisced about the past. Her spirits were lifted.

After that day, Mark rarely thought about that woman again, but he stayed alive in her memory. A decade passed, during which Mark and Heidi relocated several times, eventually settling in suburban Chicago.

Somehow this elderly woman tracked them down one Christmas and mailed them a box full of antique toys for their children, Emma Jean and Matthew. She remembered Mark because of his golden touch on her life so many years earlier, and she still felt joy because he had treated her the way he would want to be treated.

This is what God tells us through the Bible:

> Do not merely listen to the word, and so deceive yourselves. Do what it says. Anyone who listens to the word but does not do what it says is like a man who looks at his face in a mirror and, after looking at himself, goes away and immediately forgets what he looks like. But the man who looks intently into the perfect law that gives freedom, and continues to do this, not forgetting what he has heard, but doing it — *he will be blessed in what he does.*[10]

You will be blessed because you'll feel God's nod of approval for being obedient to his teaching. You'll be blessed because when you affirm the worth of someone else, you're affirming your own value. You'll be blessed when you witness the heart-melting impact of kindness and compassion on other human beings, whether it's an infant pressing against you or an elderly woman whose day is brightened by a few dollars' worth of flowers.

You'll be blessed when others are pointed to God because you've demonstrated his love for them in a very real way. And, too, there will be blessings in heaven for followers of Jesus. The Bible says, "You know that the Lord will reward everyone for whatever good he does."[11]

What's more, your simple acts of kindness may contribute to what David Steindl-Rast calls "the spiral of joy." He describes it this way:

> A mother bends down to her child in the crib and gives the baby a rattle. The baby recognizes the gift and returns the mother's smile. The mother, overjoyed with the childish gesture of gratitude, lifts the child up and gives him a kiss. *That's the spiral of joy.* Is not the kiss a greater gift than the toy? Is not the joy it expresses greater than the joy that began the exchange?[12]

What a thought—that by a single decision to reach beyond our selfishness and tangibly express love to a fellow human being, we might be able to initiate a spiral that would bless others as God is blessing us.

Such is the outrageous power of the Golden Rule.

HEAVEN IS MORE THAN WISHFUL THINKING

It was a bright and beautiful August day in 1990 when Tobin McAuley, his best friend, and their girlfriends rented a catamaran to go sailing off the coast of Mexico. Nearly two miles off shore, Tobin's buddy and the girls jumped into the warm water for a leisurely swim.

They were laughing and splashing—until suddenly Tobin's friend began shouting for help. Cramps had gripped his legs. Quickly Tobin maneuvered the catamaran as close as he could to the swimmers. The girls scrambled on board. Tobin glanced around the boat for a life jacket, but there weren't any, so he dove into the water to save his friend.

The problem was that the girls didn't know how to sail. Frantically they tried to keep the catamaran near the guys, but the current pulled the craft away faster than Tobin and his friend could swim toward it. Pretty soon the boat had drifted out of sight—and twenty-nine-year-old Tobin and his thirty-year-old friend were left behind to drown.[1]

When soldiers march off to war, they accept the risk that they may never come back. When people contract a serious disease, they understand they may not survive. But when vacationers go out on a sailing jaunt, they don't anticipate that these will be their last moments in the world.

And yet through the years I've seen time after time how death often comes calling on days that start out bright and beautiful.

DEATH STALKS THE UNSUSPECTING

On a mild autumn afternoon when I was in fifth grade, my friend Bart and I were playing on the monkey bars after school. When it was time to go home, I headed south toward my house, and Bart and his little brother rode their bicycles west toward theirs.

As they approached a busy highway, Bart's foot slipped off the pedal. He was unable to brake, and before he could regain control of his bike, it rolled directly into the path of an oncoming truck. As his helpless brother held him in his arms, Bart's lungs filled with blood and he died.

It was a sunny spring day in 1979 when my dad was driving down the highway on his way to the commuter train. Without warning he was stricken with a massive heart attack and was dead before the car came to a halt at the side of the road.

In 1982 my friend Frank got up in the middle of the night because he was feeling queasy. Since he was only in his mid-thirties, he didn't think this was anything more than indigestion. But he fell over dead, leaving behind a widow, a six-year-old son, and a four-year-old daughter.

As a journalist, I've seen hundreds of instances in which people embarked on a day that started routinely but ended tragically. They were victims of drunk drivers, muggers, drive-by shooters, carjackers, auto accidents, household mishaps, fires, medical anomalies, or airplane crashes. Each year six thousand people are killed just crossing the street!

I'm not trying to be unduly alarming. However, some people look at the national average life span and behave as though it's guaranteed to them. It's not.

There's an old saying that only two things in life are certain: death and taxes. But while you can fudge on your taxes, ultimately none of us cheats death. It is ugly, unnatural, and morbidly efficient: one out of one dies. In fact, someone cynically said that life is merely a sexually transmitted disease with one-hundred-percent mortality!

And people fear the end. One third of Americans are so afraid of death that they are emotionally unable even to ponder their own demise. They fear the pain of death, the unknown, being separated from their loved ones, and the deterioration of their body. They just can't face it.

UNPLUGGING THE REFRIGERATOR

Yet increasingly other people seem fascinated by the topic. Popular movies like *The Sixth Sense* and *Ghost* explored death and what might come afterward. Not long ago three of the top ten bestselling books dealt with these subjects. Over three hundred and fifty thousand people bought the book *How We Die*, in which a physician gave graphic details of what it's like to succumb to various diseases. Books on near-death experiences are proliferating.

Why all this interest? The most likely reason is that the leading edge of the baby boom generation turned fifty years old in 1996, and suddenly the perils of old age aren't so remote anymore. Their parents are dying, and baby boomers themselves are reaching an era in which heart attacks and cancer are starting to take their toll among people they know. Now the odds of dying aren't just an abstract mathematical long-shot but are an ever growing realistic possibility.

So more and more people are asking the same question that Job posed thousands of years ago: "If a man dies, will he live again?"[2] After all, what could be more fundamentally important than that?

Even wisecracking Murphy Brown dealt with that question. In a memorable episode of the sitcom named after the fictional television reporter, she became concerned that her son, Avery, was someday going to ask what happens after a person dies. She wanted to be ready with a response.

She thought back to what her father had told her when she asked that question as a child: "If you pull the plug on a refrigerator, does it keep running?" he said simply. That brought more confusion than clarity. "Between the ages of five and seven," Murphy mused, "I thought that when you died, the Goodwill truck hauled you away."

So Murphy went to her friends for their ideas about death—and they didn't turn out to be much help, either.

THE QUEST OF MURPHY BROWN

Murphy's colleague Frank Fontana admitted that he changes his opinion about the afterlife based on whether he's currently dating a Hindu, Buddhist, or Rostafarian. Murphy's producer, Miles Silverberg, told her, "Look, I'm Jewish, and we don't talk much about heaven and hell. We focus on the here and now. We're a lot like the Unitarians that way, except they don't have gefilte fish."

Murphy thought she might get some solid answers from anchorman Jim Dial, a devout church-attender. But when she asked what participating in Sunday services provided him in coping with life and death, Jim mustered up enough honesty to reply, "Nothing. There, I said it." He said he hopes that by immersing himself in the trappings of religion, someday he might develop a real faith that will make a difference for him.

And Corkie Sherwood, the ditzy, born-again Christian reporter, was only able to give Murphy some sugary platitudes about heaven before inviting her to a church potluck dinner where, if she was lucky, she might meet an eligible guy or win a new car.

Nobody was able to provide much guidance for Murphy Brown—until she talked with Eldon, her housepainter and confidant. "I *do* believe in life after death," he said, "but not in the way you may think. I believe you live on in the things you create. For me, that's my art. *That's* my immortality. Maybe you've got something like that, too."

Incredibly, that satisfied Murphy Brown! She thanked Eldon for his insight and—amazingly—walked away with newfound confidence. But would that satisfy *you*?

Sure, it's nice to leave behind something that will make the world a little better than before you came onto the scene. But if that's *all* there is—if we're otherwise doomed to eternal extinction, like an unplugged refrigerator—then I'll tell you what: *that's not very satisfying to me!*

That's why one of my favorite quotations from Jesus comes from when he was talking with Martha about the death of Lazarus, who was her brother and Jesus' good friend. Declared Jesus, "I am the resurrection and the life. He who believes in me will live, even though he dies; and whoever lives and believes in me will never die."[3]

In effect, Jesus was making this astonishing claim: "There *is* life after death. It's not fantasy, it's not make-believe, and it's not wishful thinking. In fact, I'll prove it to you by bringing Lazarus back to life after his four days in a tomb. And later I'll establish it conclusively by overcoming the grave myself."

For Christians who sometimes secretly wonder whether the idea of heaven is too fanciful or fantastic, and for spiritual skeptics who suspect it's probably the product of fertile imaginations rather than concrete reality, this unambiguous proclamation by Jesus is, without a doubt, one of his most outrageous.

But is it true? And if it is, how can we know?

THE RELEVANCE OF THE RESURRECTION

Gary Habermas, a bearded, hockey-loving scholar who looks more like a nightclub bouncer than a university professor, is widely recognized as one of the world's foremost authorities on the Resurrection. He received his doctorate on the topic from Michigan State University and has authored several persuasive books marshaling the evidence that Jesus rose from the dead. In 1985 he devastated the arguments of renowned atheist Antony Flew in a major debate on whether the Resurrection is an actual event of history. Of the five independent philosophers who served as judges, four voted that Habermas had won; the remaining judge was undecided.

I got to know Gary years ago when Willow Creek invited him to speak about the Resurrection in a program attended by more than five thousand people, many of them spiritual seekers. During our time together, my curiosity prompted me to ask him a question.

"You've devoted so much time and effort to researching the Resurrection and defending it as being true," I said. "What motivates you? Why is this so important to you?"

"It's very simple," he replied. "You see, every single shred of evidence for the resurrection of Jesus Christ is also evidence for *my* eventual resurrection."

When it's put that way, *all* of us have a personal stake in the issue, including Christians who long for additional assurance that their faith is well placed, and the real-life Murphy Browns of the world who aren't sure where they stand spiritually.

Of course, our everyday experience tells us that pigs don't talk, (regardless of the movie *Babe*), Santa Claus doesn't slide down chimneys (despite Tim Allen's Christmas film), and dead people don't spring back to life.

But the Bible makes the outlandish assertion that Jesus *did* return from the dead. If this is false, "your faith is futile," said the apostle Paul.[4] But if it's true, we can have hope that as Christ's followers, we also will someday conquer death ourselves and spend eternity with him.

For us, heaven hinges on the reality of the Resurrection; that's how central it is to the Christian faith. J. I. Packer said that when Christians are asked to provide evidence that their beliefs are grounded in truth, they invariably point to the Resurrection:

> The Easter event, so they affirm, demonstrated Jesus' deity; validated his teaching; attested the completion of his work of atonement for sin; confirms his present cosmic dominion and his coming reappearance as Judge; assures us that his personal pardon, presence, and power in people's lives today is fact; *and guarantees each believer's own reembodiment by Resurrection in the world to come.*[5]

With so much riding on the Resurrection, how reliable is the evidence that it really did occur? How much confidence can we have in it, really? I'm going to address that question with a query of my own.

WEIGHING THE EVIDENCE OF HISTORY

Who would you guess is the most successful lawyer in the world? Johnny Cochran? F. Lee Bailey? Mark Geragos? The attorney who filed the lawsuit against McDonald's for that famous spilled cup of scalding coffee?

There is an authoritative source to settle this sort of question, *The Guinness Book of World Records*, and it says that Sir Lionel Luckhoo is by far the most accomplished lawyer on the planet. In an absolutely amazing feat that nobody has come close to repeating, this real-life Perry Mason won 245 murder acquittals in a row, either before a jury or on appeal.[6]

What uncanny skills would be necessary for a lawyer to soar to that unprecedented level of courtroom achievement? Certainly he must be smart, he must be savvy, he must be extremely analytical so he can dissect airtight cases, and he must have world-class mastery of what constitutes reliable and persuasive evidence. All of that describes Luckhoo, who was knighted twice by Queen Elizabeth and who also served as a distinguished diplomat and justice.

Given those qualifications, wouldn't it be interesting to get Luckhoo's razor-sharp analysis of the evidence for the resurrection of Jesus? Fortunately, we have his opinion, because this one-time skeptic took the time to apply his daunting legal expertise to thoroughly studying the matter.

Here is the conclusion he ultimately reached: "I say unequivocally that the evidence for the resurrection of Jesus Christ is so overwhelming that it compels acceptance by proof which leaves absolutely no room for doubt."[7]

Thoroughly convinced that Jesus rose from the dead in an irrefutable demonstration of his deity, Luckhoo did the most logical thing he could do: he reached out to receive Christ's forgiveness and leadership of his life. "My life took a 180-degree change," he said later. "I found real peace and happiness and joy and righteousness and holiness."[8]

I appreciate Luckhoo's story, because I used to consider the Resurrection to be a laughable fairy tale. After all, Yale Law School had trained me to be coldly rational, and my years of sniffing for news at the *Chicago Tribune* had only toughened my naturally cynical personality.

But intrigued by changes in my wife after she became a Christian, I spent nearly two years systematically using my journalistic and legal experience to study the evidence for the Resurrection and the credibility of Jesus' claims to being God. Like Luckhoo, I emerged totally convinced and gave my life to Christ—and now, like Habermas, I rest in the security of knowing that Christ's resurrection is a glorious precursor of my own.

So to heighten your own confidence, I'm going to summarize some of the evidence that I found particularly persuasive, beginning with a description of how Jesus died.

DID JESUS REALLY DIE ON THE CROSS?

It's called the "swoon theory"—the idea that Jesus fainted on the cross or took a drug that made him only appear to die, and then the cool damp air of the tomb revived him and he emerged alive. Consequently, there was no miraculous Resurrection because Jesus hadn't actually perished.

Although there are no reputable scholars who currently hold this position, it was the topic of a popular book several years ago and is still frequently raised by skeptics. Frankly, I was curious about it myself when I began to sift through the possibilities, but it didn't take long for me to see the fallacy of this position.

After Jesus' trial, the eyewitness John says, "Then Pilate took Jesus and had him flogged."[9] Most people skim over this, but a physician named Dr. C. Truman Davis actually analyzed the practice of Roman beatings during the first century. His conclusion was that Jesus had been mercilessly whipped to the very edge of death.

Jesus was tied to a post and beaten at least thirty-nine times—and probably more—with a whip that had jagged bones and balls of lead woven into it. Again and again the whip was brought down with full force on his bare shoulders, back, and legs. Davis said,

> At first the heavy thongs cut through the skin only. Then, as the blows continue, they cut deeper into the subcutaneous tissues, producing first an oozing of blood from the capillaries and veins of the skin, and finally spurting arterial bleeding from vessels in the underlying muscles. The small balls of lead first produce large, deep bruises which are broken open by subsequent blows. Finally, the skin of the back is hanging in long ribbons, and the entire area is an unrecognizable mass of torn, bleeding tissue.[10]

One witness to a Roman flogging gave this description: "The sufferer's veins were laid bare, and the very muscles and tendons and bowels of the victim were open to exposure."[11] Some victims died even before making it to the cross. Undoubtedly, Jesus was in serious to critical condition before his crucifixion began. It's no wonder that history tells us he was unable to carry his own cross.

Even though Mel Gibson's movie *The Passion of the Christ* received criticism from some people because of its graphic depiction of Jesus' beating, the truth is that the actual flogging was undoubtedly worse than Gibson portrayed it. In fact, when I got a chance to interview Gibson about his film, I suggested he could have toned down the violence to avoid the criticism he was receiving. He looked at me with wide eyes and declared, "Dude—I *did* tone it down!" Had he shown the beating as it actually occurred, viewers would have fled the theaters in horror.

CHRIST'S SUFFERING FOR US

Later, five- to seven-inch spikes were driven through Jesus' wrists. Dr. Alex Metherell, another physician who has extensively studied the crucifixion, told me that this would generate an agonizing pain akin to squeezing your funny bone with a pair of pliers. So brutal was death by crucifixion that a new word was coined to describe it—*excruciating*, which is Latin for "out of the cross."

After his wrists and feet were nailed securely, Jesus was hoisted into the air to hang. Dr. Metherell said that death from crucifixion is basically a slow death by suffocation.

Because of the stress on his muscles, Jesus could inhale but couldn't exhale unless he pushed up with his feet to relieve some of the pressure on his chest. Of course, that was tremendously painful because his bloodied back was scraping against the coarse wooden cross and because of the spikes through his feet. After hours of struggling to push up and breathe, exhaustion sets in.

If the Roman executioners wanted to hasten death, they used a mallet to shatter the victim's shin bones so he couldn't push up anymore. The victim would then hang limp while his lungs would slowly fill with carbon dioxide and he would asphyxiate. That's what the executioners did to the criminals being crucified on either side of Jesus.

But when they came to him, they saw he was already dead. To confirm that, a soldier thrust a spear between his ribs, puncturing the sac around his heart and the heart itself, causing a clear fluid and blood to drain out. After that Roman experts confirmed he was dead.

Let's be unambiguous about this: Jesus did not survive the torment of the cross. "Clearly, the weight of the historical and medical evidence indicates that Jesus was dead before the wound to his side was inflicted," concluded an authoritative article in the prestigious *Journal of the American Medical Association*. "Accordingly, interpretations based on the assumption that Jesus did not die on the cross appear to be at odds with modern medical knowledge."[12]

In fact, even if Jesus wanted to go against everything he taught by intentionally deceiving people, even if he had survived the cross, even if he managed to escape from his cocoon of linen wrappings soaked with seventy-five pounds of spices, even if he could roll away the huge boulder from the mouth of his tomb—a rock so large that one ancient account said twenty men couldn't budge it—and even if he could get past the elite Roman guards, think of the condition he would have been in when he appeared to his disciples!

He wouldn't have inspired them with boldness and gotten them excited about receiving that kind of resurrection body someday. He wouldn't have prompted them to triumphantly declare his return and launch a worldwide movement on his behalf. They would have been horrified. They would have been sickened by his bloody and broken condition. They would have pitied him and gotten him a doctor.

No, the swoon theory simply doesn't make sense. There's no doubt about it: Jesus died on Good Friday. But thank God, as Tony Campolo likes to say, Sunday was a-comin'! And there are five categories of evidence that point affirmatively to the Resurrection as being an actual event of history that occurred on that day. Building on a memory device that Habermas taught me, each one begins with the letter *e*.

EARLY ACCOUNTS: THE RELIABLE TESTIMONY OF HISTORY

I used to believe that the historical documents that comprise the New Testament and describe the Resurrection were irreparably flawed because they had been written so long—perhaps one hundred years—after the events. As a professor told me in college, legend and wishful thinking developed during this interim period and hopelessly distorted the record of who Jesus was and what he did.

But I found that many scholars are concluding there never was such a big gap between the life of Jesus and the belief that he's the resurrected Son of God. The key to this is to establish an accurate date for when the book of Acts was written, since it records the spread of the early church, and then to work backward to figure out when the Resurrection accounts were recorded.

Jesus was crucified in AD 30 or 33. In his book *Scaling the Secular City*, scholar J. P. Moreland cites half a dozen compelling reasons to conclude that the book of Acts was written before the early AD 60s.

For instance, the three main figures in Acts—Peter, Paul, and James—were all put to death between AD 61 and 65, but there's no mention of that in Acts, which gives many other details of their lives. And Acts doesn't discuss Emperor Nero's persecution of the church in the mid-60s or the war between the Jews and Romans, which broke out in AD 66. Surely all of this would have been included in Acts if it had been written *after* these events, so it must have been written *before* them.[13]

Experts concur that Acts was authored by the historian Luke, and Acts explicitly states that it's the second of a two-part work. The first part is the gospel of Luke—which also affirms Jesus was the resurrected Son of God—and so we know that it was written earlier than Acts.

And most historians agree that Mark's gospel—also testifying that Jesus is the resurrected Son of God—was written before Luke, because Luke apparently incorporated some of Mark's material into his own. Consequently, Mark's account is even closer to the events of Jesus' life. In fact, there's evidence that a key source that Mark included when writing about the empty tomb can be dated no later than AD 37.[14]

Now the gap has been narrowed so much that there's nowhere near enough time for legend to have corrupted the historical record. Oxford University's renowned scholar of ancient Roman and Greek history, A. N. Sherwin-White, concluded that even the passage of *two generations* wouldn't be enough time for legend to wipe out a solid core of historical facts.[15]

What's more, there's a creed of the early church that the apostle Paul includes in 1 Corinthians and that confirms Jesus was put to death for our sins, was buried, and rose again on the third day, as was predicted in Scripture. Based on a variety of factors, some scholars date this creed as early as twenty-four to thirty-six *months* after the crucifixion—and the eyewitness accounts that underlie it go right back to the cross itself.[16] In historical terms, this is like a hot news flash!

When Paul mentioned in 1 Corinthians that the resurrected Jesus appeared to five hundred people at once, he specifically stated that many of them were still alive at the time he was writing.[17] In effect, he was saying, "Hey, this happened so recently that these witnesses are still around—ask them yourself if you don't believe me, and they'll tell you it's true!"

That's how assured he was, just as we can have confidence in the reliability of the biblical accounts of the Resurrection.

In fact, after he examined all of the relevant historical evidence, scholar William Lane Craig came to this conclusion: "Within the first two years after [Jesus'] death ... significant numbers of Jesus' followers seem to have formulated a doctrine of the atonement, were convinced that he had been raised from the dead in bodily form, associated Jesus with God, and believed they found support for all these convictions in the Old Testament."[18]

EMPTY TOMB: IT'S UNANIMOUS— THE BODY'S MISSING

During his trial, Jesus' chief accuser was Caiaphas, who, history tells us, served as high priest from AD 18 to 37. It was Caiaphas who accused Jesus of blasphemy for claiming to be God and then handed him over to Pilate for his subsequent execution.

Not many years ago archaeologists were digging in Jerusalem, when they uncovered the burial grounds of Caiaphas and his family. But although his accuser's grave has been found, nobody to this day has ever uncovered the body of Jesus himself.[19]

Jesus was laid to rest in a tomb belonging to Joseph of Arimathea, a prominent member of the Jewish council, and the vault was sealed and placed under heavy guard. However, it was discovered empty on Easter morning by—and this is very significant—several women.

The fact that the biblical record says women discovered the tomb empty lends strong credibility to these accounts. The reason: women had low status in Jewish society and didn't even legally qualify to be witnesses. So if the disciples were manufacturing or embellishing this story, undoubtedly they would have claimed that men had discovered the empty tomb because their testimony would have been considered much more credible. Recording the then-embarrassing fact that women first saw the tomb empty is just one more indication that the biblical writers were committed to accurately recording what had actually happened.

But as Habermas has pointed out, the most powerful evidence concerning the empty tomb is that nobody ever claimed it was anything *but* empty. Even Jesus' opponents admitted it was vacant on Easter. They tried to bribe the guards to say the disciples stole the body while they were asleep, which doesn't make sense because Jesus' followers lacked both motive and opportunity. Besides, how would the guards have known it was the disciples who took the body if they had been sleeping?

But the point is that when the disciples declared the tomb was empty, Jesus' opponents didn't respond by saying, "Oh no, it's not" or "You've got the wrong tomb." Instead, they admitted the grave was vacant.

The question is *how* it got empty. When I was first trying to solve this mystery as a skeptic, I went through the list of suspects but found that all of them lacked motivation. For instance, the Romans wouldn't have taken the body; they wanted Jesus dead. The Jewish leaders wouldn't have taken the body; they wanted him to *stay* dead. Either of them would have loved to have paraded Jesus' lifeless body down Main Street of Jerusalem because that would have instantly killed the growing Christian movement that they expended so much energy trying to destroy.

As for the disciples, besides the huge risks and difficulties that would have been involved in trying to steal the body, they would have had nothing to gain and everything to lose by such deception. Why would they have wanted to live a life of deprivation and suffering and then be tortured to death for what they knew to be a lie? If this had been a charade they had concocted, certainly one of them would have broken ranks under torture and told the truth.

Charles Colson can affirm that. As special counsel to President Richard Nixon during the Watergate debacle, he personally saw how conspiracies fall apart under pressure.

Is it really likely that a deliberate cover-up, a plot to perpetrate a lie about the Resurrection, could have survived the violent persecution of the apostles, the scrutiny of early church councils, the horrendous purge of the first-century believers who were cast by the thousands to the lions for refusing to renounce the lordship of Christ?.... Take it from one who was inside the Watergate web looking out, who saw firsthand how vulnerable a cover-up is: Nothing less than a witness as awesome as the resurrected Christ could have caused those men to maintain to their dying whispers that Jesus is alive and Lord.[20]

Okay, so those theories didn't work. Then I thought, "Maybe the women went to the wrong burial place—after all, the hills outside Jerusalem were pocked with tombs. Maybe they lost their way in the darkness." But that didn't withstand scrutiny, either.

Not only did Mary Magdalene and the other women find the tomb empty but Peter and John came and checked it out for themselves. What are the odds they all would have made the same mistake? And they certainly would have made sure it was the right tomb before they risked their lives proclaiming Jesus had risen. Besides, their friend Joseph of Arimathea certainly knew where his own tomb was located. And if somehow they had all come down with collective amnesia, wouldn't the Roman or Jewish authorities have gladly pointed out the real tomb to show that Jesus was still in it?

The testimony of history is unanimous: the tomb of Jesus was empty on Easter Sunday.

EYEWITNESS TESTIMONY: SEEING IS BELIEVING

Not only was Jesus' tomb empty, but over a period of forty days he appeared alive a dozen different times to more than 515 individuals—to men and women, to believers and doubters, to tough-minded people and tenderhearted souls, to groups, to individuals, sometimes indoors and sometimes outdoors in broad daylight.

He talked with people, he ate with them, he even invited one skeptic to put his finger into the nail holes in his hands and to put his hand into the spear wound in his side, to verify that it was really him. This experience was so life-changing that, according to church history, the disciple Thomas ended up proclaiming to his violent death in south India that Jesus had in fact been resurrected.

I've covered scores of criminal trials as a legal affairs journalist, and I've never seen one with anywhere near 515 eyewitnesses. To put this into perspective, if you were to call each one of them to the stand to be questioned and cross-examined for just fifteen minutes each, and you went around the clock without a break, it would take you from breakfast on Monday until dinner on Friday to hear them all. After listening to nearly 129 straight hours of eyewitness testimony, who could possibly walk away unconvinced?

Of course, as a skeptic, I tried to poke holes in their stories. For instance, could these appearances have been hallucinations? Dr. Gary Collins — former president of a national association of psychologists, a university professor of psychology for twenty years, and the author of more than forty books on psychology-related subjects — says this just isn't possible.

Hallucinations, he said, are like dreams — they're individual events that can't be shared between people. One expert said that five hundred people sharing the same hallucination would be a bigger miracle than the Resurrection itself!

But I wasn't ready to give up yet. If these weren't hallucinations, perhaps they were an example of what psychologists call "group think" — a kind of wishful thinking in which people in a group subtly encourage one another, through the power of suggestion, to see something that's not there.

But Collins said this wouldn't be possible either, because the circumstances were completely wrong. The disciples weren't anticipating a resurrection, which would have been totally alien to their Jewish beliefs, so they weren't primed for this sort of "group think" to occur. In addition, Jesus ate with them, talked back and forth with them, and appeared numerous times before all kinds of people in different emotional states—all of which runs contrary to the "group think" theory.

Besides, what about the empty tomb? If the eyewitnesses had merely talked themselves into imagining a vision of Jesus, his body would still have been in the tomb—and surely the Romans would have produced it.

One thing is certain, said Craig: "On separate occasions different groups and individuals had experiences of seeing Jesus alive from the dead. This conclusion is virtually indisputable."[21]

EMERGENCE OF THE CHURCH: FILLING A HOLE IN HISTORY

Suppose that during the politically conservative days of the Reagan administration, you left the country and lost contact with the United States for twenty years. When you returned, you learned from a history book that a radical Marxist had been elected president after Reagan's last term in office. A major question would leap into your mind: What cataclysmic event precipitated such a major social shift?

Moreland uses this illustration as an analogy for what happened in the first century when the Christian church was started by Jewish converts who abandoned or significantly modified several major tenets of Jewish tradition. This monumental change, he said, is even more dramatic than the Reagan scenario.

It would have taken something as dramatic as the Resurrection to prompt first-century Jews to switch from Saturday to Sunday worship, to abandon both the system of sacrificing animals for forgiveness of sins and adhering to the laws of Moses as a way to maintain right standing with God, and to embrace the concept of the Trinity. In doing this, those who started the church risked becoming social outcasts and, according to Jewish theology, having their souls damned to hell.

"How could such a thing ever take place?" Moreland asks. "The Resurrection offers the only rational explanation."[22]

C. F. D. Moule, a New Testament scholar at Cambridge University, put it this way: "If the coming into existence of the [church], a phenomenon undeniably attested by the New Testament, rips a great hole in history, a hole the size and shape of Resurrection, *what does the secular historian propose to stop it up with?*"[23]

The early church was fueled by the sincerity and enthusiasm of the disciples, who had shrunk back with cowardice before Easter but who after Easter boldly proclaimed to their death that Jesus had conquered the grave.

At first I wasn't persuaded by the fact that they were willing to die for their beliefs. Certainly, lots of people throughout history have sacrificed themselves for their faith. For example, why were Muslim fanatics willing to die while committing the atrocities of September 11, 2001? Newspaper articles provided the answer: because according to what they had been taught, they honestly believed that as a result of their sacrifice they would go immediately to paradise to be with their creator.

But the disciples were in a completely different situation. They were in the unique position of knowing firsthand, *for a fact*, whether Jesus had really risen from the dead. They encountered him. They talked and ate with him. They declared it was true—he *was* resurrected. And because it was true, they were willing to die for it.

Do you see the difference? Unlike the terrorists who only had faith, the disciples were able to know for sure whether their claim was true. Do you think they would have willingly let themselves be tortured to death for a lie? Nobody would do that. They were willing to die because they *knew* the Resurrection was a reality.

EXTRABIBLICAL EVIDENCE: CONFIRMATION FROM OUTSIDE THE BIBLE

While there are plenty of reasons to believe that the New Testament records about the death and resurrection of Jesus are reliable, there are other ancient historical sources that provide additional confirmation.

Habermas, who is a leading authority on these so-called extrabiblical records, has compiled twenty-two ancient sources that mention Jesus' death, and thirteen that specifically refer to the Resurrection, with an additional ten providing relevant facts surrounding it.[24]

One of the most interesting references concerns the darkness that enveloped the land during the time Jesus was hanging on the cross. As a skeptic, I read about this phenomenon in the Bible and scoffed, "There's no way the sky went dark; I don't even think Christians really believe that!" I figured that someone had added this phony incident at some later date, as a way of sensationalizing a theological point. To me, it was just one more example of why the biblical accounts couldn't be trusted.

But a first-century Greek historian named Thallus, who was not a Christian, wrote a history of the Eastern Mediterranean world in AD 52, and he actually discussed this sudden darkness. His tactic was to try to explain it away as being an eclipse of the sun, even though this would not have been possible, given the timing of the crucifixion.[25]

Again history provides more bits of affirmation that the Jesus of faith is the Jesus of history.

THE VERDICT OF HISTORY

If every shred of historical documentation for Jesus rising from the dead is evidence for our own eventual resurrection, we can face the future with confident expectancy. The hope that Christians will overcome the grave and spend eternity with God is not the desperate longing of people too afraid to face their own mortality. Instead, it's a rational and logical conclusion based on the compelling testimony of history.

"No intelligent jury in the world," said Lord Darling, the brilliant chief justice of England, "could fail to bring in a verdict that the Resurrection story is true."[26]

For the Christian, that's reassuring. For spiritual seekers, that's a challenge that should be taken seriously. I've been in both camps. On a day that started out bright and beautiful in June 1983, I was glad I was in Christ's camp.

At the time, I had been working as managing editor of a newspaper in Missouri and had brought my family to Chicago to visit my mother for a few days. Late that night, I got up feeling ill and promptly collapsed in tremendous pain.

My wife called the paramedics. As they were on their way, I was sprawled on the floor—my breathing shallow, my pulse erratic, my skin pale—fighting to stay conscious and feeling an ominous numbness creep up my arms and legs. "This is it," I thought to myself. I figured I was going to die just like my friend Frank had several years earlier.

I'll admit it: I was scared. I didn't want to die. I wanted to see my children grow up. I wanted to live a long and happy life with Leslie. But I had been a Christian for about eighteen months, and I knew with certainty that I could trust two things if I died: first, that God would watch over Leslie and the kids; second, that the moment I closed my eyes in death, I would reopen them in the presence of God.

And Jesus would put his arm around me and say to the Father, "I know this man. I love him, and he loves me. I've paid for every single sin he ever committed. On the merits of what I did on the cross, he is washed clean of all wrongdoing and clothed in my goodness—and therefore invited to spend eternity in heaven."

I was in a win-win situation: if I lived, everything would be fine, and if I died, everything would be fine. That gave me the kind of courage I needed to cope with the crisis.

Obviously I didn't die. After nearly a week in the hospital, during which doctors were never quite able to diagnose the malady that had stricken me that night, I emerged to experience lots of other bright and beautiful days. But sooner or later one of them will be my last. Death still stalks me, as it does you.

But we can proceed with bold assurance, thanks to the evidence of history that establishes with convincing clarity how Jesus not only preceded us in death but also came back from the dead and blazed the trail to heaven.

"I write these things to you who believe in the name of the Son of God," said the apostle John, "so that you may *know* that you have eternal life."[27]

JESUS IS THE ONLY PATH TO GOD

A reporter for one of the network news programs called to ask me about the resurgence of interest in spirituality around the country. We had an amiable chat for a while — until I mentioned that it was my hope that all those who were experimenting with various belief systems would eventually meet Jesus.

Instantly the conversation turned cold. "Are you telling me that two-thirds of the world is going to hell because they've never heard of Christ?" he angrily demanded. The tone of his voice made it clear: he was accusing me of being narrow-minded, bigoted, and snobbish.

He didn't linger long enough for me to defend myself, but ultimately his argument isn't with me. It's with Jesus. Because in the single most outrageous claim he ever uttered, Jesus announced, "I am the way and the truth and the life. No one comes to the Father except through me."[1]

Out of all the incredible statements by Jesus, this exorbitant assertion has the greatest tendency to outrage people. Many consider it arrogant, intolerant, and politically incorrect. Even Jesus' claim to being divine doesn't upset people the way this declaration does. In fact, while I was in India, I had an encounter that many other

Christians also have experienced there: I told some Hindus that Jesus was God, and they replied, "No problem!"

I was perplexed. "You're saying that you accept the fact that Jesus Christ is the Son of God?" I asked.

"Sure," they said. "We have millions of gods. There's no problem adding Jesus."

But when I said, "No, you don't understand—Jesus said he's the *only* Son of God, and the *only* path that leads to eternal life," that's when they got indignant and drew the line.

DO ALL ROADS LEAD TO GOD?

One reason Jesus' exclusivity claim is so controversial is because it contradicts the popularly held viewpoint that all religions are basically the same. In other words, there are a variety of paths that people can take in their spiritual journey, and they all eventually lead to the same God. When you strip them down to their essential beliefs, every religion is similar, although they may use different languages and rituals in teaching God's universal nature.

However, Jesus' outlandish claim to being the only way to God puts Christianity in a class by itself. By contending that he is the only route to God, Jesus is alleging that Christianity is unique and that it therefore cannot be reconciled with any other religion in the world. For example, it has been said:

- Other religious leaders tell people, "Follow me and I'll show you how to find truth," but Jesus says, "I *am* the truth."
- Other religious leaders tell people, "Follow me and I'll show you the way to salvation," but Jesus says, "I *am* the way to eternal life."
- Other religious leaders tell people, "Follow me and I'll show you how to become enlightened," but Jesus says, "I *am* the light of the world."

- Other religious leaders tell people, "Follow me and I'll show you many doors that lead to God," but Jesus says, "I *am* the door."

Then Jesus says, "So follow me."

Do you see the difference? For a long time people have tried to harmonize the various religions of the world. In fact, that's what one faith, Baha'i, is all about. However, there are drastic and irreconcilable theological conflicts between Christianity and all other faith systems.

DO VERSUS DONE

To use a popular illustration, all other religions are spelled *"D-O."* That is, they are based on people *doing* something, through their struggling and striving, to somehow earn the good favor of God. Adherents must go on a pilgrimage, give alms to the poor, scrupulously maintain a diet, perform good deeds, chant the right words, use a Tibetan prayer wheel, go through a series of reincarnations, or faithfully follow some other religious drills. These are the attempts of people to reach out to God.

By contrast, Christianity is spelled *"D-O-N-E,"* because it's based on what Jesus Christ has *done* for us on the cross. The Bible teaches that we're all spiritual rebels and that nobody can do anything to merit heaven, but that Jesus died as our substitute on the cross and is offering forgiveness and eternal life as a gift of his grace. Christianity, then, is God reaching out to us.

Other religious leaders can offer pithy and helpful insights, but only Jesus—because he is the unique and perfect Son of God—is qualified to offer himself as payment for our wrongdoing. No leader of any other major religion even pretends to be able to do that. "Moses could mediate on the law; Mohammed could brandish a sword; Buddha could give personal counsel; Confucius could offer wise sayings," said theologian R. C. Sproul, "but none of these men was qualified to offer an atonement for the sins of the world."[2]

This element of grace is unique to Christianity. As one scholar pointed out, the contrast becomes stark when you compare a parable taught by Jesus with a similar story found in Buddhist literature. Both stories involve sons who became rebellious and left home but later recognized the error of their way and decided to return.

In the Buddhist story, the errant son is required to work off the penalty for his past misdeeds by spending years in servitude. But the Christian parable concludes with the prodigal son receiving a warm welcome from his father and being showered with undeserved forgiveness.

The message of grace—"done"—and the message of working off past wrongs—"do"—are fundamentally incompatible. It wouldn't make sense that both could come from the same God. After all, God isn't schizophrenic. It would be unlikely that a God who embodies love and truth would go to one side of the planet and say, "Pssst! Let me tell you how you can become reconciled with me," then go to another spot on the globe and describe a completely contradictory way for humans to understand and worship him, and tell yet a third population something totally new.

Instead, it seems logical that God would provide one path for us to follow in finding him and that he would reveal that path in an extraordinary and unprecedented manner—which he did by sending Jesus Christ to enter human history.

So it *does* matter which route you take in your spiritual journey. As incredible as it sounds, Jesus is saying that all other routes are ultimately dead ends, but his is the way to God.

THE CHURCH OF ASYLUMISM

Jesus' claim of exclusivity skewers the myth that all religions are basically the same. But there's another myth, which says that even though Christianity may be different, it's just one philosophy among many, and it's only as valid as any other system of religion. This is the "you have your truth, I have mine" idea.

Sproul points out that this belief has a certain amount of appeal because, on the surface, it reflects the tolerant and pluralistic attitudes of our country. Under our Constitution, all religious opinions are equally protected; people are free to believe whatever they want. But some people jump to the erroneous conclusion that just because different religious viewpoints are equally *protected*, they therefore must be equally *valid*. That's just not the case.

The idea behind what the U.S. Supreme Court has called our "marketplace of ideas" is that truth and falsehood should be free to grapple in unhindered debate so in the end truth will prevail. While the law protects everyone who expresses an opinion, it says nothing about which viewpoints are based on truth and which are misguided or blatantly false.

For instance, the late syndicated columnist Mike Royko once wrote a tongue-in-cheek column in which he claimed membership in the Church of Asylumism. This fictional church believes that on a distant planet millions of years ago several hundred aliens ate some tainted veggie dip. Unfortunately, it contained a virus that hopelessly scrambled their brains.

When treatment failed, the victims were transported to an uninhabited planet, which would serve as an asylum where they could roam free and act goofy. That planet was Earth, and we're all descendants of these aliens. Royko said to doubters, "You want proof? Read history books. Look at the newspaper and the network news. Then tell me this isn't one big loony bin!"

I'm pretty sure Royko was kidding, but in this country people have the right to believe anything they want. The Church of Asylumism would be protected under the Constitution just as much as any other faith. However, that wouldn't mean its teachings are true.

HISTORY'S COLORFUL CONTENDERS

But how do we know Jesus was telling the truth when he claimed to be the only path to God? Anybody could make that assertion. In fact, lots of people have! David Wallechinsky and Irving Wallace have researched several of them, including Sabbatai Zebi, one of the most intriguing people to pose as the messiah.

Born in 1626, the son of a chicken farmer, Zebi was a manic-depressive with a mesmerizing speaking style. He declared he was the messiah in 1648, later married a Polish prostitute, and attracted thousands of followers with his teaching that sexual promiscuity and nudity were virtues. His message was that *he* was the only way to God.

In 1666, however, he was arrested by Turkish authorities on charges of trying to overthrow the sultan. He was given a choice: be tortured to death or become a Muslim. According to Wallechinsky and Wallace, "Without batting an eye, he renounced Judaism for the faith of Mohammed and took the name Mahmed Effendi." So much for his messianic ambitions![3]

Another example is Jemima Wilkenson, born in 1752 to a Quaker family in Rhode Island. She used to tell people she had died when she was twenty years old but God had resurrected her. She ended up with more than two hundred fiercely loyal disciples who believed that she was their ticket to God.

Wallechinsky and Wallace describe how she was on the banks of a lake one day and announced she was going to walk across the water just as Jesus did. She turned to her followers and asked, "Do you believe I can?" They chanted, "Yes! Yes!" Then she said, "Well, in that case, there's no need to actually do it," and she walked home on dry land.

I'm not sure that bolstered the faith of her flock. And it didn't help when she died in 1820 and they followed her instructions not to bury her because she was going to rise again. As her body slowly decomposed, the remainder of her sect drifted away.[4]

There were others, too. Henry James Prince claimed to be God three years after being ordained as an Anglican minister in England; despite claims of immortality, he died in 1899. Also in the 1800s, hallucinations prompted by a nervous breakdown convinced Hung Hsiu Ch'üan that he was Jesus' younger brother, sent by God to save China. He helped instigate the T'ai P'ing Rebellion, which cost millions of lives, before poisoning himself in 1911.[5]

But Jesus was different. He not only contended he was the way, the truth, and the life, but he had credentials that no other religious leader has ever had. And that gives him unique credibility.

THE CREDIBILITY OF CHRIST'S CLAIM

If I claimed to be George W. Bush, you'd say I was crazy. But if George W. Bush claimed to be George W. Bush, you'd believe him. Why? Because there would be confirming evidence—he'd look like Bush, talk like Bush, have Secret Service protection, be surrounded by a crowd of reporters, and so on. Similarly, there's plenty of confirming evidence that Jesus is God and therefore credible when he claimed to be the only way to eternal life.

And he *did* make that claim. Skeptics sometimes argue that Jesus never pretended to be God and that he was only a spiritually enlightened leader who would roll over in his grave if he thought people were worshiping him—that is, if he were still in his grave!

However, as British pastor John Stott pointed out, Jesus clearly asserted that "to know him was to know God; to see him was to see God; to believe in him was to believe in God; to receive him was to receive God; to hate him was to hate God; and to honor him was to honor God."[6]

Among the evidence that backs up those bold declarations are his miracles, which are documented by the reliable historical records that make up the New Testament. Jesus said, "Don't believe me unless I do miracles of God,"[7] because he knew that they would be strong affirmation of his identity.

He performed many miracles in broad daylight and in front of skeptics. He demonstrated power over nature by walking on water and turning water into wine, he proved his power over disease by healing people, and he showed his power over death by bringing Lazarus back to life after four days in a cold, damp tomb.

In addition, his character provides confirmation of his claim. So often when we really get close to other people, we see their flaws all the more clearly. When I was a reporter and I'd cover politicians or celebrities, the more I would interact with them, the more I could see that they had shortcomings just like everyone else.

Yet the exact opposite happened with those who knew Jesus. The closer they got to him, the more they marveled at his integrity and purity. For instance, nobody was closer to Jesus during his three-year ministry than John and Peter. What was their opinion of his virtue?

Said John, "In him is no sin."[8] Peter wrote, "He committed no sin, and no deceit was found in his mouth."[9]

Another powerful bit of corroboration came in the way that Jesus embodied the attributes of God. In other words, you can look at those qualities that make God who he is—such as omnipotence, omniscience, righteousness, eternal existence, and so forth—and you'll find evidence that Jesus fulfilled those very same characteristics.

FITTING THE FINGERPRINT

Then there's the fingerprint evidence that backs up Jesus' claim. I've witnessed many criminal trials in which fingerprints were the decisive evidence. In fact, I saw one murder case in which the defendant basically was convicted on the strength of a single thumbprint that had been found on the cellophane wrapping of a cigarette pack. A fingerprint is tremendously persuasive because science tells us that it will fit just one person on the planet.

In an analogous way, the Old Testament of the Bible contains about four dozen major predictions about the coming Messiah, and when you piece them together, they create a kind of fingerprint. The Bible says we can have absolute confidence that whoever fits this fingerprint is truly the Messiah—the Savior of Israel and the world. And of all the people who have lived down through the ages, only Jesus Christ matches the fingerprint.

The odds against anyone doing this are astronomical. University mathematician Peter Stoner, in his book *Science Speaks*, conservatively estimated that the likelihood of any one person throughout history fulfilling forty-eight of the prophecies would be one chance in a trillion, trillion, trillion, trillion, trillion, trillion, trillion, trillion, trillion, trillion, trillion, trillion, trillion![10]

To understand the magnitude of this number, I called a scientist and asked, "How small is an atom?" He replied, "An atom is so small that it takes a million of them lined up to equal the width of a human hair." Then I called another scientist and said, "Has anybody calculated the approximate number of atoms in the entire known universe?" Amazingly, the answer was yes!

Based on those numbers, I concluded that the odds of Jesus fulfilling forty-eight prophecies would be the same as trying to find one specific, predetermined atom among a *trillion, trillion, trillion, trillion, billion* universes the size of our universe! That's about as close to being impossible as you can get!

Jesus said he came to satisfy those prophecies. "Everything must be fulfilled that is written about me in the Law of Moses, the Prophets and the Psalms," he said[11]—and it was, only in him, against all odds.

As if that isn't enough confirmation, there's also the miraculous resurrection of Jesus, which he not only foretold but which the previous chapter showed is a credible event of history that conclusively established Christ as being who he claimed to be.

When you add all of this up, it's clear that Christianity isn't merely a philosophy; it's reality. It's not just a way of life; it's a faith that's uniquely grounded in history. Therefore when Jesus makes the claim that he's the only path to God, history has not snickered.

Instead, history has been changed.

CREDENTIALS AND CREDIBILITY

Although Jesus' followers are sometimes accused of being narrow-minded for believing that Jesus alone can lead us to God, it's certainly not narrow-minded to act upon the complete scope of evidence and come to the rational conclusion that his claim is true.

For example, I have some friends whose baby girl was diagnosed with a liver disorder that caused jaundice. The symptoms of this malady are a yellowing of the skin and eyes. When they took their child to a doctor, he told them that this is potentially a devastating disease but it's easily cured. All they had to do was put the baby under a special light and this would stimulate her liver to function properly.

But the parents could have responded by saying, "That sounds too simple. How about if we just scrub her with soap and water and dip her in bleach instead? If we work hard enough at it, I'm sure we could get her normal coloring back."

The doctor would have insisted, "No, there's only one way to handle this."

"How about this?" they could have responded. "What if we just ignore the problem and pretend everything is okay? If we sincerely believe that, things will work out for the best."

"You'll jeopardize your baby's life if you do that," the doctor would have said. "Look, whether you like it or not, there's only one way to cure her. You're hesitant because it sounds too easy, but look at my credentials on the wall. Do you see those diplomas? I studied for years at medical school on how to save babies. Look at this office—I've been practicing here for twenty years. I've shown time after time that my treatment works. I know what I'm talking about. Trust me!"

Would anybody accuse those parents of being narrow-minded if they trusted that doctor—a physician with credentials and credibility—and pursued the only course of treatment that was going to save their little girl? That's not being narrow-minded; that's acting logically on the basis of the evidence.

And the truth is that we all have a terminal illness called sin. The reason we cling to Christ is because he's the Great Physician who has the only medication that can cure us. Some scoff that his prescription of freely offered grace is too easy, but Jesus says it will erase the stain of sin on our lives—and he has credibility and credentials like nobody else.

THE STORY OF TWO COUNTRY CLUBS

Before he hung up after our conversation about spirituality in America, the network reporter said that it sounded "elitist" to him when he heard Christians claim that Jesus alone can bring eternal life. Unfortunately, some Christians have projected an air of arrogance in dealing with others. We need to be humble, loving, and tolerant while at the same time upholding truth. Real Christianity is anything *but* arrogant.

Imagine two country clubs. The first has a strict set of rules and only allows in people who have earned their membership. They have to accomplish something, obtain superior wisdom, or fulfill a long list of demands and requirements to qualify for entry. Despite their best efforts, lots of people just won't make the grade and will be excluded. In effect, this is what other religious systems are like.

But the second country club throws its doors wide open and says, "Anybody who wants membership is invited inside. Rich or poor, black or white, regardless of your ethnic heritage or where you live, we would love to include you. Entry is based not on your qualifications but only on accepting this invitation, because your membership has already been paid. So we'll leave the matter up to you. You decide. But remember, we will never turn you away if you seek admittance." That's what Christianity is like.

Which country club is being snobbish? Christians aren't being exclusive; they're being inclusive. They're not being haughty; they're being egalitarian. They're not pretending to be better or more accomplished than anyone else. In fact, D. T. Niles summarized Christianity this way: it's "one beggar telling another beggar where to find food."[12]

THOSE WHO HAVEN'T HEARD

What about those who live in an isolated place and who haven't had a chance to hear the Christian message? What is going to happen to them? This is one of the most commonly asked questions about Christianity—and frankly, we don't have the complete answer. God hasn't explicitly told us how he is going to deal with them. "The secret things belong to the LORD our God, but the things revealed belong to us and to our children forever," says the Bible.[13]

But we do know a few things that can help us sort through this issue. First, we know from the Bible that everybody has a moral standard written on their hearts by God and that everybody is guilty of violating that standard. That's why our conscience bothers us when we do something wrong. Second, we know that everyone has enough information from observing the created world to know that God exists, but people have suppressed that and rejected God anyway—for which they rightfully deserve punishment.

But we also know from both the Old and New Testaments that those who seek God will find him. In fact, the Bible says that the Holy Spirit is seeking us first, making it possible for us to seek him. This suggests to me that people who respond to the understanding that they have and who earnestly seek after the one true God will find an opportunity, in some way, to receive the eternal life that God has graciously provided through Jesus Christ.

I remember meeting a man who had been raised by gurus in an area of India where there were no Christians. As a teenager, he came to the conclusion that there were too many contradictions in Hinduism and that its teachings couldn't satisfy his soul. So he called out to God for answers—and in a remarkable series of events, God brought people into his life who shared Christ's message with him. Today he's a follower of Jesus.

Repeatedly we see in Scripture that God is scrupulously fair. The very first book of the Bible asks, "Will not the Judge of all the earth do right?"[14] Ronald Nash, author of *Is Jesus the Only Savior?* casts the matter this way: "When God is finished dealing with all of us, none will be able to complain that they were treated unfairly."[15] In other words, when history is consummated, we will personally marvel at how absolutely perfect God's judgment is.

And finally, we know that apart from the payment that Christ made on the cross, nobody has a chance of getting off death row. Exactly how much knowledge a person has to have about Jesus or precisely where the lines of faith are drawn, only God knows. He and he alone can expose the motives of a person's heart.[16]

However, nobody will be excluded from heaven solely because he or she has never heard the name of Jesus. The reason people will be denied admittance, said author and speaker Cliffe Knechtle, is because

all life long they have told God that they can live just fine without him. On the judgment day God will say, "Based on your own decision to live life separately from me, you will spend eternity separate from me." That's hell. God will not violate our will. If all life long we have said, "My will be done," then on the day of judgment God will say to you, "Your will be done for eternity." G. K. Chesterton put it this way: "Hell is God's great compliment to the reality of human freedom and the dignity of human choice."[17]

As for you and me, the issue isn't ignorance. We've heard the message of Jesus. If you hadn't before, you have now. It's clear that we're responsible for how we respond.

There's a famous story about comedian W. C. Fields anxiously flipping through a Bible while on his deathbed. When someone asked what he was doing, he replied, "Looking for loopholes, m'boy, looking for loopholes."

Let me tell you: I've looked. They're not there.

A PREDICAMENT OF MY OWN MAKING

Late one afternoon when I was fourteen years old, I was home by myself, painting with oil colors on a large canvas in the basement. While acrylics dry fairly quickly, oil paints seem to take forever. Quickly growing impatient, I plugged in a couple of heat lamps to hurry matters along.

Not smart.

A short time later a pile of rags soaked with turpentine went up in flames. Then the table started on fire, and soon the entire corner of the wood-paneled basement was ablaze.

I ran to the telephone to call the fire department. When I returned, I saw that the fire was out of control, with orange and yellow flames lapping the ceiling, which was directly beneath the living room. I knew that if the fire burned through, the whole house would be consumed—and then I'd *really* be in trouble.

I grabbed a bucket of water from the laundry room, dashed over to the fire, and threw it on the wall where the flames were climbing. That hardly gave the fire pause. The enclosed basement was rapidly filling with a thick, black, sooty smoke. To make matters worse, the lights had shorted out.

Choking on the smoke and acrid fumes, I was quickly becoming disoriented. I couldn't see the stairs anymore. That's when a horrible realization hit—I couldn't save myself. I wouldn't be able to find the route out of the basement before I would be overcome. I was in a life-threatening situation.

Just then a police officer arrived and opened the door to the basement. He stepped onto the top stair and began shining around a big flashlight. "Police officer!" he called out. "Anyone down there?"

RESCUED FROM DANGER—TWICE

I could have analyzed the situation intellectually. Things were serious in the basement; if I stayed down there too much longer, the chances were that I would die from the smoke and fire. But the police officer knew the only escape route. He was a trained professional and fully capable of leading me to safety. What's more, he held a big flashlight to illuminate the way for me.

But it wasn't enough just to understand all of that. I had to take a step of action. I had to put my faith in that officer—a faith based on facts—by letting him reach out and rescue me. So I followed the light, and he put his arm around me and led me to safety, away from the inferno.

Many years later I was faced with a spiritually equivalent situation. After nearly two years of investigating the claims of Jesus, I knew he had unique credentials and credibility. And based on what he said, I realized for the first time that I couldn't save myself. I was guilty of sinning against a holy God. It was an open-and-shut case. And the penalty was eternal separation from him.

I was hopelessly disoriented and lost, but Jesus was calling to me and reaching out to rescue me. He was fully capable of leading me to safety. He knew the way to eternal life. In fact, he *was* the way. And he didn't need a flashlight, because as he said, "I am the light of the world. Whoever follows me will never walk in darkness, but will have the light of life."[18]

And yet just knowing that wasn't enough. I had to act on it. I had to take a step of faith—not a blind or irrational step but one that was secure and firm because it was based on the history-proven trustworthiness of Jesus Christ.

So on November 8, 1981, I allowed him to drape his arm around my shoulder and lead me out of the darkness, away from the inferno, and into a place of safety.

Statistics show that 84 percent of Americans already believe in the credentials of Jesus Christ. They're convinced that he's God or the Son of God. Maybe you're part of that majority. But if you've never *acted* on that belief, it's my hope that you'll let him rescue you from your otherwise hopeless situation by praying to receive Christ as your forgiver and leader.

If you do, I predict that you'll discover what I did:

- Jesus *is* the way—the path to a lifetime of adventure, fulfillment, challenge, and purpose, even when we sacrifice or suffer for his sake.
- Jesus *is* the truth—and he provides us with wisdom that works for our everyday life and the turbulent times as well.
- And Jesus *is* the life. He—and he alone—can give us confidence in our future for all of eternity.

PLAYING IT SAFE IS THE MOST DANGEROUS WAY TO LIVE

He was gregarious and glib, a back-slapping, idea-a-minute salesman who had come up with yet another scheme that he was absolutely certain would make a million dollars.

Like a bee buzzing from flower to flower, this peddler of paper cups flitted from person to person at Rolling Green Country Club in suburban Chicago several decades ago, hunting for the cash he needed to get his latest enterprise off the ground. The concept: a newfangled restaurant. The investment: just $950 per franchise.

My dad was among those approached by this entrepreneur, but he was skeptical. That night, he chuckled about the venture when discussing it with my mother. "A hamburger stand!" my dad said. "How does he expect to make any money selling hamburgers at such low prices?"

So a few days later my dad politely told Ray Kroc that he didn't think it would be prudent for him to invest in this questionable fast-food business that he was planning to call McDonald's.

Of course, McDonald's ended up making *billions* of dollars, and several of my father's golfing buddies became millionaires because they took the risk of making an initial investment in Kroc's dream. Later my dad was able to laugh about this missed opportunity, but I'll tell you what: it was *years* later!

FROM KROC TO SMITH TO YOU

Life is all about risk. Doctors talk about "risk factors," business executives ponder "risk assessments," and MBA students compare "upside and downside risks." Like my dad, all of us probably have had a time in our life when we decided against taking a risk—whether a business gamble or personal matter—and lived to regret our decision.

Those businesspeople who do boldly take risks tend to win our admiration—not if they merely roll the dice and jump into a venture without thinking but if they study the market, identify a niche, analyze the odds, develop a product or service, and then risk everything in pursuit of their dream. People like Ray Kroc.

Or Fred Smith. People thought Smith was crazy when he conjured up the idea for an overnight package delivery company in 1973. As a student, Smith described the concept for his economics professor, but his paper came back with a C scrawled on top and with lots of scribbling in the margins explaining why the idea would never get off the ground.

But Smith believed in his project. At age twenty-eight, he risked his entire family inheritance of four million dollars to put together a small fleet of corporate jets and launch his company under the name Federal Express.

That first night, it looked as if the skeptics might be right: only six packages were handled, one of them a birthday gift that Smith was sending to a friend. But Smith persevered, and Federal Express ended up creating an entirely new multibillion-dollar industry in overnight package delivery.

What prompts people like Smith to be risk takers? What causes any of us to take a risk, whether it's starting a new business, accepting a different job, or moving to a new part of the country? Usually people take risks because it's the only way to grow. It's ironic but true: playing it safe can be the riskiest way to live!

As a competitive golfer, my mother found that her biggest mistake in a tournament was when she would jump off to a big lead and then decide to play it safe. Inevitably, she would lose the edge, forfeit her momentum, and wind up in danger of losing.

We've got to keep moving to keep getting ahead. Quipped Will Rogers, "Even if you're on the right track, you'll get run over if you just sit there."

THE JOY OF FAILURE

Finally a young moviemaker had come face-to-face with his idol, a critically acclaimed director he had admired from afar for years. At the time, the youthful producer had several successful comedy films to his credit, and he described some of them to the renowned director. The director nodded, then asked whether any of his movies had failed.

"No," he said proudly. "Not one of them."

The director shook his head. "Oh," he replied sadly, *"that's too bad."*

What did he mean by that? He wasn't suggesting that failure, in and of itself, is noble. Instead, he was making the point that unless this producer took a risk and broke out of his comfort zone, he would never attain his full potential. He meant that if people never fail, it probably means they have never tried to stretch themselves.

That encounter changed the producer. He could have continued to crank out his formula comedies once a year for the rest of his life, with half his creativity tied behind his back. But after that director's comments, he decided to take some risks, do some experimenting, and accept some new challenges to see whether he could expand his boundaries.

It wasn't too long before he had his first flop—but in the long run he also achieved more than he had ever imagined he could. To succeed, he had to accept the risk of failure. He had to become a risk taker.

Risk takers share some common characteristics: they envision potential gains and rewards, they courageously seize opportunities, they exploit chances to grow and expand their horizons. Sure, they consider the potential losses, but they're more than willing to overlook the downside if the end result is worth it. "You don't concentrate on risks," said test pilot Chuck Yeager. "You concentrate on results."

THE REWARDS OF SPIRITUAL RISK TAKING

When we take a risk, we're stretching beyond what we think are our limits in order to reach for a goal. Inevitably, that involves overcoming some sort of fear—fear of the unknown, of physical harm, of failure, of humiliation, even of success. And it involves adventure.

When I was in college, a friend often lent me his Kawasaki motorcycle, which was primarily designed for off-road use. When I'd ride thirty miles an hour down the smooth residential streets toward campus, it was safe but boring. Wind whipped my hair but my heart didn't quiver. However, when I'd go zipping off the road, through tall weeds, down twisting dirt trails, dodging trees and bushes, around boulders and up steep inclines—places where I was facing some risk—*that* was exciting.

The same could be said for living a life of faith. It's when we overcome our fears and take spiritual risks that we really experience the adventure of Christianity. Jesus said, in effect, that those who risk their whole life for him will find it, but those who hang on to their life—those who shrink back from risk—will be the losers.

After all, faith and risk are intertwined. As we stretch our faith—as we increasingly follow Christ even when his wisdom collides head-on with the thinking of our culture—we're taking calculated risks based on our conviction that God can be trusted.

When we follow God's teaching on honesty despite our fear that we'll pay a price, when we ask God to open doors for us to make a difference in the lives of others despite our fear of the unknown, when we talk to someone about God despite our fear of embarrassment, when we follow the Holy Spirit's nudgings despite our hesitancies—those are spiritual risks. Those are the times when we leave the boring residential street for the thrill of the unmarked trails.

And we risk most when we pray. As a skeptic, I used to think that prayer was an empty exercise for weak-willed people who babbled into their folded hands because they were afraid to take any action on their own. Boy, was I wrong!

When we come to the realization that there's actually someone on the receiving end of our prayers—an omnipotent someone who wants us to grow and mature and develop and learn and become more and more like Jesus—then prayer becomes a great adventure. Then we're blazing new trails. Then our heart quivers.

Through the years, I've noticed that two prayers in particular are among the riskiest a person can pray. At least, they're risky from our limited human perspective. One prayer is for those who are just checking out Christianity; the other is for followers of Jesus. Both are just one sentence in length. Both are a mere seventeen words. And both have the potential to change everything—if you'll take a risk.

Ready to explore them? Let's spend the next few pages talking about the risky prayer for the spiritually curious.

OPENING UP TO GOD

In a best-selling book, Generation X guru Douglas Coupland tracks a young man through a troubled era. He's remorseful over his mistakes. His marriage has stagnated. He's ensnared in a meaningless job. Instead of deep friendships, he endures what he calls "halfway relationships." He's worried that he doesn't *feel* life the way he used to. He peers into his future with uncertainty.

The book's title: *Life after God.*

But after 358 pages of aimlessness and frustration, this was his conclusion:

> Now—here is my secret: I tell it to you with an openness of heart
> that I doubt I shall ever achieve again, so I pray that you are in
> a quiet room as you read these words. My secret is that I need
> God—that I am sick and can no longer make it alone. I need God
> to help me give, because I no longer seem to be capable of giving;
> to help me be kind, as I no longer seem capable of kindness; to
> help me love, as I seem beyond being able to love.[1]

Like Coupland's character, maybe you have a secret, too. Perhaps your own circumstances are causing you to conclude that maybe—*just maybe*—you need God to breathe hope and life into your world.

Or maybe you need him to knock the crust off a heart that's corroded with self-interest and cynicism. Or maybe you need him because … well, to be honest, you're not sure why. You just sense that there's got to be more to your existence than a job, three meals a day, and the gnawing feeling that something's missing.

So you've been casually checking out Christianity. Nothing too serious yet. You've leafed through a book or two—including this one. Questions are swirling through your mind. You'd like to get at the truth, but you're not sure how to—and you're a little afraid of what you might find.

Or possibly you already know a lot about the *idea* of God, but you're realizing that you really don't know *him*. You've wrestled with the concept of a deity yet never embraced Jesus himself. You went to church as a youngster and even went through religion classes, but they seemed to have numbed you toward God more than sensitized you toward him. If someone asked, you'd say that you were a religious person, although the truth is this: a heartfelt, life-changing, soul-satisfying faith has always eluded you.

This prayer is for you. Seventeen words that can start a revolution. Pray them at your own risk:

"God, open my eyes to who you really are, and then I'll open my life to you."

From Spectator to Seeker

For you, that prayer might seem fraught with risk. Because if you pray it sincerely, it catapults you from the status of an observer to the status of someone who's really intent on getting to the truth about God. You're entering unchartered territory. That old saying pops into your head: "Be careful what you ask for; you might get it."

You might be afraid that you'll end up stuffed inside a moral straitjacket that would bind and suffocate you. Your freedom would be choked by a proliferation of restrictive regulations at a time when you see your life as needing fewer rules, not more.

Perhaps you see a risk of being turned into something you don't want to be—a polyester proselytizer who punctuates every sentence with "Amen!" or forfeits fun in favor of faith.

Or it could be that you see a risk to your self-image if you're forced to admit some things about yourself that you'd rather not talk about. Isn't it healthier to focus on all the positive things you've done, instead of dredging up your mistakes?

On January 20, 1980, I prayed a prayer like this, even though these worries loomed large with me. And God answered. Through research and relationships, I investigated God, encountered him, and then responded to him on November 8, 1981, receiving Jesus Christ as my forgiver and leader. Today I can look back at the revolution that has happened in my life and say with complete candor that those initial risks I imagined were tremendously overblown.

Finding Freedom and Fulfillment

Instead of feeling suffocated through living by God's game plan, I've found liberation and security. In fact, my experience substantiates what the apostle John said about God: "His commands are not burdensome."[2] That has been a theme woven through this entire book—that God's guidelines make sense, they benefit us, and his wisdom works in our everyday life, like the rules I've established for my own children.

I don't impose capricious restrictions to squeeze the fun out of my kids' lives; they're rules that flow out of my fatherly love for them, to protect them from danger, to help them develop character, to help them live in harmony with others, and to help them reach their full potential. They're rules that grow out of a relationship in which there's trust, forgiveness, communication, and loving discipline—and that's how God operates.

Freedom isn't doing whatever we want; freedom is fulfilling what we were created to become. I can drive from Los Angeles to Chicago because there are highways, stoplights, traffic signs, and rules of the road. These aren't there to hinder my freedom; they facilitate freedom of travel. And because they come from the one who created us, God's commandments give us freedom by developing an environment in which we can flourish.

Instead of God squeezing me into a mold and stripping me of my uniqueness, I found that he wants to maximize the person he intended me to be. It's like the biblical account of the time a shepherd named David volunteered to fight the dreaded warrior Goliath. The authorities tried to prepare David by shoehorning him into the stereotype of a soldier — they slapped a suit of armor on him, put a bronze helmet on his head, and handed him a sword. That's the way warriors were expected to go into battle during those days.

But the armor weighed him down and restricted his movements. The helmet pinched. The sword felt awkward in his hand. David walked around and said, "Whoa! I can't fight this way. I'm not used to all this. This isn't me! I've got to be who I am!" So he stripped off the standard battle gear, put his shepherd clothing back on, grabbed his sling and five smooth stones, and went off to fight. He battled Goliath in a way that reflected who he authentically was, and God used him to defeat the enemy.[3]

Similarly, God won't force you to become something he never designed you to be. He created you. God wants to take *your* personality, *your* temperament, *your* talents, *your* experiences and give you a new character, new attitudes, new abilities, and the guidance of the Holy Spirit so you can reach your full potential.

Who I am today is a much better reflection of God's intention for my life than my years as a carousing, profane, and heavy-drinking cynic. In the end, all I was really risking by this prayer was the shedding of those things that were, in reality, weighing me down instead of freeing me up.

And that was no risk at all.

The Risk of Repentance

I also saw a risk in repentance, which is a word people don't use much anymore. Actually, it's the combination of two words that mean "change" and "mind." Repentance means confessing that we're spiritual rebels — that we've ignored God and broken his rules — and then literally changing our mind by turning around and going in the other direction, with God's help.

In the Bible, repentance isn't optional; it's mandatory. In fact, the very first words out of Jesus' mouth in his public ministry were, "The time has come," he said. "The kingdom of God is near. Repent and believe the good news!"[4]

But I saw big risks to my ego and self-image with that. I didn't relish the idea of admitting I had done anything wrong. I didn't want to face the possibility that I was a moral failure. I didn't want to dwell on my bad motives, my half-truths, my twisted desires, or the times I averted my eyes from those in need, shaved ethical corners, cursed God, or wished the worst upon others. I had become an expert in rationalizing my behavior and covering my tracks.

And I wasn't alone. One of the lures of popular thinking is that we're all essentially good and evolving into better and better people—a premise thoroughly contradicted by the evening news on any given day. This bogus belief feeds into what psychologists call our "self-serving bias," which is our tendency to emphasize the positive side of our lives.

For example, several years ago a drug dealer was being sentenced in Chicago for masterminding a giant drug operation and committing—and this is no exaggeration—*hundreds* of felonies, including plotting to murder a federal agent. At his sentencing he looked the judge in the eye and said with complete sincerity, "I may be a drug dealer, but I'm not a bad person." Talk about a self-serving bias!

Contrast that with how the British writer G. K. Chesterton came face-to-face with the depth of his own sin and the way it was poisoning others around him. When the *London Times* invited readers to write on the topic "What's wrong with the world?" this is the complete text of what he submitted:

> Dear Sirs,
>
> I am.
>
> Yours truly, G. K. Chesterton[5]

Like it or not, when we strip away our self-serving bias, we're left with the reality that all of us have fallen short of God's standard for our lives. In addition, the Bible says that all of the good deeds we perform are like "filthy rags."[6] Compared with the holiness of God, they're torn and tattered efforts stained by mixed and self-serving motives.

God gave us the Law, which we call the Ten Commandments, as a way of helping us realize that we can't possibly live up to his ideals for us. Martin Luther said,

> God wants to teach man to know himself through the Law. He wants him to see how false and unjust his heart is, how far he still is from God, and how entirely impotent his nature is…. Thus man is to be humbled, to creep to the cross, to sigh for Christ, to long for his grace, to despair of himself, and to base all his confidence on Christ.[7]

When we refuse to take the personal risk of admitting our failures and turning away from our wrongdoing—when we keep all that bottled up inside—it slowly eats away at us like rust devouring an old car. King David said in Psalm 32, "When I kept silent [about my sin], my bones wasted away through my groaning all day long. For day and night your hand was heavy upon me; my strength was sapped as in the heat of summer."[8]

While it may seem to be a risk to our self-image to admit our own sinful nature, that's nothing compared with the rewards we receive when we candidly confess our wrongs and seek God's help in putting our lives on a healthier course. The Bible says there is forgiveness, cleansing, healing, and a sense of release that flows into us when we come to God for forgiveness. The very next words King David wrote in Psalm 32 were these: "Then I acknowledged my sin to you and did not cover up my iniquity. I said, 'I will confess my transgressions to the LORD'—and you forgave the guilt of my sin."[9]

In place of a proud, ego-oriented self-esteem, our healthy new self-image is based on the Bible's amazing declaration, "God demonstrates his own love for us in this: While we were still sinners" — *that is, even in the midst of committing our most vile act or thinking our most disgusting thought* — "Christ died for us."[10]

Such is the outrageous depth of God's love.

Life Lesson from a Little Girl

If you think there's a risk in coming clean with God, let me tell you a story about something that happened to me several years ago. An acquaintance called with what he said was an embarrassing request: his little girl had been caught shoplifting from our church bookstore, and he wanted to know if I would represent the church so she could come and apologize. He said he wanted to use this incident as a teaching moment. I agreed — but I had a bigger lesson in mind.

The next day, the parents and their eight-year-old daughter trooped into my office and sat down. "Tell me what happened," I said to the little girl as gently as I could.

"Well," she said as she started to sniffle, "I was in the bookstore after a service and I saw a book that I really wanted, but I didn't have any money...." Now tears formed in her eyes and spilled down her cheeks. I handed her a tissue. "So I put the book under my coat and took it. I knew it was wrong. I knew I shouldn't do it, but I did. And I'm sorry. I'll never do it again. Honest!"

"I'm so glad you're willing to admit what you did and say you're sorry," I told her. "That's very brave, and it's the right thing to do. But what do you think an appropriate punishment would be?"

She shrugged her shoulders. I thought for a moment, then said, "I understand the book cost five dollars. I think it would be fair if you paid the bookstore five dollars, plus three times that amount, which would make the total twenty dollars. Do you think that would be fair?"

She nodded sadly. "Yes," she murmured. She could see the fairness in that. But now there was fear in her eyes. Twenty dollars is a mountain of money for a little kid. Where would she ever come up with that much cash?

I wanted to use this moment to teach her something about Jesus. So I pulled open my desk drawer, removed my checkbook, and wrote out a check on my personal account for the full amount. I tore off the check and handed it to her. Her mouth dropped open.

"I'm going to pay your penalty so you don't have to. Do you know why I'd do that?" Bewildered, she shook her head. "Because I love you. Because I care about you. Because you're valuable to me. And please remember this: that's how Jesus feels about you, too. *Except even more*."

I'll tell you what: I wish I could find the words to describe the look of absolute relief and joy and wonder that blossomed on her face! She was almost giddy with gratitude.

And that's a bit like what Jesus is offering to do for you. By his suffering and death on the cross, he paid the complete penalty for your wrongdoing, as your substitute, so you wouldn't have to. Out of his love for you, he's offering that payment as a pure gift—which you're free to accept or reject.

Your choice.

There's no real risk in doing what that little girl did. She admitted her wrongdoing because it was true and she was sorry. She accepted the check because she was powerless to pay the penalty herself.

And her reaction was the same one I often see on the faces of people who have prayed that seventeen-word prayer and ended up having a subsequent life-changing encounter with Jesus: there's delight, there's thankfulness, and most of all there's amazement over his outlandish grace.

Yes, there is a risk in all this, but it's probably not the one that first sprang into your mind. The real risk is *not* praying that prayer.

Embarking on a Spiritual Adventure

The comic strip "B.C." showed a character praying, "God, if you're up there, give me a sign!" Then he's startled when suddenly— *whomp!*—a giant, gaudy neon sign plunged to earth in front of him, flashing, *"I'm up here! I'm up here!"*

When you seek God, do so with confidence: he isn't hiding from you. The very fact that you're able to seek him is because he has already started doing something inside you. In fact, your seeking is actually a response to the subtle tuggings of the Holy Spirit. So trust that God will help you along your spiritual journey. "Ask and it will be given to you," Jesus said. "Seek and you will find; knock and the door will be opened to you."[11]

And seek sincerely. Keep an open mind as you explore the Bible (reading, for instance, *The Journey*, a Bible specifically formatted for spiritual seekers). Talk with Christians, read Christian books, listen to Christian tapes, and visit a church that encourages seekers and is sensitive to their needs.[12] My friend Judson Poling, coauthor of *The Journey*, also encourages these specific steps:

- Spend time in nature, observing and experiencing God's creation.
- Know your presuppositions—the things you already believe—and try not to let them interfere with your quest for the truth.
- Know your personal issues; your past will profoundly influence your present ability to be objective.
- Determine to seek for a specific period of time, and continually evaluate your progress. Then try to reach an appropriate conclusion.
- Remember that you don't have to know *everything* to know *something*.[13]

In short, seek wholeheartedly. Make this a priority in your life. Devote time and energy to it. So much depends on this spiritual quest that it makes sense to approach it enthusiastically. "You will seek me and find me when you seek me with all your heart," promises the Bible.[14]

TAKING LIFE'S BIGGEST PLUNGE

Then there's the other risky prayer that I told you about a few pages back. It's for those who have already found Christ, received his gift of forgiveness and grace, and been securely adopted forever into his family.

It's a prayer that invites God to stretch you beyond your comfort zone, to open new horizons of faith, and to inaugurate a fresh era of adventure and expectancy. If expressed sincerely, these seventeen words can be a launching pad not just for thrills but for thrills that fulfill:

"God, here I am, fully submitted to you; use me as you have never used me before."

I was thinking about this kind of prayer while I was watching the Olympic diving competition on television. The event reminded me of when I was a youngster and first climbed that seemingly endless ladder to the high dive at the swimming pool.

I remember taking hesitant steps down that narrow, sandpaper-like board, and the farther I walked, the more the shivers rippled through my body. When I reached the end, I peered over the edge and gasped. The water was so far below that it looked like one of those canyons in a *Road Runner* cartoon—a million miles down, *minimum*!

Even though I knew it was safe to jump, that the physical risk was small, that my friends had leaped off the board before me and survived, my natural reaction was to inch backward and grab the railing. The instant I did that, my heart rate decreased and I could breathe a little easier.

Some Christians feel that their spiritual life is boring, bland, and routine, that it has become predictable and safe — and the reason is, they're clutching a railing like that. They're wondering why their heart doesn't beat fast for spiritual matters anymore, and the simple explanation is this: no risk, no adventure.

What this prayer does is invite God to walk with you back out toward the end of the board, where you feel a bit of the risk and where life has an edge to it. When your toes curl over the end and the height causes you to catch your breath, that's when your prayer life *really* gets serious, that's when you cling tighter to God, that's when your adrenaline gets pumping, and that's when — if I push this analogy to its limit — God can really begin to use you to make a splash with your life!

This prayer is telling God, "I want to dive into *your* work. Use me as you never have before, to make a difference in the world, one person at a time. Use me to bring your message of hope to someone mired in despair. Use me to influence a teenager for you. Use me to solve someone's problem. Use me to soothe someone's pain. Use me to answer someone's prayer. Use me to feed someone who's hungry.

"Use me to encourage someone who's desperate. Use me to ease someone's loneliness. Use me to raise a godly family. Use me to deepen someone's faith. Use me to cheer somebody on. Use me to help a broken person understand how infinitely valuable he is in your sight. Use me to touch a life in your name. I'm tired of being a railing clutcher; I'm tired of paddling around the shallow end of life. I want to plunge into the deep waters! I want you to use me as your eyes and ears and hands and feet in a world that needs you more and more each day."

If you say that prayer and mean it, there *will* be action. And the chances are that from time to time you're going to face circumstances in which your heart will leap into your throat from fear, the odds will seem insurmountable, obstacles will appear hopelessly daunting, your sacrifices will be painful, and failure will seem inevitable.

And you will never regret it.

God Can Use Us When We Feel Useless

If you're like me, you will pray a prayer like that with a bit of doubt lingering in the back of your mind. A voice will whisper, "C'mon, who are you trying to kid? Why would the all-powerful God of the universe want to make use of a puny person like you? You'd better hold tight to that railing, buddy, because otherwise you're in for a big fall."

Maybe you too feel vulnerable to those voices that remind you that you're no Bible scholar, you're no Mother Teresa, you're no Billy Graham, or that your age, inexperience, or background somehow disqualifies you from making a difference.

When I fall into the trap of taunting myself with those kinds of messages, one way I bolster my courage is to look at the lives of others who probably thought the same things and yet were empowered by God in remarkable ways.

Like a fifteen-year-old girl who was shoved into the spotlight many years ago, whose knees knocked with fear and whose palms perspired with anxiety, and yet who was used by God in an extraordinary manner—just because she made herself available.

The story involves John Sung, who came to the United States from China to study science and turned out to be a tremendously gifted student of chemistry and physics. He won scholarships, gold medals, and other accolades; he was voted Phi Beta Kappa, newspapers lavished praise on him, and in 1926 he earned his doctorate from Ohio State University.

Despite his academic achievements, Sung was spiritually troubled. Although he had grown up in a Christian family, he still hungered for a relationship with God. However, his spiritual journey took a meandering route. He tried chanting Buddhist scriptures but he still felt empty. He toyed with Taoism but God still seemed distant. He fell into depression, writing at one point that he felt as if his soul were wandering in a wilderness. And I suspect that this was when he prayed a prayer similar to the "seeker prayer" that I mentioned earlier.

Then Sung heard that a brilliant Christian was visiting the university and was scheduled to deliver a speech on the faith. Finally, he thought, an intellectual equal, someone with credibility whom he could respect for his incisive mind and academic credentials. Maybe this person could tell him something meaningful about God.

Sung arrived at the lecture hall that evening with great expectancy. He chose a seat with a good view and waited for the program to start. But soon an announcement was made: the speaker was unable to come. Sung sighed with disappointment.

As he was getting up to leave, the organizers of the event walked over to a high school freshman and asked if she would substitute as the main speaker. I have no doubt that as she timidly walked onto the platform, she quickly prayed that God would use her as he had never used her before.

But what could a shy teenager teach a towering intellectual like John Sung? What could this young Christian say that would be significant to someone who was already knowledgeable about so many faith systems?

What she chose to do that evening was very simple: she merely talked with sincerity and childlike honesty about the revolutionary difference that Jesus Christ had made in her young life. With a purity born of her innocence and with a love inspired by God, she spoke about the very thing that John Sung had been hungering for.

The truth is that he didn't need another intellectual to speak to his mind; what he needed most was an authentic Christian to speak to his heart. And God took her words and used them to transform John Sung that night.

He turned into a committed and growing Christian who gave his life to ministry. Eventually John Sung ended up going back to the Far East, where he rejuvenated hundreds of Chinese churches and helped tens of thousands of spiritually starved people discover the forgiveness and compassion of Jesus. In fact, he would come to be called one of China's greatest evangelists.[15]

All because God chose to use a young teenager whose name has been forgotten by history.

A Children's Crusade

There's no shortage of stories like that. For instance, there was the barely literate shoemaker who was forced to step into the pulpit at a tiny London church after a snowstorm stranded the pastor. A teenager entered the sanctuary that morning to escape the frigid weather, heard what he later called one of the worst sermons ever delivered—and gave his life to Christ right then and there.

That youngster was Charles Haddon Spurgeon, who later became "the Prince of Preachers" and brought a new evangelistic zeal to England's largest city.

Then there was a "children's crusade" northwest of Chicago in the 1970s. A group of young people ached so much for their spiritually lost friends that they started a new kind of seeker-oriented church, designed to reach them with the message of Jesus that had so radically transformed the group members.

Inspired by a grandfatherly professor of theology, their fledgling ministry mushroomed into one of the most attended church in the United States—a ministry that brought me, my wife, my children, and untold thousands of others into a relationship with Christ.

I believe that God didn't use those youngsters at Willow Creek Community Church *despite* their inexperience; I think he used them *because* of their inexperience.

With youthful abandon, they offered their lives unreservedly to God. They joyfully handed him their time, talents, and treasures. Their young age made them open to fresh approaches and daring strategies for creatively communicating Christ's message to seekers. In their idealism they took risks that others would have avoided. Because they didn't have much of their own experience to lean on, they learned to lean on Jesus. And they refused to let those internal voices of doubt quench their God-given dream.

The Power of One Life

To observe its twentieth anniversary, Willow Creek had to rent the largest indoor arena in Chicago—the United Center, home of the Chicago Bulls—to accommodate twenty thousand of its attenders. As each person entered that evening, he or she was given a tiny flashlight.

Near the end of the evening, Nancy Beach—one of the original teenagers who founded the ministry, and still a key leader—requested that the arena be darkened. Then she asked everyone who had become a follower of Jesus Christ through the ministry of Willow Creek to turn on their light.

There was a brief pause ... and then in an instant the cavernous auditorium was transformed into a veritable constellation, with thousands upon thousands of lights glimmering in a joyous celebration of what God can do when his risk-taking followers make themselves wholly available to his work. There were "Oooohhhs" and "Aaaahhhhs" as people looked around—and then spontaneous praise for God.

That's when an absolutely remarkable incident occurred. A photographer had stepped onto the platform to preserve the scene on film. At the precise split second that he snapped his photo, someone on the main floor took a random flash-picture of the audience.

Amazingly, the light from that flash registered on the photo being taken by the first camera, onstage — and when the image was printed, out of the vast ocean of faces in the United Center that night, only one of them was lit.

It was Dr. Gilbert Bilezikian, the elderly theology professor who had cast the vision for creating this church to reach spiritually lost people. The camera caught him sobbing like a baby — *because suddenly, at that moment, it was all worth it.*

All the risk. All the criticism from those who didn't understand. All the work and prayer and sacrifice and pain. All the planning and meetings and services. All the hours and years. It was all worth it for the thousands of flickering lights representing individual human beings whose lives have been revolutionized and whose eternal destinies have been rewritten. *It was worth it all — for them.*

One of the church's mottoes is "What a ride!" And there's no doubt about it: when you submit yourself wholly to God and his work in your life — when you open your arms wide and invite him to use you as he never has before — watch out!

You're in for the ride of a lifetime.

NOTES

An Introduction to God's Surprises
1. Jer. 29:11 NRSV.

Outrageous Claim #1
There's Freedom in Forgiving Your Enemies
1. Matt. 5:43–44.
2. Luke 11:4.
3. Terry Anderson, "Small Graces," *Guideposts* (September 1993), 2–5, emphasis added. For a more complete account, see Anderson's book *Den of Lions: Memoirs of Seven Years* (New York: Crown, 1993).
4. Rom. 5:8.
5. Prov. 23:7 NASB.
6. Luke 23:34.
7. For more complete accounts of the story of the Morrises and Tommy Pigage, see "Could They Forgive Their Son's Killer?" *Reader's Digest* (May 1986), 136–40, and "Seventy Times Seven," *Guideposts* (January 1986), 2–6.
8. Robert Smith Thompson, *The Missiles of October* (New York: Simon & Schuster, 1992), 320–21.
9. David S. Dockery and David E. Garland, *Seeking the Kingdom* (Wheaton, Ill.: Harold Shaw, 1992), 68.
10. Matt. 18:23–35.
11. Matt. 6:15.
12. Matt. 5:46.
13. Rom. 12:18.
14. Matt. 5:44.
15. William Barclay, *The Gospel of Matthew*, vol. 1 (Philadelphia: Westminster, 1975), 176.
16. Luke 6:27.
17. Luke 6:28.

18. James 5:16.
19. Eph. 5:1.
20. John Stott, *The Message of the Sermon on the Mount* (Downer's Grove, Ill.: InterVarsity Press, 1985), 119, emphasis added.
21. Acts 7:60.
22. Acts 7:55.
23. Gal. 5:22–23.

Outrageous Claim #2
You Can Even Learn to Forgive Yourself

1. "Artswatch," *World* (April 7, 1990), 15.
2. Rom. 8:1.
3. Chris Thurman, *The Truths We Must Believe* (Nashville: Nelson, 1991), 23–24.
4. David Stoop, *Hope for the Perfectionist* (Nashville: Nelson, 1991), 81, emphasis added.
5. Mark 12:13–17.
6. LaGena Lookabill Greene as told to Paula Spencer, "I Am What AIDS Looks Like," *Aspire* (January 1996), 14–19, emphasis added.
7. 1 John 1:9.
8. 1 John 4:21.
9. Rom. 12:18, emphasis added.
10. "Offerings at the Wall," *Chicago Tribune Magazine* (May 28, 1995), cover.
11. James 5:16.
12. Arthur Freeman, *Woulda, Coulda, Shoulda* (New York: William Morrow, 1989).
13. Phil. 3:13–14.
14. Rom. 8:28.
15. Matt. 6:33.

Outrageous Claim #3
You Can Survive the Rat Race Without Becoming a Rat

1. Lee Strobel, *Reckless Homicide: Ford's Pinto Trial* (South Bend, Ind.: And Books, 1980), 75–92, 184.
2. Warren Wiersbe, *The Integrity Crisis* (Nashville: Nelson, 1988), 21.
3. Doug Sherman and William Hendricks, *Keeping Your Ethical Edge Sharp* (Colorado Springs: NavPress, 1990), 26.
4. Job 4:8.
5. Albert Carr, "Is Business Bluffing Ethical?" *Harvard Business Review* (January-February 1969), 153.

6. Jack Eckerd and Charles Paul Conn, *Eckerd: Finding the Right Prescription* (Old Tappan, N.J.: Revell, 1987), 189.
7. Prov. 10:9.
8. Prov. 20:7 NASB.
9. Robert Solomon and Kristine Hanson, *It's Good Business* (New York: Atheneum, 1985), xiii–xiv, emphasis added.
10. Eckerd and Conn, *Eckerd: Finding the Right Prescription*, 190.
11. Matt. 6:24.
12. Mark 10:21.
13. 2 Tim. 4:7–8.
14. Prov. 3:32 NASB.
15. 1 Peter 2:20 TEV.
16. Paul Reiser, *Couplehood* (New York: Bantam, 1995), 226–27.
17. Laura Nash, *Believers in Business* (Nashville: Nelson, 1994), 45–46.
18. Ibid., 37.
19. Ibid., xiv–xv.
20. Ps. 119:105.
21. Rom. 12:2.
22. Sherman and Hendricks, *Keeping Your Ethical Edge Sharp*, 153–54.
23. Prov. 27:17.

Outrageous Claim #4
You Can Make a Difference That Will Last for Eternity

1. Matt. 5:16.
2. Terry C. Muck, *Those Other Religions in Your Neighborhood* (Grand Rapids, Mich.: Zondervan, 1992), 150–51, emphasis added.

Outrageous Claim #5
God Can Give You Power as Power Is Needed

1. 2 Tim. 1:7.
2. John 16:33 NASB.
3. Heb. 4:15.
4. 1 Cor. 10:13.
5. Gal. 4:19.
6. 2 Cor. 12:9.
7. 1 Chron. 16:11–12.
8. Josh. 1:9.
9. John 15:5.
10. James 4:2.
11. John 19:30.

12. Heb. 11:6.
13. Rom. 12:18.
14. Brother Andrew with Verne Becker, *The Calling* (Nashville: Moorings, 1996), 26–27.
15. Ps. 37:5–6 NASB, emphasis added.
16. See Judg. 6–8.

Outrageous Claim #6
You Gain When You Give Yourself Away

1. Matt. 20:28.
2. Eugene H. Peterson, *The Message* (Colorado Springs: NavPress, 1993), 491.
3. John 13:15.
4. D. James Kennedy, *What If Jesus Had Never Been Born?* (Grand Rapids, Mich.: Zondervan, 1994), 36.
5. David Jeremiah, *Acts of Love* (Gresham, Ore.: Vision House, 1994), 102–4.
6. Matt. 5:16.
7. Heb. 6:10.
8. Kenneth Leech, *True Prayer: An Invitation to Christian Spirituality* (San Francisco: Harper & Row, 1980), 73.

Outrageous Claim #7
A Dose of Doubt May Strengthen Your Faith

1. C. S. Lewis, *Mere Christianity* (New York: Macmillan, 1952), 123.
2. Os Guinness, *In Two Minds: The Dilemma of Doubt and How to Resolve It* (Downers Grove, Ill.: InterVarsity Press, 1976), 25.
3. Karl Barth, *Evangelical Theology: An Introduction* (New York: Holt, Rinehart, and Winston, 1963), 124.
4. Lynn Anderson, *If I Really Believe, Why Do I Have These Doubts?* (Minneapolis: Bethany House, 1992), 25–26.
5. Gary R. Habermas, *Dealing with Doubt* (Chicago: Moody Press, 1990), 15. His thinking on this topic has greatly influenced my approach.
6. John 1:29.
7. Mark 1:11.
8. John 1:34.
9. Luke 7:20.
10. Luke 7:22.
11. Luke 7:28.
12. Mark R. Littleton, "Doubt Can Be a Good Thing," *The Lookout* (March 17, 1991), 5.
13. Henri Nouwen, *Reaching Out* (New York: Doubleday, 1957), 128.

14. 1 Thess. 5:21.
15. Rufus Jones, *The Radiant Life*, quoted in Gary E. Parker, *The Gift of Doubt: From Crisis to Authentic Faith* (San Francisco, Harper & Row, 1990), 71.
16. Parker, *The Gift of Doubt*, 69.
17. Anderson, *If I Really Believe*, 31.
18. Daniel Taylor, *The Myth of Certainty* (Grand Rapids, Mich.: Zondervan, 1992), 16.
19. Eccl. 7:25.
20. Paul C. Vitz, "The Psychology of Atheism," *Truth: An International, Interdisciplinary Journal of Christian Thought*, vol. 1 (1958), 29.
21. Guiness, *In Two Minds*, 70.
22. R. C. Sproul, ed., *Doubt and Assurance* (Grand Rapids, Mich.: Baker, 1993), 22.
23. John 8:44.
24. 1 John 4:4.
25. Sproul, *Doubt and Assurance*, 24.
26. Mark 9:24.
27. James 5:16.
28. Howard Hendricks and William Hendricks, *Living by the Book* (Chicago: Moody Press, 1991).
29. Ps. 34:8.
30. Parker, *The Gift of Doubt*, 142.
31. Based on 1 Corinthians 13:12, adapted from *The Living Bible*, Copyright © 1971. Used by permission of Tindale House Publishers, Inc., Wheaton, Ill. 60189 USA. All rights reserved.

Outrageous Claim #8
God Has a Cure for Your Secret Loneliness

1. Marla Paul, "Help Wanted: Everyone Has Time for Everything—Except Making Friends," *Chicago Tribune* (May 21, 1995).
2. Marla Paul, "Lonely? Don't Feel Like the Lone Ranger," *Chicago Tribune* (August 20, 1995).
3. David W. Smith, *Men Without Friends* (Nashville: Nelson, 1990), v.
4. Smith, *Men Without Friends*, 24–31.
5. James Wagenvoord, *Men: A Book for Women* (New York: Avon, 1978), 165.
6. Smith, *Men Without Friends*, 47–48.
7. Gen. 2:18.
8. C. S. Lewis, *The Four Loves* (New York: Harcourt, Brace, 1960), 169.
9. Prov. 18:24.
10. Lee Iacocca, *Iacocca: An Autobiography* (Boston: G. J. Hall, 1985), 138.

11. 1 Sam. 18:1 NASB.
12. Gary Inrig, *Quality Friendship* (Chicago: Moody Press, 1981), 54.
13. Ibid., 26.
14. Rom. 15:7.
15. Ted Engstrom, *The Fine Art of Friendship* (Nashville: Nelson, 1985), 17.
16. Inrig, *Quality Friendship*, 52–53.
17. Smith, *Men Without Friends*, 214.
18. Prov. 17:17.
19. Gal. 6:1 NASB, emphasis added.
20. Inrig, *Quality Friendship*, 53.
21. Matt. 26:38.
22. Gerard Egan, *Interpersonal Living* (Monterey, Calif.: Brooks/Cole Group, 1976), 45.
23. Judson Swihart, *How Do You Say "I Love You"?* (Downers Grove, Ill.: InterVarsity Press, 1977), 46–47.
24. Rom. 12:10.
25. Engstrom, *The Fine Art of Friendship*, 131.
26. Prov. 27:17.
27. Jim Conway, *Making Real Friends in a Phony World* (Grand Rapids, Mich.: Zondervan, 1989), 164.
28. Ibid., 171–74.

Outrageous Claim #9
God's Rules on Sex Can Liberate Us

1. Joyce Huggett, *Dating, Sex, and Friendship* (Downers Grove, Ill.: InterVarsity Press, 1985), 76, emphasis added.
2. Robert T. Michael et al., *Sex in America: A Definitive Survey* (Boston: Little, Brown, 1994), 103.
3. Gen. 2:24.
4. Peterson, *The Message*, 346.
5. 1 Cor. 7:5.
6. John Ankerberg and John Weldon, *The Myth of Safe Sex: The Tragic Consequences of Violating God's Plan* (Chicago: Moody Press, 1993), 65.
7. David Reardon, *Aborted Women: Silent No More* (Westchester, Ill.: Crossway, 1987), 119–20.
8. Paul Fowler, *Abortion: Toward an Evangelical Consensus* (Portland, Ore.: Multnomah Press, 1987), 196.
9. 1 Cor. 6:18.
10. Isa. 59:2.
11. Ankerberg and Weldon, *The Myth of Safe Sex*, 94.
12. Phil. 4:8.

13. Al Haffner, *The High Cost of Free Love* (San Bernardino, Calif.: Here's Life, 1989), 101.
14. Ibid., 107.
15. Tom Minnery, ed., *Pornography: A Human Tragedy* (Wheaton, Ill.: Christianity Today, Inc. & Tyndale House, 1986), back cover.
16. Ibid.
17. Bill Hybels, *Christians in a Sex-Crazed Culture* (Wheaton, Ill.: Victor, 1989), 97.
18. Ibid., 93–94.
19. 1 Cor. 10:12.
20. Ray E. Short, *Sex, Love, or Infatuation: How Can I Really Know?* (Minneapolis: Augsburg, 1978), 83–90.
21. Robert Moeller, *To Have and to Hold: Achieving Lifelong Sexual Intimacy and Satisfaction* (Portland, Ore.: Multnomah Press, 1995), 162–63.
22. Michael, *Sex in America*, 124–25.
23. Ibid., 127.
24. Ibid., 127, 130.
25. Ibid., 113.
26. Ps. 51:2.
27. 1 John 3:1.

Outrageous Claim #10
Random Acts of Kindness Aren't Enough

1. Stuart Hample and Eric Marshall, *Children's Letters to God* (New York: Workman, 1991).
2. Matt. 7:12.
3. D. A. Carson, *The Sermon on the Mount: An Evangelical Exposition of Matthew 5–7* (Grand Rapids, Mich.: Baker, 1982), 112.
4. Rom. 8:7.
5. Gal. 6:2.
6. Mark 12:30–31.
7. Gal. 5:22–23.
8. 1 John 4:19.
9. Kathryn Spink, *The Miracle of Love* (San Francisco: Harper & Row, 1981), 124–25, emphasis added.
10. James 1:22–25, emphasis added.
11. Eph. 6:8.
12. Don Postema, *Space for God* (Grand Rapids, Mich.: CRC Publications, 1983), 70–71, emphasis added.

Outrageous Claim #11
Heaven Is More Than Wishful Thinking

1. Abigail Van Buren, "Think Ahead, Avoid Boating Tragedies," *Chicago Tribune* (June 28, 1995).
2. Job 14:14.
3. John 11:25–26.
4. 1 Cor. 15:17.
5. Gary Habermas and Antony Flew, *Did Jesus Rise from the Dead?* (San Francisco: Harper & Row, 1987), xi, emphasis added.
6. Donald McFarlan, ed., *The Guinness Book of World Records* (New York: Bantam, 1991), 547.
7. Ross Clifford, ed., *The Case for the Empty Tomb*: *Leading Lawyers Look at the Resurrection* (Claremont, Calif.: Albatross, 1991), 112.
8. Ibid.
9. John 19:1.
10. C. Truman Davis, "The Crucifixion of Jesus," *Arizona Medicine* (March 1965), 185, quoted by Josh McDowell, *The Resurrection Factor* (San Bernardino, Calif.: Here's Life, 1981), 43.
11. McDowell, *The Resurrection Factor*, 44.
12. William D. Edwards et al., "On the Physical Death of Jesus Christ," *Journal of the American Medical Association* (March 21, 1986), 1463.
13. J. P. Moreland, *Scaling the Secular City*: *A Defense of Christianity* (Grand Rapids, Mich.: Baker, 1987), 152–53.
14. Michael J. Wilkins and J. P. Moreland, eds., *Jesus Under Fire*: *Modern Scholarship Reinvents the Historical Jesus* (Grand Rapids, Mich.: Zondervan, 1995), 150.
15. William Lane Craig, *Reasonable Faith*: *Christian Truth and Apologetics* (Wheaton, Ill.: Crossway, 1994), 285.
16. Moreland, *Scaling the Secular City*, 150–51; Wilkins and Moreland, *Jesus Under Fire*, 43.
17. 1 Cor. 15:6.
18. Wilkins and Moreland, *Jesus Under Fire*, 43.
19. Ibid., 41.
20. Charles Colson, *Loving God* (Grand Rapids, Mich.: Zondervan, 1987), 69.
21. Craig, *Reasonable Faith*, 284.
22. Moreland, *Scaling the Secular City*, 179–80.
23. Ibid., 181, emphasis added.
24. Gary Habermas, *The Verdict of History*: *Conclusive Evidence for the Life of Jesus* (Nashville: Nelson, 1988), 169–72.
25. Ibid., 93–94.

26. Val Grieve, *Verdict on the Empty Tomb* (London: Church Pastoral Aid Society, 1976), 26.
27. 1 John 5:13, emphasis added.

Outrageous Claim #12
Jesus Is the Only Path to God

1. John 14:6.
2. R. C. Sproul, *Reason to Believe: A Response to Common Objections to Christianity* (Grand Rapids, Mich.: Zondervan, 1981), 44.
3. David Wallechinsky and Irving Wallace, *The People's Almanac #3* (New York: Bantam, 1981), 581–82.
4. Ibid., 582.
5. Ibid., 582–84.
6. John Stott, *Basic Christianity* (Downers Grove, Ill.: InterVarsity Press, 1964), 26.
7. John 10:37 LB.
8. 1 John 3:5.
9. 1 Peter 2:22.
10. Peter W. Stoner, *Science Speaks* (Chicago: Moody Press, 1969), 109.
11. Luke 24:44.
12. D. T. Niles, quoted by Paul Little, *Know Why You Believe* (Downers Grove, Ill.: InterVarsity Press, 1988), 145.
13. Deut. 29:29.
14. Gen. 18:25.
15. Ronald H. Nash, *Is Jesus the Only Savior?* (Grand Rapids, Mich.: Zondervan, 1994), 165.
16. 1 Cor. 4:5.
17. Cliffe Knechtle, *Give Me an Answer* (Downers Grove, Ill.: InterVarsity Press, 1986), 42.
18. John 8:12.

Outrageous Claim #13
Playing It Safe Is the Most Dangerous Way to Live

1. Douglas Coupland, *Life after God* (New York: Pocket Books, 1994), 359.
2. 1 John 5:3.
3. 1 Sam. 17:38–50.
4. Mark 1:15.
5. William L. Craig, *Knowing the Truth about the Resurrection* (Ann Arbor, Mich.: Servant, 1988), 6.
6. Isa. 64:6.

7. Ewald M. Plass, ed., *What Luther Says*, vol. 2 (St. Louis: Concordia, 1959), 757.
8. Ps. 32:3–4.
9. Ps. 32:5.
10. Rom. 5:8.
11. Matt. 7:7.
12. For a list of seeker-oriented churches near you, contact the Willow Creek Association, P.O. Box 3188, Barrington, IL 60011–3188 or call (847) 765–0070.
13. Judson Plina and Bill Perkind, *The Journey: A Bible for Seeking God and Understanding Life* (Grand Rapids, Mich.: Zondervan, 1996), xiv.
14. Jer. 29:13.
15. Ruth A. Tucker, *Stories of Faith* (Grand Rapids, Mich.: Zondervan, 1989), 20; John T. Seamands, *Pioneers of the Younger Churches* (Nashville: Abingdon, 1967).

> *"My road to atheism was paved by science. . . . But, ironically, so was my later journey to God."* — *Lee Strobel*

The Case for a Creator:

A Journalist Investigates Scientific Evidence That Points Toward God

Lee Strobel, Author of The Case for Christ and The Case for Faith

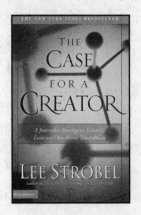

During his academic years, Lee Strobel became convinced that God was outmoded, a belief that colored his ensuing career as an award-winning journalist at the *Chicago Tribune*. Science had made the idea of a Creator irrelevant — or so Strobel thought.

But today science is pointing in a different direction. In recent years, a diverse and impressive body of research has increasingly supported the conclusion that the universe was intelligently designed. At the same time, Darwinism has faltered in the face of concrete facts and hard reason.

Has science discovered God? At the very least, it's giving faith an immense boost as new findings emerge about the incredible complexity of our universe. Join Strobel as he reexamines the theories that once led him away from God. Through his compelling and highly readable account, you'll encounter the mind-stretching discoveries from cosmology, cellular biology, DNA research, astronomy, physics, and human consciousness that present astonishing evidence in *The Case for a Creator*.

Hardcover: 0-310-24144-8   Unabridged Audio Pages® CD: 0-310-25439-6

ebooks:

Adobe Acrobat eBook Reader®: 0-310-25977-0   Palm™ Edition: 0-310-25979-7

Microsoft Reader®: 0-310-25978-9   Unabridged ebook Download: 0-310-26142-2

The Case for Faith

A Journalist Investigates the Toughest Objections to Christianity

In his best-seller *The Case for Christ*, Lee Strobel examined the claims of Christ, reaching the hard-won yet satisfying verdict that Jesus is God's unique son.

But despite the compelling historical evidence that Strobel presented, many grapple with doubts or serious concerns about faith in God. As in a court of law, they want to shout, "Objection!" They say, "If God is love, then what about all of the suffering that festers in our world?" Or, "If Jesus is the door to heaven, then what about the millions who have never heard of him?"

In *The Case for Faith*, Strobel turns his tenacious investigative skills to the most persistent emotional objections to belief, the eight "heart" barriers to faith. *The Case for Faith* is for those who may be feeling attracted toward Jesus, but who are faced with formidable intellectual barriers standing squarely in their path. For Christians, it will deepen their convictions and give them fresh confidence in discussing Christianity with even their most skeptical friends.

Hardcover 0-310-22015-7   Evangelism Pack 0-310-23508-1
Softcover 0-310-23469-7   Mass Market 6-pack 0-310-23509X
Audio Pages® Abridged Cassettes 0-310-23475-1

Pick up a copy today at your favorite bookstore!

ZONDERVAN™

GRAND RAPIDS, MICHIGAN 49530 USA

WWW.ZONDERVAN.COM

We want to hear from you. Please send your comments about this
book to us in care of zreview@zondervan.com. Thank you.

GRAND RAPIDS, MICHIGAN 49530 USA

WWW.ZONDERVAN.COM